DANTE AND THE CITY

DANTE AND THE CITY

CATHERINE KEEN

TEMPUS

First published 2003

Tempus Publishing Limited
The Mill, Brimscombe Port,
Stroud, Gloucestershire, GL5 2QG

British Library Cataloguing in Publication Data.
A catalogue record for this book is available from the British Library.

ISBN 0 7524 2836 5

Typesetting and origination by Tempus Publishing Limited
Printed in Great Britain by Midway Colour Print, Wiltshire

CONTENTS

ACKNOWLEDGEMENTS

In completing this book, I am conscious of a debt of gratitude to a large number of people and institutions for their support to my research. First and foremost, Robin Kirkpatrick has sustained me with his scholarship and encouragement from the beginning of my interest in city ideas in Dante, and has been unfailingly generous with guidance and criticism. A number of other Dante scholars have helped the development of my ideas and I would like to thank them, and others who have read and commented on drafts of all or parts of the book, for their generosity with their time and ideas: Patrick Boyde; Ann Caesar; Virginia Cox; Maria Sofia Fusaro; David Gibbons; Simon Gilson; John Henderson; Maurice and Mary Keen; Anna Lawrence; Joe Maiolo; Prue Shaw; and Quentin Skinner. I am grateful for their assistance, and for the friendship and support of my colleagues and the stimulus of my students, in the Universities of Cambridge and Leeds, as I have worked on this book. The flaws and errors that remain in the book, both of fact and of interpretation, are of course of my own making. I must also record my gratitude for financial support during the course of my research from the British Academy; St John's College, Cambridge; and the University of Leeds.

TEXTS

Throughout this book, standard abbreviations are used to refer to Dante's works. Quotations from the *Commedia* are taken from *La Commedia secondo l'antica vulgata*, ed. Giorgio Petrocchi, 4 vols (Milan: Mondadori, 1966–1967). Quotations from the minor works in Italian, and from the Latin *Epistles*, are taken from the Ricciardi editions of the *Opere minori* listed in the bibliography. For the remaining Latin works, both the Latin text and the English translations are taken from *Monarchia*, ed. Prue Shaw (Cambridge: Cambridge University Press, 1995), and *De vulgari eloquentia*, ed. Steven Botterill (Cambridge: Cambridge University Press, 1996). All other translations are my own.

For the convenience of the English reader, the Bible is quoted in English in the Authorised (King James) Version, and the works of Aristotle, Cicero, Ovid, Virgil and other classical authors are where possible cited, using standard abbreviations and references, from the Loeb bilingual editions of the texts published by Harvard University Press. Medieval texts are cited following the editions that appear in the bibliography and the translations are my own.

I have drawn extensively on the articles and bibliographies of the *Enciclopedia Dantesca*, ed. Umberto Bosco (6 vols, Rome: Istituto della Enciclopedia Italiana), for biographical information about the historical figures discussed in chapters 4 to 6 (as for much else).

INTRODUCTION

Almost as soon as Dante's masterpiece, the *Commedia*, was finished, it became the object of serious critical study, which continues today. The literally universal scale of the poem, its vivid and inventive language, and its compelling first-person narrative, have captured the attention and imagination of its readers from the fourteenth century onwards. As was recognised immediately, the text offers challenges to its readers at innumerable levels; a starting point for many readers is to define who Dante is. Almost inevitably, a modern audience encounters Dante first through the *Commedia*, and is drawn into its narrative through the immediacy of its first-person presentation of the journey as genuine autobiographical fact, whereby the manifest incredibility of an account of travelling to the afterworld is counter-balanced by the simplicity of Dante's claim that 'I was there'. Critical discussion of the *Commedia*, therefore, compels us to distinguish between two Dantes: the Dante-poet who writes the text and the Dante-protagonist whose adventures it narrates; this convention will be adopted throughout the present study.[1] Beyond either of these, we may wish to distinguish a third Dante: Dante the historical man, who was not only an immensely gifted and original writer, but whose life was intriguing and adventurous in itself. Before turning to Dante's writing, we should give some brief consideration to the known facts of his biography: for Dante is one of the most personal of writers, whose historical existence unavoidably impinges on his texts.[2]

Born in Florence in 1265, Dante Alighieri spent his youth in one of the largest and wealthiest cities of contemporary Europe. In his twenties, he became a prominent figure in a circle of avant-garde writers based predominantly in Florence, pursuing linguistic and stylistic experimentation in the medium of vernacular poetry. Before he was thirty years old, he had written an apparently autobiographical love story, the *Vita Nova*, which combines experiments in content and in form that would no doubt guarantee him a literary reputation even in the absence of the *Commedia*.[3] Around the same time he had begun also to pursue an active political career, and within five years rose to hold what was then the highest office in the government of the Florentine Republic, the priorate; but only a few years later, the complexities of the city's faction-based politics earned him political disgrace and a sentence of perpetual exile when he was still only in his mid-thirties.[4] The final twenty years of his life were spent moving between cities and courts in central and northern Italy, gaining the patronage of several politically prominent families and splitting his energies between creative writing, intellectual pursuits and occasional incursions back into the arena of politics. The facts of Dante's historical career are, then, sufficiently varied to merit attention – but his achievements in the realm of autobiography, or rather of autobiographical fiction, are still more commanding. Across a span of nearly thirty years, Dante pursued experiments in self-representation, from the *Vita Nova* to the *Commedia*. The reader of these narratives is compelled to address complex questions of continuity, change and comparison with regard to the 'Dantes' encountered in and through each of his texts, as his ideas shift, develop, and recur in constantly evolving guises.

The present study proposes the investigation of a single thread in the complex web of themes and issues that Dante weaves as an author, but one that is of very obvious continuity of importance to the one, two, three or more 'Dantes' whom his readers may identify. This theme is that of the city. Broadly speaking, this means that the book's primary concerns are with political questions – and, as will be seen in the arguments that follow, political matters embrace for

Dante a wide range of ethical, philosophical, historical and linguistic matters.

It may seem surprising, in an investigation of broadly political issues in Dante, to focus on the small community of the city, rather than on empire or at least on Italy. These, after all, are the political entities that Dante places explicitly to the fore in his formal theoretical works, especially in the political philosophy of *Convivio* and *Monarchia*. Scholars of medieval political thought recognise these treatises as making substantial contributions to contemporary debates over the nature, source and extent of the power exercised by the secular and religious institutions of the day. On the basis of the evidence of these two works, it is conventional to stress Dante's interest in monarchical theory and to emphasise the privileged position that he accorded to the empire of Rome, both in theory and, to a large extent, in all the practical political activity of his post-exile career.[5]

His interest in cities, and specifically in his native city of Florence, is never denied: but is often dealt with summarily, the town being dismissed as a building block within the greater edifice of empire, on which he expressed such vehement theoretical views. In this book, however, the city will be the primary object of concern, in a study that attempts in part to understand how Dante conceived the institutional function of the city in theoretical terms.

More urgently, however, this book is concerned with ideas about the city as communicated poetically in the *Commedia*. In many studies of Dante's political thought, evidence from the poem is used mainly to corroborate Dante's arguments in the prose treatises, which take pride of place as formal works of political theory. This study proceeds differently, placing Dante's *magnum opus*, the *Commedia*, at the centre of the investigation.[6] While recognising the value and the importance of *Convivio* and *Monarchia* as expressions of definite views on specific political debates, it accords greater significance to evidence from the work on which Dante's enduring fame rests – evidence presented not in the form of philosophical argument but of a verse narrative, where linguistic interests and poetic practice provide contributions equally significant to his political thinking as the formal arguments of the prose treatises. Dante's very choice to commit his most sustained creative energies to a work composed in vernacular Italian verse, has political implications. Rather than addressing himself exclusively to learned, Latin specialists, the *Commedia*'s form and idiom ensure the dissemination of his ideas on both secular and spiritual matters to the popular, vernacular audience found on an Italian city *piazza*.[7] In composing a 'comic' poem, too, Dante signals his intention to make his material accessible to a wide audience: in medieval rhetorical thought, *commedia* is a genre where style and subject matter can be employed with a flexibility close to the all-embracing accessibility of the *sermo humilis* used in scripture to reach the widest possible audience.[8] Dante's work, which he emphatically terms a '*poema sacro*' ('holy poem': *Par.* XXVI. 1), thus opens up to a wide audience its message about human life on earth and in eternity. Consequently, the political ideas about the organisation of human society into cities, kingdoms and empire, that form so clear a strand in the *Commedia*, are communicated in a language, form and style that their author made immediately accessible and relevant to an Italian, urban audience; an audience that is invited to engage with and to act on the poem's message of moral and political reform.

Within the poem, the city, a small-scale political environment of knowable human and physical extent, becomes an essential paradigm in political matters. It is a type of community deeply familiar to Dante the man via his experiences in Florence and in other Italian cities. In his writings, the city – both as a general concept and through the examples of specific historical cities – provides him with a constant point of reference in his examination of how and why individuals and societies achieve success or failure, in political and secular terms as well as spiritual and eschatological ones. As Dante-author moves from the relative objectivity of philosophical analysis to a mode of representation in the *Commedia* that places himself, as Dante-protagonist, at the centre of the action, he reminds his readers that political matters are not abstract affairs but are vitally important to the personal and social interests of real historical individuals such as Dante himself, or themselves. The city appears in the *Commedia* as a polity where such interests can find full expression – though for bad as well as for good – in a forum neither so large that institutions overwhelm individuals, nor so small that individuals can retreat into self-sufficiency, but rather where civic and individual needs can, and ideally do, coincide in all manner of ways.

The importance of the city to Dante has long been recognised: Alexander Passerin D'Entrèves long ago noted that 'the municipal spirit pervades the whole of Dante's work', and that 'the core of his political philosophy remained essentially *civic*'.[9] Critics have especially noted the significance to Dante's political thinking of his attachment to his native city: hence studies that investigate Dante's thinking about the city often focus all but exclusively on his view of Florence. Dante represents the experience of exile from Florence as intensely traumatic, but retains an enduring interest in Florentine fortunes, evidence of an imagination still profoundly involved with the affairs of a particular, specifically urban community. The overall picture painted by studies of Dante's relationship to Florence tends, however, to be negative, based on the numerous anti-Florentine statements of Dante's exile years and especially on evidence from the *Commedia*, where he felt justified in consigning a large number of fellow-citizens to hell and even in asserting that Florence had been founded by the devil himself (*Par.* IX. 127–129). Ricardo Quinones, for instance, has recently produced a book-length study in which Dante's attitude towards Florence is closely linked to the story of Cain, the fratricide who according to the Bible founded humanity's first fixed, urban settlement.[10] Although some scholars also highlight the positive images of Florence that emerge from *Paradiso* in particular, the fact that Dante relegates his city's period of greatest moral prosperity and civic harmony to the distant past is normally seen to undermine optimism about the city in general, or at least about Florence – an argument with which I shall take issue later in this book.[11]

In seeking a historical city to counterpoise the negative urban image of Florence, scholars often turn to Dante's admiration for Rome, the city that is also the seat of an empire endowed with universal authority, a community genuinely *urbis et orbis*. Encouraged by the enthusiasm for Rome evinced in the political theory of *Convivio* and *Monarchia*, critics can also show that the *Commedia* offers extensive evidence of Dante's enthusiasm for the political and moral achievements of Rome and of Roman culture. Both Nancy Lenkeith and Charles Davis have produced book-length studies of the political significance to Dante of the 'legend' (Lenkeith) or the 'idea' (Davis) of Rome; while Peter Armour and John Scott are only two of the most recent scholars to have paid prolonged attention to Dante's conception of Rome, in their studies of his political thought in relation to empire and to Church.[12] Since Dante's thinking about Rome and about empire is so densely intertwined in *Convivio*, *Monarchia*, and the *Commedia*, references to that city litter the numerous studies of Dante's imperial theories, allowing an urban element to run alongside the more global perspective of empire.

In the past two decades, a number of stimulating studies of Dante's political thought have appeared that accord pride of place to evidence from the *Commedia*. These recognise the importance of Dante's poetic imagination, according lesser significance to the emphatic, sometimes schematic, statements of formal political philosophy in the *Monarchia*. Scholars such as Joan Ferrante and Giuseppe Mazzotta have traced different aspects of the political thought of the poem. Their studies return to and extend Eric Auerbach's notion of Dante as 'poet of the secular world', exploring how Dante conceives of the function and organisation of human existence in the temporal world of history.[13] They remind us of the importance of paying due attention to the *Commedia* in any assessment of Dante's thinking on social and political matters – as indeed, on most other topics, for the poem is undoubtedly the text to which he accorded most time, energy and significance in the course of a highly prolific career. Such insights have informed my decision to give primary importance to analysis of the *Commedia* in this book.

As the previous remarks indicate, there is no shortage of critical studies of Dante's views on politics. Scholarship on Dante's broad conception of 'a city' or 'the city' is, however, lacking; my book sets out to address this void. Thus, in discussing *Monarchia* and *Convivio*, relatively little attention will be accorded to statements about empire, but I will pursue the question of how these texts represent the city and the nature of citizenship at some length. Above all, the *Commedia* will be the source that provides the principal evidence about Dante's conception of the city and about the conduct, the language and the aspirations appropriate to successful urban existence. Although Dante's poem overwhelmingly presents his ideas about the city through the citation of individual, historical examples, this book attempts to identify broader conceptions applicable to city life in general in Dante's thought. Much of my evidence is drawn from consideration of Dante's remarks on specific, historical cities. Alongside what may be considered the paradigmatic urban communities of Dante's poetic imagination, Rome and Florence, more neutral centres such as Lucca and Bologna will be discussed, towns that have no predetermined emotional or intellectual connotations for Dante and so allow us to move towards more general conclusions about the city. Claire Honess, the only other scholar recently to have engaged extensively with the concept of the city in Dante, has chosen to avoid the Florentine or Roman over-determination of her urban theme by taking Jerusalem as a model in her important investigation of the city as a structuring device in the *Commedia*.[14] My own choice is to focus on other local, Italian townships as the counterweights to Rome and Florence, so as to stress the importance of Dante's engagement with the city in the secular context of historical time – for Jerusalem carries biblical and theological connotations as the City of God that I do not wish to pursue here.

By exploring his representations of city life and citizenship both in theoretical analysis and also in the poetic representation of specific urban communities, my study aims to gain insights into matters of practical interest for Dante: questions about how to achieve political peace and harmony, and about how to discover and express feelings of fellowship with one's peers and neighbours. My contention is that Dante shares the 'urban imaginary', as Jacques Le Goff calls it, typical of medieval Italy, and that he takes the city as the normative human community, despite his concern with empire.[15] The cardinal position of the city in the *Commedia*, which will be seen in my book's detailed analysis of individual episodes, provides the clearest possible evidence of the significance of city concerns within all Dante's expressions of political consciousness. It is my hope that the study will cast new light on to the city as a point of continual reference in Dante's thought, with urban concerns providing interconnections between disparate works in verse and prose and in Latin and the vernacular, throughout his writing career.

To describe some of the realities covered by the term 'city' for the poet, my first chapter investigates the urban and socio-political history of Duecento Florence. It examines the way that the citizen of medieval Florence – taken as a more or less typical example of the medieval Italian city – built up a complex sense of urban patriotism. Dante continuously draws on such feelings in his depictions of city life and in his judgements on moral and political success, in both his philosophical and his poetic works. The chapter also investigates the political writing concerned with city government produced in late Duecento Florence. The great political debates of the thirteenth century concentrated on the competition for power between papacy, empire, and national monarchies, but within Italy texts relating to *comune* government were produced that, as will be seen, reveal aspects of the distinctive political culture of the independent cities and represent their first approaches towards constitutional analysis. The chapter concludes with the examination of episodes from the *Inferno* in which Dante passes judgement on leading figures from his city's recent past, condemning both the actions and the ideas that have left his polity riven by faction and corruption. The chapter takes Florence as a 'case study', to illustrate how Dante experienced and conceived of city life, using the example of his native city to sketch some of the realities that most immediately influenced his broader thinking on the city in general.

Dante's own reaction to philosophical and practical failures in contemporary politics, in Florence and other Italian *comuni*, is revealed in part in his argumentative prose treatises. In these philosophical texts, Dante analyses what political structures are necessary to enable justice and peace to be actuated in human society and discusses the role that linguistic developments can play in fostering political improvements in the community. In Chapter 2, I examine Dante's formal contributions to political debate in the treatises *Convivio* and *Monarchia*, both texts which display a strong concern with cities and the virtues of citizenship. The chapter takes due account of Dante's pronouncements on empire, but argues that it is conceived as the cohesive framework within which smaller, city-based associations may best flourish. Studies of political thought in the *Convivio* inevitably highlight the significance of the chapters in its last book that discuss Rome and its empire, and which define the broad remit of imperial power. My investigation, after examining the role of the city in these sections of the text, also turns to material later in the book that deals with nobility and political virtue. I argue that the civic precepts that Dante enunciates in these closing chapters of the *Convivio* have obvious practical relevance to city life, and highlight in particular the apostrophes that Dante addresses to contemporary Italian states and rulers, which demonstrate his local, urban concerns.

Chapter 3 turns to *De vulgari eloquentia*, emphasising the political importance of its linguistic conceptions. This treatise's concern with the history of human speech, from the creation of Adam to the crisis of Babel and on to Dante's own age, brings ethical and political concerns into the linguistic arena. Surveying the linguistic and political fragmentation of the contemporary Italian peninsula,

Dante argues that a move towards linguistic unity in poetry may materially affect practical life and help create the will to build political structures with unifying potential. In the last section of this chapter, I analyse additional aspects of his linguistic and poetic theories in the close reading of a *canzone*, *Tre donne intorno al cor mi son venute*, which allegorises the importance of justice and of appropriate language for the proper functioning of human communities.

The second half of the book moves on to the *Commedia*. Across the three *cantiche* of *Inferno*, *Purgatorio* and *Paradiso*, the poem provides a narrative development of concerns with secular as well as spiritual problems. My last three chapters investigate urban themes through the analysis of individual episodes taken from each of the three *cantiche*, building up a detailed picture of how Dante speaks of the city. The chapters cross-reference concerns that have emerged from the previous chapters with the *Commedia*'s evidence, stressing the interconnections between different texts, and showing how Dante's poem, through its accessible form and language and its use of individual example, brings the theoretical conclusions of the prose treatises to life.

The *Commedia* itself opens not with the city but the wilderness, with the description of an allegorical landscape that represents a moment of despair and confusion in its narrator's inner life as a journey into a dark wood, undertaken in his autobiographical *persona* as Dante-character:

> *Nel mezzo del cammin di nostra vita*
> *mi ritrovai per una selva oscura,*
> *ché la diritta via era smarrita.*
>
> (*Inf.* I. 1–3)

Midway in the journey of our life I found myself in a dark wood, for the straight way was lost.

The image draws on traditions already ancient in Dante's age that associated woodland and wilderness symbolically with confusion, sin and sterility in the human soul – though the desert was also seen as a place of self-discovery and conversion.[16] As Dante-character seeks to escape this wasteland, the ghost of Virgil appears to guide him, bringing the reassuring presence of Roman order – both urban and imperial – onto the scene, and promising him a journey that will culminate eventually in a paradisal realm that is portrayed as both city and empire. From the outset of the *Commedia*, then, Dante lets the reader know that God rules over a heaven made not only in the image of a universal institution but also in a civic mould, '*la sua città*' ('his city': *Inf.* I. 128). At the end of the journey, the pilgrim is welcomed to '*nostra città*' ('our city': *Par.* XXX. 130) by his beloved Beatrice and by all the citizens of heaven. An overarching paradigm of urban beatitude thus frames the whole narrative, with the goal of the journey always represented in specifically civic terms, as well as regal or religious ones. For a Florentine struggling to get out of a dark wood, the city provides the conceptual counterweight to present confusion, reminding us from the outset of the narrative of the urban instincts and imagination that colour Dante's political, social and moral thought.

In Chapter 4, I follow the protagonist's movement from the wilderness of the *selva oscura* into the more puzzling and disturbing wilderness of the city, or cities, of hell. The *Inferno*'s vision of the city is often simultaneously negative and hopeful: encounters with failed civic speakers and actors build up a detailed image of the consequences of abusing social ties, but also indicate the means by which regeneration needs to proceed, using historical examples to provide concrete evidence for Dante's ideas. The reflections and interconnections that Dante traces between the failed leadership of the *Inferno*'s urban politicians and the paradoxical anti-city of hell, provide powerful arguments against earthly political corruption; they also stress the justice and order that lie beneath terrestrial and infernal chaos, allowing positive, as well as negative, political lessons to be drawn from this stage of the *Commedia*'s journey.

More obviously optimistic suggestions about human nature and human society emerge from the encounters of *Purgatorio* and

Paradiso, discussed in chapters 5 and 6. The *Purgatorio* emphasises the connections between linguistic and political concerns already identified in *De vulgari*. In sequences both early and late in the *cantica*, Dante depicts groups of princes and poets whose ready collaboration fulfils the treatise's notion that small societies contain the potential for unified endeavour, facilitated by the use of fitting language. Dante explores the interests of the city and of the court, both political and literary, to emphasise the notions of service and self-abnegation that form an important part of his political ethic. The prominence given to two classical epic poets, Statius and Virgil, adds chronological and literary weight to the *cantica*'s concerns, aligning contemporary Italian issues within the same pattern as ancient, imperial ones. By exploring the achievements of both ancient and modern poets, Dante underlines the importance of his own poem and of its moral and political goals.

Chapter 6 turns to the *Paradiso*, to find the culmination of Dante's interest in the city spelt out, with emphatic prominence, in the central *canti* of this concluding section of the poem. It is in this *cantica* that Dante's sense of a providential order in history is most fully revealed. A pivotal encounter with his supposed ancestor, Cacciaguida, stresses that city life and city communities may lie at the heart of the pattern (*canti* xv–xvii). The varying moral *fortuna* of Florence and of her inhabitants is shown to exemplify different extremes of social wellbeing or corruption. Here politics and ethics unmistakably combine, in the small-scale context of city life. Linguistic, historical, and even domestic matters are found to fall within Dante's sphere of interest and to contribute to the wellbeing of all the members of the civic community. The ideal model of citizenly experience depicted in the *Paradiso* tells us even more about Dante's political values than do his theoretically based idealisations of the empire in *Convivio* or *Monarchia*, by bringing the realities of individual human example into the picture through the vividly nuanced medium of poetic language.

In the chapters that follow, then, comparison and contextualisation will be constantly used to investigate the nature of Dante's thinking on civic communities, as expressed in prose and verse, Latin and vernacular, at different points in his authorial career. The presentation of his concerns varies according to formal and linguistic considerations and is developed and modified over time, making the urban theme appear in many different guises. Overall, though, Dante maintains a continuous engagement with political issues that makes him return repeatedly to the image of the city, as the exemplar of a community in which the best and the worst of human behaviours make perhaps their most telling mark.

I

DANTE AND HIS CITY

THE URBAN EXAMPLE OF FLORENCE

For the last twenty years of his life, Dante followed his signature on personal and political letters with the words '*Florentinus et exul inmeritus*' ('a Florentine and undeservedly in exile').[1] The words indicate the depth and complexity of his feelings about his native town, reminding us of how far his thinking on cities was shaped by personal experience. Dante passed almost all of his life in the towns of northern and central Italy: in Florence, and later in Bologna, Verona, Ravenna and other cities in Tuscany, Lombardy and the Veneto.[2] Florence was, undoubtedly, the most important of these in forming Dante's civic consciousness. No other city apart from Florence, with the possible exception of Rome, is mentioned so frequently in Dante's writings, or spoken of with so much variation between love and loathing. Florentine citizens and Florentine monuments are mentioned repeatedly throughout the *Commedia*, which is written in a form of Florentine vernacular and places two Florentines, Dante and his beloved Beatrice, at the centre of its drama of conversion and salvation. The youthful story of the relationship between these lovers, the *Vita Nova*, unfolds within a city that, although unnamed, is clearly recognisable as Florence. Virtually everything that Dante wrote after his political exile makes some reference to that banishment, emphasising his Florentine origins and often urging his patriotic attachment to the city and his desire to return, although at other times expressing revulsion towards Florence on the grounds of its corrupt social and political *mores*.

Dante himself, therefore, points unavoidably towards Florence as his fundamental example of city life, making it the logical starting point for this chapter's investigation of how medieval urban realities inform Dante's verse and prose engagements with the idea of the city. It was Florence that provided the poet with his first, and most lasting, impressions of 'the city'. Thus an investigation of the specific political experiences and ideas of his native town will help isolate elements that became significant to Dante's views of the city as an entity in general.

With this purpose in view, I have divided this chapter into four sections. In the first, the principal theme is the myths of the foundation and early history of Florence current in Dante's day, which contributed to the Florentines' idea of themselves and of their city. The second examines the more recent history of Florence, and looks at the rise of factional discord in the Duecento and the constitutional efforts to restrain it which form the background to Dante's own brief career in Florentine politics. The third section of this chapter considers a different, but related, subject: the cultivation of rhetoric as part of the art of city government in Duecento Italy. Using excerpts from two well-known works, this section shows how writers in this tradition had developed a view of civic life and its ends that was largely independent of Aristotle, and that was primarily concerned with the problem of factional discord. Dante was well aware of such ideas, and this chapter's fourth and final section considers his largely negative reactions to them, which helped to shape his own, different approach to essentially the same problem – an approach that will be explored more fully in later chapters.

FLORENCE AND ROME: MYTHS OF ORIGIN AND ORDER

Florence in the later Duecento was in many ways a boom town, and contemporary commentators such as the chroniclers Giovanni

Villani and Dino Compagni record the excitements and the tensions of life in the constantly changing metropolis. The city was one
of the largest in Italy, indeed in Europe, and a centre for interna-
tional trade and banking. Its two most successful products,
Florentine cloth and Florentine currency, were in demand throughout Italy, France, England and beyond. Waves of immigration from
the countryside had brought both artisans and landowners into the
city to profit from its economic growth. The demographic surge
had led to urban expansion into new settlements beyond the old
city walls, and during Dante's youth a rash of new building projects
sponsored by the civic authorities, trade guilds, religious orders and
private individuals was changing the city's external appearance and
stamping it as a modern, prosperous conurbation. During the 1290s,
work began on a new cathedral, a new government palace, new
paved streets and *piazze*, and on new city walls, all providing visible
affirmations of Florence's wealth and importance. Although the city
had no university, its religious houses were in contact with the the-
ologians of Paris, and well-to-do Florentines could easily travel to
Bologna to study in its famous faculties of law and rhetoric. Its
home-grown, vernacular culture was also particularly rich, with
writers in both verse and prose experimenting with new forms and
styles, and drawing on both courtly literary traditions and intellectual disciplines: figures such as Guido Cavalcanti and Dante himself
kept Florence at the literary *avant-garde* in the 1280s and 1290s.[3]

Dino Compagni, an almost exact contemporary of Dante's,
introduces his *Cronica* of contemporary Florentine history with a
description of the city that emphasises its attractions, but also
reveals a darker side:

> *E acciò che gli strani possano meglio intendere le cose advenute, dirò la
> forma della nobile città, la quale è nella provincia di Toscana, edificata
> sotto il segno di Marte, ricca e larga d'imperiale fiume d'acqua dolce il
> quale divide la città quasi per mezo, con temperata aria, guardata da
> nocivi venti, povera di terreno, abondante di buoni frutti, con cittadini
> pro' d'armi superbi e discordevoli, e ricca di proibiti guadagni, dottata e*

temuta, per sua grandeza, dalle terre vicine, più che amata. [...] La
detta città di Firenze è molto bene popolata [...]; i cittadini bene cos-
tumati, e le donne molto belle e adorne; i casamenti bellissimi pieni di
molte bisognevoli arti, oltre all'altre città d'Italia.

(*Cronica* I. i)

And so that foreigners may better understand the events which
took place, let me describe the form of that noble city in the
province of Tuscany, built under the sign of Mars, rich and
ample with an imperial river of fresh water which divides the
city almost in half, temperate in climate, sheltered from harm-
ful winds, poor in land, abundant with good products, its citizens bold in arms, proud and combative, and rich with
unlawful profits, suspected and feared for its greatness by the
nearby cities, rather than loved. This city of Florence is very
populous. Its citizens are well-bred and its women lovely and
adorned; its buildings are beautiful and filled with many useful
crafts, more than any other city in Italy.

Compagni's pride in the attraction of his city's people and buildings is counterbalanced by unease over its territorial ambitions, its
turbulent politics and the dubious morality of the usurious profits
of its financial activity. A similar ambivalence appears in many of
Dante's own remarks on Florence, heightened by an experience of
political exclusion that has removed him from all the physical and
psychological comforts but also from the dangers of life inside the
city walls.

A famous articulation of Dante's feelings of patriotic and personal disorientation when banished from the city of Florence
appears in the *Convivio*:

Poi che fu piacere de li cittadini de la bellissima e famosissima figlia
di Roma, Fiorenza, di gittarmi fuori del suo dolce seno — nel quale
nato e nutrito fui in fino al colmo de la vita mia, e nel quale, con
buona pace di quella, desidero con tutto lo cuore di riposare l'animo

stancato e terminare lo tempo che m'è dato − [...] peregrino, quasi mendicando, sono andato, mostrando contra mia voglia la piaga de la fortuna.

(*Cvo* I. iii. 4)

Since it has pleased the citizens of Rome's most beautiful and famous daughter, Florence, to cast me out from her sweet bosom − where I was born and nourished until my full maturity, and where, with her gracious consent, I desire with all my heart to rest my weary mind and complete my allotted span − I have made my way a homeless wanderer reduced almost to beggary, and showing against my will the wound inflicted by fortune.

This extravagant praise of Florence allows Dante to evoke the city's civilised attractions, and to highlight the contrasting pathos of exile. It also serves to emphasise elements in the city's past, as well as its present, that can be linked significantly to his wider political thought.

The passage draws attention to the fact that Florence was founded by Rome. Elsewhere in the treatise (*Cvo* IV. iv–v), Rome is hailed as the seat of an empire providentially ordained to maintain political and social order; the close kinship that Dante imagines between Rome and Florence at the start of the *Convivio* thus implies that his heartfelt patriotic allegiance to the latter is compatible with his evolving imperial interests. In portraying Florence as the daughter of Rome, moreover, Dante is making use of a local historiographic tradition that suggested a particularly close and privileged relationship to have subsisted between the two cities in antiquity. Although few of his contemporaries allowed accounts of an imperial past to influence present political choices, these local, Florentine legends may have helped bolster Dante's conviction of the compatibility of the urban interests of cities *in general* with the stable governance of an idealised Roman empire. Although this passage offers only a generic reference, there is plenty of evidence from other works, especially the *Commedia*, that Dante was familiar with the details of the legend of Florence's Roman foundation.

According to legend, Florence was founded by Julius Caesar, in the period of Catiline's conspiracy against the Roman Republic, and shortly before Caesar's own rise to supreme power.[4] A mythical Roman general, Florinus or, in the vernacular, Fiorino, was killed while besieging Catiline in Fiesole. Caesar led the Roman retaliation, sacking Fiesole and resettling its inhabitants in a new town in the Arno valley. In the *Commedia*, Dante shows his knowledge of this element of the tale in referring to a part of the population '*che discese di Fiesole ab antico*' ('who of old came down from Fiesole': *Inf.* XV. 62). The new settlement that Caesar founded was built on a site associated with the war-god Mars, and named Florentia (in vernacular, Fiorenza) in commemoration of the murdered general.[5] Various Roman patricians sponsored the construction of different civic amenities (city walls, aqueducts, baths, and so on) copied from models in the mother-city, and settlers from Rome's leading families arrived to populate the city alongside the Fiesolan refugees. The chroniclers are careful to stress the topographical and demographic similarities between Rome and Florence in their triumphalist account of the latter's martial and patrician origins and associations. Dante too, in one of his letters, notes the founders' intention that Florence should bear a significant physical resemblance to Rome, '*que ad ymaginem suam atque similitudinem fecit illam*' ('which made her [i.e. Florence] in her own image and after her own likeness': *Ep.* VII. 25)

The foundation legends, however, have also to accommodate a narrative of civic disaster that they claim struck Florence after several centuries of prosperity, when the city, in an episode clearly based in part on the history of Rome, was destroyed by a malevolent barbarian king, '*Totila flagellum Dei*' ('Totila the scourge of God': the confusion with Attila is evident).[6] The story stresses Totila's determination to re-found Fiesole, the settlement symbolic of the defiance of Rome and of good governance; it also tells how he destroyed Florence and numerous other Roman settlements in

Tuscany, Romagna, Lombardy and the Marches.[7] Barbarian victory over Italian urban culture, though devastating, was nonetheless short-lived. The legends go on to tell how the Romans, after Totila's death, re-founded Florence, this time using astrological calculations to ensure a propitious future for the revived city. Dante's familiarity with this part of the story is demonstrated in his allusions to '*que' cittadin che poi la rifondarno | sovra 'l cener che d'Attila rimase*' ('those citizens who afterwards rebuilt it [i.e. Florence] on the ashes left by Attila': *Inf.* XIII. 148–149). Once again, the legends recount that noble Roman families settled the town and built new city monuments to mimic Roman ones, this time constructing churches that corresponded to the basilicas of Rome, with the church of the revived Christian city's patron, St John the Baptist, in pride of place.[8] Eventually, Florence grew strong enough to lead another victorious attack upon Fiesole, culminating once again in the latter's destruction and the Fiesolans' resettlement in Florence.

These legends of Florentine foundation and re-foundation ascribe aristocratic origins to the city, achieving glamour through the intervention of Julius Caesar and of the Roman patriciate in the various crises of civic fortunes and dignifying the city's topography by stressing its Roman aspect. Medieval Florentines often described their city as a second Rome: for instance, an inscription placed on the façade of the city governor's palace around 1265 boasted that, '*Est quia cunctorum Florentia plena bonorum, | […] que mare, que terram, que totum possidet orbem; | […] tamquam Roma sedet semper ductura triumphos*' ('Florence is full of all goods, she possesses the sea, the land and the whole globe, like Rome she presides over triumphs always').[9] As the city achieved increasing territorial and financial pre-eminence, the chronicler Giovanni Villani was even able to claim that Florence had outdone the mother-city, observing that by 1300, '*la nostra città di Firenze, figliuola e fattura di Roma, era nel suo montare e a seguire grandi cose, sì come Roma nel suo calare*' ('our city of Florence, daughter and creature of Rome, was on the rise and pursuing great things, just as Rome was in decline': *Nuova cronica* IX. 36).[10] Various civic monuments were confidently (though often mistakenly) identified as Roman in origin, such as old city walls or defence towers, the remains of the amphitheatre area, or more improbably, the Baptistery. The church was supposedly built on the site of, or even converted from, the pagan cult temple of Mars; the supposed cult idol was also superstitiously preserved near the Ponte Vecchio.[11] These notionally antique remains appeared to offer visible corroboration of the stories about the Roman grandeur of Florence's foundation and re-foundation.

But although the city's foundation legends provided justification for claims to civic glory, the heritage they outlined also contained more ambiguous elements. The city's early association with Mars, the pagan god of war, suggested to the mid-Duecento commentator Brunetto Latini that Florentines had a natural propensity towards violence:

> La place de tiere ou Florence est fu jadis apelee chiés Mars, c'est a dire
> maisons de batailles. [...] Por ce n'est il mie merveille se li florentin
> sont tozjors en guerre et en descort, car celui planete regne sor aus.
>
> (Tresor, I. xxxvii. 2–3)

> The site where Florence is was formerly called the field of Mars, that is, the house of war. For this reason, it is not surprising that the Florentines are always at war and in discord, for this planet rules over them.

Compagni too, as we saw, mentioned the influence of Mars over the city as well as commenting on the Florentines' combative nature.[12] Others – Giovanni Villani, for instance – viewed the settlement of the Fiesolans at Florence as introducing the permanent potential for unrest in the city, by producing a mixed population of whom half owed sympathy to Rome but the other half to Rome's bellicose enemies, Catiline and Totila.[13]

In various works, Dante too alludes to both the genealogical and the astrological explanations for Florence's tendency towards civil war. In *Inferno*, the ghost of a Florentine suicide alludes to Mars as

Florence's *'primo padrone | [che ...] sempre con l'arte sua la farà trista'* ('first patron, who with his art will ever make her sorrowful':XIII. 144–145), while in *Paradiso*, a vendetta murder carried out in the vicinity of the supposed cult statue of Mars is described as the city's sacrifice of a ritual victim to the war-god (XVI. 145–147). Interestingly, when Dante makes the shade of Brunetto Latini refer to Florentine bellicosity, he turns not to the astrological theory proposed by the historical Brunetto in the *Tresor*, but to the legend of Fiesolan resettlement, denouncing the *'ingrato popolo maligno | che discese di Fiesole'* ('thankless, malignant people who came down from Fiesole': *Inf.* XV. 61–62) or *'bestie fiesolane'* ('Fiesolan beasts': l.73), who persecute the descendants of *'la sementa santa | di que' Roman che vi rimaser'* ('the holy seed of those Romans who remained there': ll.76–77). Outside the *Commedia*, Dante's comment on the foreign Prince Charles of Valois, whose alliance with his faction-enemies led to the poet's own exile, casts Charles in the role of Fiesole's barbarian ally Totila: *'eiecta maxima parte florum de sinu tuo, Florentia, nequicquam Trinacriam Totila secundus adivit'* ('the greater part of your flowers, O Florence, having been snatched from your breast, the second Totila advanced in vain towards Trinacria': *DVE* II. vi. 4). In his letter of reproach to the Florentines for holding out against the forces of the Holy Roman Empire in 1311, Dante casts the struggle as a replay of the Fiesolan–Roman tensions of the legendary past: *'O miserrima Fesulanorum propago, et iterum iam punita barbaries!'* ('O most wretched offshoot of Fiesole, barbarians now punished once more!': *Ep.* VI. 24). His message seems to be that whenever the Fiesolan Florentines get the upper hand over the Roman ones – who clearly include himself – destruction ensues.

Just as in the *Convivio* passage cited above (I. iii. 4), so in these examples Dante's interpretation of the legends of Florentine origins stresses the kinship between Florence and Rome, suggesting that Florentine governance is ideally compatible with that of the Rome of its founder, Caesar, and of the imperial authority inherited by the contemporary Holy Roman Empire, and that disaster follows whenever the Rome–Florence tie is broken. The Florentine foundation legends, therefore, provide a logical background to his wider conviction that the aims and ideals of city life are compatible with acceptance, and indeed enjoyment, of imperial authority.

LA CITTÀ PARTITA: DIVIDING UP MEDIEVAL FLORENCE

Dante's engagement with the myths of origin leads him to represent Florence as a city often divided within itself – a '*città partita*', as he puts it (*Inf.* VI. 61). Division was indeed a characteristic feature of medieval Florentine experience: and not only in the city's political structures but also, in a broader sense, in most of the city's social and topographical ones. It was not hard for rivalry to emerge between different parts of the population when the built environment of the city was divided into distinct neighbourhoods and its inhabitants channelled the majority of their activities through associative sub-groupings of an often exclusive kind. Administrative, military, commercial, familial and religious ties bound the citizens of medieval Florence to one another; but also exerted competitive pressures between them.[14] Trade guilds, for instance, created bonds between individuals exercising the same craft or profession, but the guilds also served to concentrate and extend the power and prominence of their members, who were often viewed askance by aristocratic families accustomed to influence and mistrustful of mercantile values (although there were also aristocrats who plunged enthusiastically into trade). Spatial division of the city into neighbourhoods – six separate *sestieri* in Dante's age – made for administrative convenience, but wealthy families could build up territorial holdings and patronage patterns within one *sestiere* to menace central control. Visually, the often fortress-like buildings, crowned with aggressive towers, used by lineage groups, guilds, political parties and the city authorities, presented a threatening aspect and were decorated with symbols and coats of arms that appealed to particular (and often conflicting) loyalties, building incitements to rivalry or violence into the cityscape.[15]

Competition between different elements in the population manifested itself in many ways, but most notoriously in the rivalry for political power that dominated Florentine public life throughout the thirteenth and fourteenth centuries, and which deeply troubled Dante. Similar rivalries also afflicted many other Tuscan and Italian towns, so that once again the Florentine experience could be translated into his broader analysis of city life in general. In these urban centres, political life was dominated by clashes between groups of citizens variously aligned according to social background, lineage interests and alliances, or notional ideological affiliation to the wider causes of the empire or the papacy. Family and ideological interests were, indeed, often hard to distinguish; Florentine historiography in fact drew direct connections between them. In the chronicles that continued the story of Florence from the Roman period towards more contemporary times, accounts of how organised political factions first evolved in Florence ascribed the cause to tensions between aristocratic families in the early Duecento.

This tradition asserted that around 1215, the young nobleman Bondelmonte dei Bondelmonti abruptly broke off his betrothal to a daughter of a branch of the Amidei family, and married into the Donati family instead. The outraged Amidei, supported by members of other noble houses, murdered Bondelmonte in revenge, and thus initiated a cycle of vendetta.[16] Dante makes several allusions to the story, linking it in *Paradiso* XVI to the domination of Mars over Florence, and assigning a place in hell to Mosca dei Lamberti, the Amidei ally who allegedly instigated the first murder with his advice, "'*Capo ha cosa fatta*'" ("'A thing done has an end'": *Inf.* XXVIII. 107). The chroniclers agree that the vendetta-oriented family alliances developed into organised political factions, concentrating local rivalries into two opposing groups that became aligned with the broader contemporary hostilities between the Emperor Frederick II and the papacy. The Bondelmonti faction thus became known as the Guelfs, supporting the pope and the Angevin claimants to Frederick's kingdom in southern Italy; the pro-imperial faction led by the Amidei and their chief allies the Uberti, was labelled Ghibelline.

Whatever the original cause of the Guelf–Ghibelline conflict, it certainly absorbed much of the energies of the Florentine ruling classes in the 1230s and 1240s, as the struggle between Frederick II and the papal–Angevin alliance grew more intense. The factions – often forming alliances with sympathetic forces from outside the city – competed to control the councils of the republican *comune*, and to ensure that the outsider annually elected to govern the city as *podestà* came from their own party. In *Inferno*, Dante makes the ghost of the great Ghibelline leader, Farinata degli Uberti, celebrate his party's triumphant expulsions of the Guelfs from Florence in 1248 and 1260, but Dante-character in turn recalls the retaliatory Guelf banishments of the Ghibellines in 1250 and 1266 (*Inf.* X. 48–51). Dante's frequent condemnations of the activities of both parties suggest a strong degree of scepticism about their notional ideological motivations. When, in *Paradiso*, he describes what he sees as the city's era of greatest prosperity, he looks back to a time before 1215 when a pro-imperial but non-partisan government led by the urban aristocracy governed Florence harmoniously, before familial competition had introduced vendetta among the city's leaders.

Political division in Duecento Florence encompassed not only rivalries between powerful aristocratic families, but also social competition between the established ruling élite and the so-called 'new men' or *popolani* whose wealth derived from trade and professional activities. In 1250, when Ghibelline control of Florence was destabilised by the death of Frederick II, these new men formed the backbone of the *Popolo* movement that toppled the government of Farinata and his allies and instituted a programme of reform aimed at unifying the city, eliminating organised factions, and representing and promoting the interests and status of the non-aristocratic citizenship – hence the name *Popolo*, 'the people'. The *Popolo* organised neighbourhood militias to circumvent vendetta by policing the city and containing public disturbances, and they instituted their own governor, the *Capitano del*

Popolo, whose authority overrode the *podestà*'s.[17] As a symbol of the new regime's authority, the city's first purpose-built government palace was constructed, the Palazzo del Capitano del Popolo (today called the Bargello). It was to the façade of this imposing building that the inscription boasting of Florence's Rome-like supremacy on land and sea (mentioned earlier) was subsequently affixed – although by then, the palace was occupied by the *podestà*, government having reverted to aristocratic control.

The decade of relative stability achieved by the *Popolo* regime came to be viewed by many Florentines of Dante's generation as a kind of golden age (Dante, however, located the golden age in a more remote era) of civic peace and of a material prosperity symbolised by the inauguration of the golden florin currency in 1252. The *Popolo* experiment however collapsed in 1260, under a resurgence of factionalism, and the city returned to aristocratic government headed once again by a *podestà* and controlled first by the Ghibellines (1260–1266) and then by the Guelfs (1267–1280). In 1280, after extensive negotiations presided over by Cardinal Latini of Rome, the Guelfs and the Ghibellines were formally pacified and the latter re-admitted to the city (though some particularly detested families, such as the Uberti, remained excluded) – but under conditions that guaranteed the survival of Guelf political predominance.

By 1282 the kind of groups who had contributed to the *Popolo* movement returned to the political foreground, when a new governmental reform instituted a constitution based on the membership of the guilds. Control of the *comune* shifted from the *podestà* to six priors elected from the most powerful guilds, and representing the different *sestieri*. The priors' legislative programme, like the *Popolo*'s, attempted to foster unity and prevent civil strife, and particularly to protect the less privileged classes (the *popolo minuto*, or 'little people') from the arrogance of the most powerful aristocratic families and their mercantile associates (the *popolo grasso*, or 'fat people'). These families, however, still supplied most of the candidates for the priorate: growing resentment over their high-handed conduct of government culminated with a further reform to the city constitution, embodied in the Ordinances of Justice of 1293, instigated by the popular leader Giano della Bella (himself, ironically, from the ancient nobility). The Ordinances made eligibility for government conditional not only on membership of a guild, but also on the practical exercise of its trade, while members of families from the knightly caste, the so-called 'magnates', were debarred from government.[18]

In 1295 della Bella was toppled from government, and the reforms relaxed. Figures like Dante himself, who was a member of a minor, non-magnate noble family and was enrolled in the Guild of Physicians and Apothecaries but never practised any branch of its trades, became eligible for office. Dante was quick to take advantage of the new situation, and by the end of 1295 was serving on different government councils and contributing to policy debates.[19] By the time he wrote the *Paradiso*, Dante would comment with some contempt on della Bella's abandonment of the '*milizia e privilegio*' ('knighthood and privilege': *Par.* XVI. 130) of his aristocratic ancestry to range himself '*con popol*' ('with the people/the *Popolo*': l.131), and was anxious to claim ancient and privileged origins for his own family, the Alighieri, by making his great-great-grandfather a knight, a crusader, and a loyal companion of the Holy Roman Emperor (*Par.* XV. 134–148). Yet in 1295 he sat on the committee dedicated to overseeing reforms to the election of the priors – admittedly under the less radical rules of the post-della Bella regime – and in 1296, is recorded as approving legislation defending office-holding *popolani* against insults or attacks from magnates, suggesting that at this period he was a willing supporter of the consensual, mercantile outlook embraced (at least in theory) by the guild-based government.

Although the reforms of the 1290s seem to have represented genuine attempts at recapturing the stability of the mid-century *Popolo* movement – della Bella's regime even became known as the *Secondo Popolo* – the decade also saw the resurgence of organised factionalism and open rivalries among members of the aristocratic caste. As in the original Guelf–Ghibelline confrontations of the early

Duecento, groups of families banded together around two young and ambitious rivals, Vieri dei Cerchi and Corso Donati. Giving the lie to the apparent unanimity of Florentine Guelfism, they split into two distinct factions, the Cerchi supporters known as Whites and the Donati as Blacks. Historians can offer few clear social, economic or ideological distinctions between the two faction groups, which each attracted support from *popolani* and aristocracy to their side. As in the legend of Bondelmonte's murder in 1215, personal and familial interest probably played the greatest part in the polarising of the ruling clans, although eventually the Black faction came to be seen as standing for the kind of convinced support for papal and Angevin politics that had originally been associated with pure Guelfism, while the Whites adopted an attitude of greater independence from the papacy (though not, at least as yet, being associated with Ghibelline-style out-and-out imperialism).[20] Dante, whose political career continued to flourish, became aligned with the more moderate position of the Whites, and generally took a sceptical line over papal demands in his recorded interventions in public debates and in the policies pursued when he served as one of the priors, in July and August 1300.[21]

After several years of growing tension between the two factions, the governments of 1299–1300 attempted to calm the situation by exiling both Black and White leaders from the city and by accepting the papal appointee Cardinal Aquasparta as peacemaker between the factions – however, the latter's pro-Black bias (inevitable in a papal representative) made peace uneasy. During 1300, despite the call to Christian peace and reconciliation associated with Pope Boniface VIII's pronouncement of a Holy Year or Jubilee, both Black factionalism within Florence and papal ambitions beyond continued to gather strength. Despite White embassies to the pope in 1300 and 1301, the latter at least probably including Dante in its number, Boniface continued his partisan policy, appointing Aquasparta and also his French ally Charles of Valois, to missions of so-called pacification aimed in fact at achieving Black domination of the priorate and other government offices.

After several months of rioting, this policy was realised. Sentences of exile were pronounced against numerous White politicians including, in January 1302, an edict banishing Dante along with several other recent office-holders on the charges of barratry (financial corruption), and of opposition to papal and Angevin policies in Tuscany and Sicily. The exile proved permanent: Dante was never to return to Florence. The city, however, continued to preoccupy his political interests and imagination – the urgency of his exile writings on the vexed issues of political faction and of civic unity reveal a political outlook that retains the marks of Florentine experience, even when engaged with far wider-ranging philosophical issues.

THE MYTH OF COMMUNITY:
POLITICAL RHETORIC AND CONCEPTS OF THE CITY IN
DUECENTO WRITING ON GOVERNANCE

Given the continual constitutional and ideological upheaval that Dante had known in Florence between 1265 and 1302, it is small wonder that when he looked back at his native city from exile he should label it '*la città partita*' ('the divided city': *Inf.* VI. 61) *par excellence*. He could refer to its perilous inheritance of bellicosity and political intolerance through reference to the legends of Mars's astrological influence, and of tensions between descendants of Fiesole and of Rome. In the theoretical remarks on government that he recorded in exile both in *Convivio* and *Monarchia*, a heartfelt interest in the elimination of such civic discord as he had known in Florence seems to lie behind his enthusiasm for an emperor's central authority to maintain the rule of law. Yet these tracts continue to display a keen awareness of the importance of city life, and a concern that citizens should not rely passively on imperial direction but participate responsibly and reflectively in the public life of their local communities. This suggests that he retained the imprint of much of the civic rhetoric of the Duecento *comune* (especially of its *Popolo* and guild-based regimes), which repeatedly promoted an

ideal of consensus, participation and civic brotherhood, despite –
or perhaps because of – the glaringly obvious divisions within the
citizen body. The same political ideals, moreover, were advocated
not only in Florence but also in the majority of other Italian free
comuni, forming a kind of shared civic ethos. A brief consideration
of such typical civic rhetoric will provide a useful conclusion to
our discussion of the urban forms that helped shape Dante's civic
consciousness.

Republican *comuni* such as Florence, admitting no direct allegiance to any superior secular or ecclesiastical power, were relatively common in Italy in the thirteenth century, but
constitutionally anomalous in the wider European context. Legally
speaking, the position of cities governing and legislating for themselves ran counter to all the principles of the Roman *Corpus Iuris
Civilis* and also to the Lombard and feudal systems of law that had
been brought to Italy since the barbarian invasions, all of which
presupposed a political administration based broadly on monarchical hierarchy.[22] The cities themselves were often content with *de
facto* rather than *de iure* independence, but when opportunities arose
– as at the Peace of Constance in 1183 – they were keen to obtain
imperial recognition of their rights to self-government. The opin-
ion of academic jurists at Bologna and other Italian universities was
unanimous in upholding the authority of the Roman civil code,
with inevitably pro-imperial consequences – at least until Bartolus
formulated the precept of the '*civitas sibi princeps*' ('city acting as
emperor unto itself'),[23] and arguably even afterwards – but at the
same time, other branches of academic study in Italy were developing disciplines with more immediate applicability to *comune* life.

The study of rhetoric, in particular, developed along lines that
carried it ever further towards practical use in the arena of republican politics, and even produced some, perhaps rather elliptical,
attempts to define the distinguishing characteristics of the city as a
political form.[24] In the thirteenth century, Italian instruction in
rhetoric focused on the *ars dictandi* (art of epistolary rhetoric) and
the *ars arengandi* (art of public speaking), both skills eminently fitted

for use in the public life of the *comuni*, where the frequent exchange of letters and the even more frequent practice of public oratory and council debate gave rhetorical studies obvious practical application. The widely practised *podestà* system, which placed city government under the control of a non-native elected for a year, or even just for six months, developed a need for standardised rhetorical and governmental formulae adapted to city use, given the rapid turnover of a personnel constantly imported from the outside; conciliar debate between the citizens provided a further context for the exercise of formal rhetoric at all levels of the administration. Participants in government needed oratorical skill in the courtroom and the council chamber, but also in relations with the city at large. It was important to use public oratory to remind the disenfranchised majority of the population about the high-minded principles governing the city, the party in power and the individuals holding office.[25] As is attested by the fairly substantial body of literature on city government aimed at *podestà* in particular that survives, rhetoric played a central part in the public life of the cities; it constituted one of the main defences against factionalism envisaged by those who first set out to instruct Italian citizens on how to tackle the characteristic challenges of *comune* government.[26]

Dante could well have known two of the most famous of these texts, directly or indirectly, as they had a direct Florentine connection. Giovanni da Viterbo composed his *Liber de Regimine Civitatis* (*Book on City Government*) while serving in the *podestà's* retinue at Florence some time around the 1250s or 1260s, while Brunetto Latini tells us that he composed his *Livres dou Tresor* (*Book of Treasure*) in the French vernacular during his exile from Florence in the 1260s; he brought it back with him when he returned to resume his highly successful political career in 1267.[27] The third book of Brunetto's encyclopaedic 'treasury' of knowledge is dedicated to '*politike, ki ensegne coment on doit governer la cité*' ('politics, which teaches how one should govern a city': III. i. 1). The material is divided into two sections, the first a '*Livres de bone parleure*' ('Book of good speech': III. 1–LXXII) on rhetoric, while the second

is essentially a manual for prospective *podestà*, entitled '*Dou gov-
ernement des cités*' ('On city government': III. lxxiii–cv), and probably related to Giovanni da Viterbo's Latin text.[28] Latini makes it
clear that the two parts of Book III are fundamentally connected,
citing Cicero in his assertion that:

> *la plus haute science de cité governer si est rectorique, c'est a dire la sci-
> ence du parler; car se parleure ne fust cités ne seroit, ne nus establisse-
> mens de justice ne de humaine compaignie.*
>
> (*Tresor*, III. i. 2)

> the highest art of city government is rhetoric, that is the art of
> speaking; for cities would not exist were it not for speech, nor
> any regime of justice or of human fellowship.[29]

Latini's identification of rhetoric as the highest civic art is
backed up by his appropriation of the narrative of political origins
set out by Cicero in the rhetorical treatise *De inventione* (I. ii. 2–3).[30]
This tells how humanity is rescued from a state of nature, living '*a
loi de bestes*' ('after the manner of beasts'), by enlightened counsel:

> *Uns sages hom bien parlans [...] tant consilla les autres et tant lor
> moustra la grandour de l'ame et la dignité de la raison [...], qu'il les
> retraist de ces sauvegines, et les aombra a abiter en .i. lieu et a garder
> raison et justice.*
>
> (*Tresor*, III. i. 7)

> A wise man and good speaker so counselled the others and
> demonstrated to them the greatness of the soul and the dignity
> of reason that he drew them away from this wildness and gath-
> ered them to live in one place and to respect reason and justice.

Significantly, the same story also appears earlier in the *Tresor*, during
the second book's discussion of vices and virtues, where it occurs
in a chapter on justice (II. lxxxxi. 1). Thus Latini makes rhetoric

fundamental not only to government, but to *just* government – and this helps mitigate the problematic moral neutrality of rhetoric, the pliable art of persuasion that Brunetto acknowledges can be a *'mauvaise art'* ('evil art') if exercised *'sans sapience'* ('without wisdom': III. i. 9). By stressing the necessity that the civic rhetorician possess wisdom and justice, Brunetto can assume that he will exercise his art beneficially and avoid committing such *peccata linguae* as encouraging discord – even though his rhetorical section includes instructions on persuading an audience to accept *'vilh matire'* ('vile subjects': III. xxi) and *'douteuse matire'* ('dubious subjects': III. xxii).[31]

The *Tresor*, to be sure, also offers a brief Aristotelian account of the origins of political organisation: *'naturele chose est a l'home k'il soit citeins et k'il se converse entre les homes [...]; et contre nature seroit habiter es desers ou n'a point de gent'* ('it is natural to man to be a citizen and to live together with other men; and it would be against nature to live in the desert where there are no other people': II. v. 2). Brunetto's awareness of at least Aristotle's *Nicomachaean Ethics*, which was just beginning to circulate in Latin translation, is demonstrated by a number of references throughout the *Tresor*; indeed, a large section of Book II is effectively a vulgarisation of this work (II. ii–xxxxviiii).[32] However, Latini is clearly more attracted by the Ciceronian account of the coercive origins of political life, and of the almost heroic discovery of reason, justice, and wise eloquence – perhaps because the story's emphasis on the natural mutual hostility of human beings accords better with his experience of Florentine politics. Certainly, the introduction to the governmental section of Book III stresses the idea of the state as a *remedium peccati*:

> *Des lors ke gens commencierent premierement a croistre [...] et ke li pechié dou premier home s'enracina sor son linage et ke li siecles enpira durement si ke li un covoitoient les choses a lor voisins [...] il covint a fine force ke cil ki voloient vivre de lor droit et eschiver la force des maufeteurs se tornaissent ensamble en .i. lieu et en .i. ordre.*
>
> (*Tresor*, III. lxxiii. 2)

Ever since humanity first began to grow and the sin of the first man became embedded in his lineage and the world declined so much that people envied their neighbours' goods, it has perforce been necessary that those who want to live under their own laws and avoid malefactors should come together in one place and under one disposition.[33]

And in another comment that confirms, subliminally, the links between both rhetoric and government as responses to sin, a reference to the story of Nimrod and Babel, normally associated with ideas about *linguistic* diversity, is used to explain how it is that different *political* forms have developed in different societies.[34]

These remarks lead into Brunetto's analysis of different types of polity, which culminates with a brief description of the distinguishing characteristics of the Italian *comune* regime. First, he gives a quick sketch of different European forms of rule: kings and princes rule for life through dynastic inheritance; the pope and emperor are elected to exercise lifelong power; city officials are nominated or elected to rule for a single year. Of the latter, Brunetto asserts that princes normally sell city governorships for cash, and seldom have the citizens' welfare in mind when appointing the official. But in the Italian cities,

> *li citain et li borgois et li communité des viles eslisent lor poesté et lor signour tel comme il quident qu'il soit plus proufitables au commun preu de la vile et de tous lors subtés.*
>
> (*Tresor*, III. lxxiii. 6)

the citizens and the burghers and the *comune* of the cities elect their *podestà* and their lord as they believe will be most profitable to the common good of the city and of all their subjects.

His analysis emphasises the *comune*'s powers of self-determination, and also the moral bond of citizenly interdependence that forces the republican citizen to reflect on the common good, unlike the self-serving and profit-driven attitude of a prince to his subject cities. Giovanni da Viterbo too, although less analytical than Brunetto of constitutional matters, notes that *'civitates hodie vivunt ad constituta, que sibi faciunt'* ('cities today live according to constitutions, that they make for themselves': 136), and stresses, in a passage lifted bodily from Cicero's *De Officiis* (I. 85), that:

> *duo precepta [...] tenenda sunt prelatis, unum ut utilitatem civium [...] tueantur [...]; alterum est ut totum corpus civitatis curent, ne dum partem aliquam tueantur reliquas deserant.*
>
> (*De Regimine*, 130)

> city leaders should remember two rules: one, to protect the good of the citizens; the other, to look after the whole of the body politic, so that in serving one part they should not neglect the remainder.

Giovanni shares Brunetto's concern with government as service of the common good, but his citation of *De Officiis* also confronts the bugbear of non-commonality, or political faction. Both Giovanni and Brunetto in fact acknowledge regretfully the fact that *podestà* will, more often than not, have to deal with situations of civic discord: the protective walls and laws of the city often fail to restrain the underlying savagery of the Ciceronian natural man. Giovanni three times notes that *'vix enim aliqua reperitur hodie civitas, que inter se non sit divisa'* ('today one can scarcely find a city that is not divided against itself': 72, also II. 73), and Brunetto presents this as a typically Italian problem: *'guerre et haine est si multepliee entre les ytaliens au tans d'ore, [...] k'il a devision en trestoutes les viles et enemistié entre les .ii. parties des borgois'* ('war and hatred have so multiplied among Italians in our time, that there is division in almost every town and enmity between the two parties of the burghers': III. lxxv. 15.) The *podestà* is urged to combat factionalism through rhetoric, re-enacting the role of the Ciceronian *'sages parleour'* ('wise speaker': III. lxxxii. 15) in public addresses that stress the horrors of war and that use historical example to bring the message home: '*die comment concorde essauce les viles et enrichist les borgois, et guerre les destruit; et ramentevoir Romme et les autres bonnes viles ki por la guerre dedens sont decheues et mal alees*' ('he should say how concord elevates the city and enriches the burghers, and war destroys them; and recall Rome and other good cities that due to civil war have been brought low and come to grief': III. lxxxii. 9). Both Brunetto and Giovanni agree that the *podestà* should devote considerable energy to the task of encouraging citizenly concord;[35] but Brunetto also warns that pacification attempts can be dangerous:

> *Se la vile se descorde u dedens u dehors, il se doit molt travillier por avoir la pais, se ce ne fust de tel maniere que si citain ne voelent pas k'il s'en melle; car li sires se doit mout garder k'il ne chie en la haine ou en la suspection de sa gens.*
>
> (*Tresor*, III. lxxxiii. 5)

> If the city is in disaccord, for either external or internal rea-
> sons, he must work hard to procure peace, unless the situation
> is such that the citizens don't want him to interfere; for the
> lord must take care not to fall under the hatred or suspicion of
> his people.

The public prominence of the city governor is what exposes him to possible suspicion, but also lays on him the necessity of speaking and acting at all times so as to serve the common good. Giovanni and Brunetto remind prospective *podestà* repeatedly that they are to provide models of good conduct to the populace, and restrain human iniquity as much by example and precept, as by action. Both writers offer detailed checklists of the personal qualities the *podestà* should cultivate or repress so as best to fulfil his role, Giovanni not-ing that '*cessantibus virtutibus in preside, cesset bonus effectus regiminis*' ('when the virtues of the governor are lost, the good effects of his rule are also lost': 11). Governance, Brunetto remarks, is upheld by '*trois pilers, c'est de justice et de reverence et d'amor*' ('three pillars, that is, by justice, by reverence, and by love': III. LXXIIII. I). Mutual respect and love are fundamental to the civic bond tying governor and subjects together; they are acquired and guaranteed by the wise leader's understanding of justice, that civilising, Ciceronian virtue, propagated by law and by the rhetoric that provides the very *raison d'être* of the body politic in Brunetto's view.

In the connections that they trace between the exercise of rhetoric, wisdom, justice and law, and in their emphasis on government as service of the common good, Brunetto and Giovanni articulate an admirably orderly vision of how city government should be exercised by the *podestà*. Giovanni da Viterbo, whose text is composed in Latin, probably addresses himself to a fairly specialised, professional audience (even though he claims that '*rudes vero et indoctos in eodem opusculo fideliter edoceri non pigeat*', 'I do not hesitate to offer faithful instruction to the rude and inexpert in this work', *De Regimine*, Introduction). Brunetto, however, is writing in a vernacular language that he states to be widely accessible, its form of French being '*plus delitable et plus commune a tous langages*' ('the most pleasant and the most commonly comprehensible of all languages': I. i. 7), and by inserting his remarks on cities and government into a broader, encyclopaedic work, he seems to be seeking a wide audience for his political ideas. The text was translated into Florentine, as the *Tesoro*, after Brunetto's return to Italy in 1266, thus helping to propagate in his native town the vision of peace, concord and justice that Latini so urgently proposes as the keynotes of city government.[36] Brunetto's own terms in office as a civil servant, chancellor and prior likewise provided plenty of opportunity for the practical exercise, and hence public dissemination, of the political rhetoric codified in the *Tresor*. However, given the turbulent conditions in Florence during his public career – given, indeed, that factionalism forced him to spend six years in exile – his belief in the redeeming powers of rhetoric seems over-optimistic, with the governmental section of the *Tresor* sitting somewhat at odds with the frank acknowledgements, elsewhere in the text, of the political instability of Florence and the Florentines (I. xxxvii, cited above), and of the Italian cities in general (III. xxv. 15, above).

CIVIC RHETORICIANS IN THE *COMMEDIA*

In the *Commedia*, Dante famously includes an encounter in hell, between his narrative *persona* and the ghost of Brunetto Latini, in which the latter urges him to read '*il mio Tesoro*' ('my *Treasure*': *Inf.* XV. 119). Dante-character greets the great politician with affection and reverence, commenting on how he has remembered Brunetto and his moral or intellectual guidance, cherishing '*la cara e buona imagine paterna | di voi quando […] | m'insegnavate come l'uom s'etterna*' ('the dear, kind, paternal image of you when you taught me how man makes himself eternal': ll.83–85). Brunetto in turn, using the powers of partial prophecy available to the dead, tells Dante-character that his faction-enemies in Florence are going to persecute him, calling the city a '*nido di malizia*' ('nest of wickedness': l.78), but that an honourable fortune ultimately awaits him (ll.55–78). Despite this exchange of compliments, it is impossible to overlook the fact that Brunetto is in hell and that he carries the outward markers of sin on his naked and disfigured body, burnt by the fiery rain of this circle. The episode is notoriously hard to interpret, with even the identification of Brunetto's fault hotly disputed among scholars;[37] indisputably, however, the overall effect of the passage is to create tension around the figure of Brunetto, the ostensibly respectable Florentine politician so shockingly condemned to hell.

The encounter with Brunetto forms part of a series of encounters in *Inferno* between Dante-character and leading figures from recent Florentine history, with whom he exchanges reflections on Florentine political values. These politicians, all active between the 1240s and the 1290s, are associated with the period of political transformation in Florence that saw the emergence of the *Popolo* movement and the gradual decline of the power of *podestà*, whose nominations were increasingly controlled by the political factions. Although the *Primo Popolo* and the later guild regimes advocated new means of social control, the chief aims articulated by their leaders – protection of the people, service of the common good and repression of civil discord – conformed closely to those of *podestà* rule as expressed in Brunetto's and Giovanni's texts. Public speaking continued to hold great importance in the different regimes, and justice, concord and peace remained key terms in the political rhetoric of all sides. Dante's representation in *Inferno* of leading figures from these regimes invites reflection on the words and the deeds that had shaped Florentine political experience over the previous fifty years. Through these Florentine examples, Dante begins to explore the typical points of tension that can bring disorder into the society of *any* city.

In his very first meeting in hell with a fellow citizen, though he is an obscure one – the historical identity of Ciacco the glutton remains unclear – Dante-character eagerly asks about the destiny of Florence. He learns that its two parties *'verranno al sangue'* ('will come to blood': l.65), in further faction-fighting. Looking back to the past, the protagonist next asks the eternal fate of a number of Florentine politicians of high reputation, who *'fuor sì degni, | [...] e [...] a ben far puoser li 'ngegni'* ('were so worthy and who set their minds on doing good': ll.79–81). Ciacco however tells him that those he names were all sinners now confined to hell, indeed *'tra l'anime più nere'* ('among the blackest souls': l.85). Dante-character will encounter their shades as the journey progresses.

The first one he meets is the Ghibelline leader, Farinata degli Uberti: as mentioned earlier, his exchanges with Dante-character focus mainly on the linked issues of party and family ancestry and allude explicitly to faction violenceof the past, present and future. An element of rhetorical interest may perhaps be found in Farinata's praise for Dante's honourable manner of speaking (*'onesto'*: *Inf.* X. 23) and ready identification of his Florentine linguistic origins; more significantly, Farinata alludes proudly to the rhetorical skill with which he personally dissuaded his Ghibelline allies at the council of Empoli from their proposed destruction of Florence (ll.91–93).[38] Later on, and immediately after the meeting with Brunetto Latini, three other Florentines appear, whose reputations Dante-character once again praises: *'sempre mai | l'ovra di voi e li onorati nomi | con affezion ritrassi e ascoltai'* ('always have I rehearsed and heard with affection your deeds and honoured names': *Inf.* XVI. 58–60). The political practice of two of the spirits is reviewed, one, Tegghiaio Aldobrandini, being attributed rhetorical skill that perhaps went unappreciated – *'la cui voce | nel mondo sù dovria esser gradita'* ('whose voice should have been prized up in the world': ll.41–42) – while his companion Guido Guerra exercised his rhetorical and martial skills more effectively:*'fece col senno assai e con la spada'* ('he did much with counsel and with sword':l.39).[39] In answer to the query whether *'cortesia e valor'* ('courtesy and valour':l.67) are still practised in Florence, Dante-character replies that such qualities have been abandoned, thanks to the supremacy of *'la gente nuova e i sùbiti guadagni'* ('the new people and the sudden gains':l.73).

The worthy deeds that Dante-character's remarks to Ciacco initially associated with the leadership of an earlier generation begin to be deconstructed through these encounters. Each episode shows some interest in rhetorical matters, as well as in discussing whether Florence's future is likely to be prosperous or marred by faction-conflict. Dante-author makes both Brunetto and Farinata refer to rhetorical performances in which they defended non-partisan civic values: respectively, the *Tresor*, with its long section on virtuous government providing a written manifesto for service of the common good, and the speech at Empoli that protected Florence's physical integrity against faction-motivated destruction. Yet outside the pages of the *Commedia*, the two men are historically associated with intensely partisan politics, having taken leading positions in aggressively Guelf and Ghibelline administrations. As for what we learn about Tegghiaio Aldobrandini and Guido Guerra, the former seems to be indicated as an ineffective rhetorician, while the latter relied not only on words but also on acts of violence, executed with the sword. Historically, both men were prominent within the Guelf party and active in the same faction-clashes between Guelf and Ghibelline forces as Farinata and Brunetto. The inclusive, public-spirited speech conventions of the *comune* have in fact in all of these cases, not just Guerra's, been allied to the sword, and have failed to achieve the suppression of natural vice envisaged by Brunetto in the *Tresor* as one of the principal aims of political oratory and of good governance.

In the *Inferno*'s probing of Florence's history, thirteenth-century unrest is traced back by the ghost of Brunetto to the very origins of the city. In his speech, the power of a myth of predestined civil discord, set out in Florentine foundation legend, eclipses the myth of community promoted by the thirteenth-century *podestà* and priorate. However, we should not forget that these historical, political, and rhetorical reflections, like those of Farinata, Tegghiaio, and Guerra, have been placed in the mouth of the damned: the parodically Pentecostal tongues of fire that flicker around each speaker perhaps carry a warning against taking their words as authoritative.[40] In representing the imperfections of rhetorical performances by these shades of the political leaders of the 1240s to 1290s, Dante can offer a critique of the re-orderings of the Florentine polity attempted both by the *Popolo* and by the regimes of the immediate past. None of them managed to find long-term solutions to civic discord, and all can be seen to have succumbed to some social or political bias that destabilised their authority. The governments that Dante himself historically served inherited the rhetorical optimism of their predecessors, and continued to experiment with changing political forms in their search for administrative security; but they also ultimately failed to neutralise party spirit and social tension. Dante-author, representing the encounter of his active political self of 1300, Dante-character, with those who had formatively shaped the structures and the rhetoric of the Florentine polity that he knew, passes severe judgement on their achievements and on the traditions that they represent.

The *Inferno* thus points towards the need to break the interpretative mould of convention and to seek a fresh encounter with the history, politics and rhetoric of Florence and of civil society at large. The city politics of Florence provide an urgent illustration of wider problems on the contemporary Italian scene, where political life was dominated by jealousies and competition both between rival cities and between factions within the cities themselves. In reflecting on a half-century's experiences within a particular community, Dante moves towards a wider understanding of the mainsprings of political failure within the social fabric of the city in general. The following chapters will trace some of his attempts to find more enduring solutions to the problems of urban existence that he recognised so clearly.

THEORIES OF GOVERNMENT, CITIZENSHIP AND HAPPINESS

CONVIVIO AND *MONARCHIA*

Dante's practical experience of government in Florence between 1295 and 1300 was brief, but had decisive personal and intellectual consequences. His exile from Florence was the product of having become involved in the civic administration. Leonardo Bruni, the fifteenth-century humanist and Florentine chancellor, writes in his biography of Dante about a letter from the poet, not surviving today, which lamented: '*tutti li mali e tutti li inconvenienti miei dalli infausti comizi del mio priorato ebbono cagione e principio*' ('all my ills and all my misfortunes had their cause and beginning in the unhappy duties of my priorate').[1] In reflecting on the causes of his banishment, Dante did not only feel concern with his own career. As the previous chapter indicated, his experience of participation in government and his subsequent exile also led him to examine broader historical and political questions. Perhaps in revulsion from the formulaic pieties of Florentine governmental rhetoric, Dante embarked on a review of the first principles of political organisation in two serious philosophical texts, first in a set of chapters within the *Convivio*, and later in a full-blown political treatise, the *Monarchia*.

A determination to break with formula is presented as a primary motivation in the very opening lines of *Monarchia*:

> *Longe [...] ab offitio se esse non dubitet qui, publicis documentis imbutus, ad rem publicam aliquid afferre non curat; non enim est*

*lignum, quod secus decursus aquaram fructificat in tempore suo, sed
potius perniciosa vorago semper ingurgitans et nunquam ingurgita
refundens. Hec igitur sepe mecum recogitans, ne de infossi talenti culpa
quandoque redarguar, publice utilitati non modo turgescere, quinymo
fructificare desidero, et intemptatas ab aliis ostendere veritates.*

(*Mon.* I. i. 2–3)

The man who is steeped in the teachings which form our
common heritage, yet has no interest in contributing something to the community, is failing in his duty: let him be in no
doubt of that; for he is not 'a tree planted by the rivers of water,
that bringeth forth his fruit in due season,' but rather a destructive whirlpool which forever swallows things down and never
gives back what it has swallowed. Thinking often about these
things, lest some day I be accused of burying my talent, I wish
not just to put forth buds but to bear fruit for the benefit of all,
and to reveal truths that have not been attempted by others.

His investigation leads him to address questions about the origins
of the state, and about justice, peace and the common good that
share some of their principal terminology with the writers on city
government active in Duecento Florence whom we encountered
in the previous chapter. Dante's methods of investigation and his
conclusions are, however, distinctly different from theirs, both in
the *Monarchia* and in the political material that is addressed in
Convivio, Book IV.

The *Convivio* has something in common with Brunetto Latini's
Tresor, in that it is a treatise composed in the vernacular (in this case,
Florentine Italian) intended to offer access to a range of philosophical knowledge to an audience not qualified to undertake the serious reading, in Latin, that was necessary to any formal intellectual
enterprise in medieval Europe. Like Brunetto's, Dante's book is
very much a product of exile, for he embarked on its composition
shortly after his expulsion from Florence, around 1303 or 1304. In
other respects, however, it differs substantially from Brunetto's

work. Structurally, the treatise is organised as a collection of lyric poems (*canzoni*), composed by Dante himself, accompanied by prose exegesis. Following the central metaphor of the work's title, Dante offers his readers a banquet (*convivio*) of different appetising dishes (the *canzoni*), accompanied by the bread (the prose commentary) that Italians still consider indispensable to any meal today (I. i. 14–15). Originally intended as a fifteen-book enterprise, the work was in fact abandoned at Book IV, after only three poems had been discussed, probably because Dante had by this stage (1307 or 1308) conceived and begun to compose the *Commedia*. The final book of the extant treatise contains the political material that this chapter will discuss: the *canzone* and its commentary address the themes of nobility and the virtues of the active, or political, life; two chapters (the fourth and fifth) deal with theoretical questions regarding the origins of the state, and the authority of the Roman empire.

These theoretical questions addressed in *Convivio* IV. iv–v are taken up again in the *Monarchia*, a treatise dedicated exclusively to political questions, as its title, 'Monarchy' (by which Dante means 'Empire'), indicates. The work is divided into three books: the first discusses the broad question of the necessity of monarchical government to the good of humanity; the second and third deal with the more specific questions, respectively, of the right of Rome to exercise such monarchy and of whether monarchical authority derives directly from God, or depends on a papal (or any other) intermediary. The treatise was probably composed in or after 1314, as can be established by a clear reference to *Paradiso* V in Book I.[2] The final part of the work has traditionally attracted the closest scholarly attention, for the arguments about imperial–papal relations that Dante rehearses there provide a contribution to one of the liveliest and most controversial debates in Italian political life of the period.[3] Book I, however, presents the material most closely relevant to the purposes of our discussion, since it is here that Dante sets out to investigate the origins of civil society and to reflect on the different forms and hierarchies of states, including considerations on the nature and purposes of the city.

The overall conclusions of the *Monarchia* place the authority of the Holy Roman Emperor, inherited directly from the classical Roman empire, at the pinnacle of the secular hierarchy, and remove all temporal authority from the pope. Broadly speaking, these are the same conclusions as were outlined a decade earlier, in the *Convivio* (which, however, omits any direct comment on the position of the papacy). Not even the *Monarchia* represents Dante's final word on political matters – for instance, a reaffirmation of his concern with imperial politics occurs as late as *Paradiso* XXX, where he states that a throne is reserved in heaven for Emperor Henry VII (ll. 133–138). *Convivio* and *Monarchia*, however, represent Dante's most formal and theoretical reflections on questions of political organisation. Together, the two texts provide evidence that Dante sustained a continuous interest in the question of empire from a rather early period of his exile, and that his main conclusions when considering the authority of the empire, and its relationship to the papacy, remained substantially the same, though evolving in matters of detail.[4]

The *Monarchia* presents a political programme far more fully articulated in theoretical terms than the *Convivio*. The *Convivio*, however, raises other political issues that the *Monarchia* in turn neglects. Its discussion of nobility, for instance, produces pronouncements on personal conduct and social organisation that have eminently political implications and that are ensured wide dissemination because articulated in the vernacular, rather than in the Latin conventional for political philosophy. The treatise makes a polemical point, indeed, of its dedication to an audience debarred from the systematic pursuit of Latin learning precisely because occupied with *'cura familiare o civile'* ('domestic or civic duties': I. i. 13). This audience could be expected to respond readily to such social and political issues as the review in the *canzone* and commentary of Book IV, of claims by the ruling élites to possess nobility on the grounds of genealogy and socio-political prominence. Dante's investigation concludes that nobility is a matter of personal virtue, not of social or economic distinction; his conclusion has obvious practical relevance to the political life of Italian city-states such as Florence where, as we have seen, the involvement of an aristocratic caste in government had been increasingly questioned in the later Duecento. (A generation after Dante, the great jurist Bartolus of Sassoferrato recognised the political importance of the poet's arguments, though largely refuting his conclusions, by quoting *Convivio* IV in a tract defending the legitimacy of civil, rather than personal, nobility.)[5] Thus when *Convivio* and *Monarchia* are read side-by-side, their combined reflections on moral and political questions reveal that Dante's concern with the universal political structure of empire is linked in fact to an equally strong concern with the life of ordinary urban society and of its individual members.

THE ORIGINS OF THE STATE: ARISTOTELIAN ENQUIRY

As we saw at the start of this chapter, Dante tells the readers of the *Monarchia* that his intention in the treatise is to discuss truths that have not been attempted by others ('*intemptatas ab aliis veritates*'). He goes on to declare that he can only address his chosen subject, secular monarchy, by going back to first principles and defining his field of enquiry: this has been identified as an essential philosophical preliminary by Aristotle, whom Dante refers to simply as 'The Philosopher' ('*Phylosophum*': I. iii. 1), and who represents the principal scientific authority cited throughout the *Monarchia*.[6] The new availability of Aristotelian texts in Latin had, over the thirteenth century, produced an explosion of scholarly commentary and interpretation, especially associated with ecclesiastical scholars such as St Albert the Great and St Thomas Aquinas. Their commentaries, synthesising the ancient philosopher's insights with orthodox Christian beliefs, remained essential in introducing lay enthusiasts such as Dante to Aristotle's methods and conclusions. At the start of the fourteenth century, the new philosophy had still not been fully absorbed outside intellectual circles. Dante is thus reasonably justified in suggesting that his principles of political enquiry break new ground. Even though scholars such as Aquinas in Paris, or in Florence the lesser-known Dominican Remigio dei Girolami, had been working with Aristotelian political philosophy for some time, Dante is one of the earliest laymen of the Italian city-states to make such an attempt.[7]

Over the past centuries, questions about Dante's use of Aristotelian or Thomistic philosophy, about the authorities cited in the *Monarchia*, and about the extent of the *Monarchia*'s innovations, have been the objects of extensive and contentious critical discussion. Dante's adherence to Aristotelian philosophy, for instance, was assumed by early twentieth-century critics like Giovanni Busnelli to be substantial. Subsequent scholarship has modified such views and raised questions about what kind of Aristotelian he may have been – a 'safe' Thomist, or a holder of more radical, unorthodox views? Also, crucially, modern scholarship has recalled the importance to Dante's thinking of the more established Augustinian or Neo-Platonist philosophical traditions of Western Christendom.[8] Modern Dante scholars have reminded us that he followed no formal philosophical training (as far as we know), and was unlikely to have been able to keep abreast of the vanguard of contemporary intellectual debate. Instead, his self-directed intellectual endeavours followed eclectic paths, new discoveries and insights being accommodated into an outlook also shaped by Florentine experience, and by deep saturation in conventional Christian belief, in vernacular courtly and chivalric literature, and in what is now called popular culture.[9] As regards *Convivio* and *Monarchia*, there can be no doubt that Dante draws on a wide range of other authorities besides Aristotle to shape and colour his arguments. For instance, besides the Bible and the Christian Fathers, both texts draw extensively on Virgil, and it has been suggested that *Convivio* IV's heavy use of the *Aeneid* shows a close contact with the text that may have directly inspired Dante to abandon philosophical prose and embark on his own Christian epic poem.[10] *Monarchia*'s second book is rooted in Virgil, while the whole treatise is also filled with passages of quasi-prophetic exhortation that carry a strong biblical and mystical flavour. Aristotle however, as filtered through scholastic interpretation and commentary, is accorded a primary position in both texts as shaping the *method* of enquiry.

Both *Monarchia* and *Convivio* open their enquiries into empire using an explicitly Aristotelian, teleological method, asserting that the necessity of any particular form of government can only be understood by asking what the purpose of human society is in general terms. The term that Dante uses for humanity in the collective is '*umana civilitade*' (*Cvo* IV. iv. 1) or '*humana civilitas*' (*Mon.* I. iii. 1), and he identifies its single distinctive goal in Aristotelian terms. In *Convivio*, the argument in Book IV that '*la umana civilitade [...] a uno fine è ordinata, cioè a vita felice*' ('human society as a whole is directed to a single goal, that is, to a life of happiness': IV. iv. 1), makes a logical connection with a statement about individual human happiness from the start of the whole treatise:

> Sì come dice lo Filosofo nel principio de la Prima Filosofia, tutti li uomini naturalmente desiderano di sapere. [...] Ciascuna cosa, da providenza di prima natura impinta, è inclinabile a la sua propria perfezione; onde, acciò che la scienza è ultima perfezione de la nostra anima, ne la quale sta la nostra ultima felicitade, tutti naturalmente al suo desiderio semo subietti.
>
> (*Cvo* I. i. 1)

As the Philosopher says at the beginning of the *Metaphysics*, all men naturally desire to possess knowledge. All beings are instinctively impelled by their own natures to seek their own perfection; so that since knowledge is the highest perfection of our souls, in which our highest happiness lies, we all are naturally impelled to desire it.[11]

Monarchia also stresses that every human being desires happiness, and that this is achieved through the powers of the intellect:

Si enim consideremus unum hominem, [...] cum omnes vires eius ordinentur ad felicitatem, vis ipsa intellectualis est regulatrix et rectrix omnium aliarum: aliter ad felicitatem pervenire non potest.

(*Mon.* I. v. 4)

If we consider a single person, while all the faculties are directed towards happiness, it is the intellectual faculty which guides and directs all the others; otherwise happiness is unattainable.

In *Monarchia*, however, Dante draws a distinction between the goals of individuals and of all humanity (I. iii). Humanity's collective task is to ensure the maximum realisation of all its intellectual potential ('*potentia sive virtus intellectiva*': I. iii. 7), considered as the sum of each individual's intellectual activity as exercised in theoretical speculation and/or in practical doing and making. In the course of these remarks on the goal of all humanity, Dante cites Averroes (I. iii. 9), the great Muslim commentator on Aristotle. Averroes interpreted *De Anima's* remarks on humanity's possible intellect so as to posit a single, eternal intellectual faculty for all mankind, rather than the separate, individual possession of an immortal soul – a position unacceptable to orthodox Christian belief, and fiercely condemned by St Thomas Aquinas. Later commentators on this passage, starting with the papal propagandist Guido Vernani, who directed a vehement attack against *Monarchia* in 1329, have periodically accused Dante of Averroistic tendencies, amounting perhaps to heresy.[12] In fact, Dante's insistence on the separation of goals for different orders of society, from the single individual through to universal humanity, allows him to avoid denying human beings their own intellectual and spiritual individuality. His remarks emphasise the multiplicity of intellectual endeavour required of humanity as a sum of single beings, rather than positing any unity of human intellect. The controversial nature of this passage, however, illustrates Dante's determination to conduct his political enquiry from an independent position, starting from first principles and drawing on even the most unexpected of authorities in his examination of questions that he felt had not been satisfactorily answered by contemporary theoreti-cians of government.

Another Aristotelian principle fundamental to Dante's political enquiry, and which sets him apart from traditional lay writers on government, is his absolute acceptance of the dictum that '*l'uomo naturalmente è compagnevole animale*' ('man is naturally a social ani-mal': *Cvo* IV. iv. 1).[13] Unlike Brunetto Latini, with his view of the state as a coercive construct, Dante assumes that human beings are instinctively sociable and co-operative:'*l'uomo è animale civile, per che a lui si richiede non pur a sé ma altrui essere utile*' ('man is a social ani-mal, and so it is required of him that he not only seek his own ben-efit, but that of others also': IV. xxvii. 3). This explains why the associative instinct extends beyond an immediate circle towards larger social forms, enabling the exchanges of goods and services that are necessary to a truly happy existence – the pursuit of happi-ness being, as we have seen, another instinct innate to humankind.

This tightly linked series of philosophical propositions lies behind Dante's earliest outline, in *Convivio*, of the reasons why empire is a desirable political form:

> *Lo fondamento radicale de la imperiale maiestade, secondo lo vero, è la necessità de la umana civilitade, che a uno fine è ordinata, cioè a vita felice; a la quale nullo per sé è sufficiente a venire sanza l'aiutorio d'alcuno, con ciò sia cosa che l'uomo abbisogna di molte cose, a le quali uno solo satisfare non può. E però dice lo Filosofo che l'uomo natural-mente è compagnevole animale.*
>
> (*Cvo* IV. iv. 1)

The foundation and root of imperial authority, truly under-stood, is the need for human society in the collective [*l'umana civilitade*], which is directed towards a single goal, that is, to a life of happiness. No-one is capable of reaching this goal by himself, without the help of others, since men have many needs, which a single individual cannot satisfy on his own. It is for this reason that the Philosopher tells us that man is naturally a social animal.

This opening statement leads directly into an analysis of the different political structures, that supply companionship and satisfy wants, which each individual requires in order to realise the happiness of *l'umana civilitade*. Following the sequence envisaged in Aristotle's *Politics*, these extend from the '*compagnia dimestica di famiglia*' ('domestic society of a family') to a larger '*vicinanza*' ('neighbourhood') and on to '*la cittade*' ('the city': IV. iv. 2).[14] Dante goes on to enumerate forms not included in the *Politics*, the kingdom ('*regno*'), and finally universal empire or '*Monarchia*' (IV. iv. 2–4). At each expansion of the community, Dante shows that its inhabitants collectively experience different needs '*a sua sufficienza*' ('for their own satisfaction'). This phrase or a close equivalent is used to describe the need an individual has for a household, a household for a neighbourhood, and a neighbourhood for the city: no such wording appears in the outline of the need cities have for kingdoms, or kingdoms for empire. Yet only when he reaches the level of empire can Dante identify a state where all needs can be satisfied, since this final form encompasses all of human society.

Monarchia outlines a similar series of human communities, each stated to have a different goal (I. iii. 2). As we saw above, the individual man, as in *Convivio*, is born for the purpose of living happily. The goals of the larger social groups are all related intimately to this requirement of the individual. The household (*domus*) for instance is intended '*domesticos ad bene vivere preparare*' ('to prepare its members to live the good life': I. v. 5), and the goal of a neighbourhood or village (*vicus/vicinia*) is to achieve '*commoda tam personarum quam rerum auxiliatio*' ('neighbourly support in relation both to people and to goods': I. v. 6). The distinctive aim of the city is '*bene sufficienterque vivere*' ('to be self-sufficient in living the good life': I. v. 7): significantly, this is the goal that Aristotle's *Politics* makes fundamental to the need for a state.[15] Beyond the level of a city, the individual kingdom ('*unum regnum particulare*') has the supplementary function of maintaining the good life of these towns: '*finis est* is qui civitatis *cum maiori fiducia sue tranquillitatis*' ('its purpose is *the same as that of a city*, but with greater confidence that peace can be maintained': I. v. 8, my emphasis).

Significantly then, whereas up to the level of the city each community has goals that add something extra to individual wellbeing, larger political forms have a less primary, purely protective function. Happiness – the Florentine analyst concludes – is fully realisable within the city.

In *Convivio* too, although different goals are not ascribed to the different types of polity, Dante outlines a qualitative difference in the way that they serve the *vita felice* that alters perceptibly at the level of the city. The *Convivio* envisages that cities may benefit from establishing relationships with each other:

> *Ancora la cittade richiede a le sue arti e a le sue difensioni vicenda avere e fratellanza con le circavicine cittadi; e però fu fatto lo regno.*
>
> (*Cvo* IV. iv. 2)

> The city also needs, for the purposes of trade and of defence, to generate mutual ties and brotherly relations with its neighbouring cities, and so the kingdom was established.

While not strictly necessary to the community's happiness, these relationships enhance civic wellbeing in military, diplomatic and economic terms: the kingdom encompasses and facilitates such exchanges. The kingdom, however, is also the political form where the *Convivio* first locates the possibility of serious political discord.

It is curious that a fourteenth-century Florentine citizen like Dante should not comment on political competition and violence in relation to the city, given that he came from a spectacularly factional *città partita*. Perhaps, however, another political reality informs his desire to locate the sources of political discord outside the society of a city in his outline of political theory, given his conviction that the anti-imperial alliance of the papacy with the kingdom of France had been a major cause of the Florentine and Italian upheavals of 1300 and, therefore, of his own exile. His comments on the causes of political violence reveal unease over the kingdom as a political construct and make a suggestive reference to lived experience ('*esperienza*'):

Con ciò sia cosa che l'animo umano in terminata possessione di terra non si queti, ma sempre desideri gloria d'acquistare, sì come per esperienza vedemo, discordie e guerre conviene surgere intra regno e regno, le quali sono tribulazioni de le cittadi, e per le cittadi de le vicinanze, e per le vicinanze de le case, e per le case de l'uomo; e così s'impedisce la felicitade.

(*Cvo* IV. iv. 3)

Since the human spirit cannot be satisfied with limited territorial possession, but always desires the glory of acquiring more, as we see by experience, war and discord necessarily break out between one kingdom and another. These bring affliction to the cities, and through the cities to neighbourhoods, and through neighbourhoods to households, and through households to the individual; and in this way, happiness is denied.

It certainly seems indicative of a Florentine *forma mentis* that the ill effects of war are viewed so firmly in the context of damage to the city and to its self-sufficient provision for each individual's pursuit of happiness. It is to counter competitive violence between kingdoms and their princes that empire is required since, as was stated at the start of the political enquiry, the root and foundation ('*fondamento radicale*') of empire is its ability to provide happiness for all of *umana civilitade*.

The *Convivio* thus outlines a political hierarchy in which, up to the level of the city, expansion of the political community brings positive benefits that facilitate the individual's goal of attaining happiness. At the level of kingdom, and even of empire, such expansion is desirable on the more negative grounds of defending against harm. It appears, therefore, that peace rather than happiness is the goal of kingdom and empire. Nuances in the language with which Dante describes the chain of connections extending down from emperor to individual, enhance the impression that his political concerns concentrate significantly upon the city. The emperor himself is guaranteed against destructively acquisitive instincts by the universal nature of his rule; he can therefore oversee other rulers and keep them satisfied within the boundaries of their own states ('*li regi tegna contenti ne li termini de li regni*': IV. iv. 4). This in turn guarantees peace and repose to the cities ('*pace*' and '*posa*'). The social bonds of city life are however described with considerably more emotional emphasis: the town, neighbourhoods and households are linked together by love ('*amore*') in their cultivation of life's necessities. Mutual love and support are thus the hallmarks of city life, the means to the ultimate end of political life: this being, that '*l'uomo viva felicemente; che è quello per che esso è nato*' ('the individual may live happily; which is the goal for which he is born': IV. iv. 4). Once again, the city represents a peculiarly privileged form of polity, in which the strong bonds of love and dependence, as well as an equable climate of peace, knit together the members of the community.

THE MONARCH: GUARANTOR OF EARTHLY HAPPINESS

Both *Convivio* and *Monarchia* place the city at a pivotal position in the political hierarchy: it can provide all the conditions for the good life where individuals attain happiness. However, it can only fulfil this function properly under conditions of peace (*pace, posa, tranquillitas*). The kingdom, but above all the over-arching empire, provides the best defence against any threat to this peace. In *Convivio*, as we have seen, Dante envisages peace as a condition of happy equilibrium where economic and military norms are maintained at city level through trade and defence, and where warfare is eliminated through the protection of the empire and the kingdom. Similarly, several chapters of *Monarchia*'s Book I stress the administrative benefits of imperial peace: Chapter X, echoing *Convivio*, discusses how an emperor can resolve disputes between two rival kingdoms, and Chapter xiv shows how imperial law establishes universally agreed principles that create a common framework for all local legislation. Other arguments about peace in *Monarchia* I offer a wider-ranging and more mystical vision of peace, using scriptural rather than political evidence to make their case. Thus, as Dante works towards his definition of first principles in the opening chapters, he states that human happiness is designed to be attained under conditions of peace, proving his point from the Gospels, where the angels of the Nativity promised "*"pax hominibus bone voluntatis"*" ("*"peace to men of good will"*": I. iv. 3), and Christ's customary greeting was "*"Pax vobis"*" ("*"Peace be with you"*": I. iv. 4). These greetings demonstrate that peace, rather than riches, status, or other desirables, makes the best contribution to human happiness (*'pax [...] est optimum eorum que ad nostram beatitudinem ordinantur'*: I. iv. 2). Book I culminates, too, with an evocation of the peaceful condition of the Pauline "*"plenitudinem temporis"*" ("*"fullness of time"*": I. xvi. 2) that was reached with the Incarnation, the secular *Pax Romana* that ushered in the spiritual Prince of Peace. The connection between peace and happiness is once again drawn explicitly, in the statement that *'tunc humanum genus fuerit felix in pacis universalis tranquillitate'* ('mankind was then happy in the calm of universal peace': I.xvi.2). Thus Dante finds religious authority for his assertions that, although separate goals have been assigned to the life of the individual and that of all humanity, the peace provided by imperial rule is necessary to both.

The final chapter of *Monarchia* returns to this same connection between political peace, individual happiness, and the intellection required of humanity in the collective, in its closing discussion of the respective roles of the pope and the emperor with regard to universal humanity. Here Dante comments that the two powers are responsible for two distinct forms of happiness required by human beings: an active, political and earthly happiness; and a contemplative, spiritual and heavenly happiness. These are attained respectively via *'phylosophica documenta'* ('the teachings of philosophy') and *'documenta spiritualia'* ('spiritual teachings': III. xvi. 8), and are figured respectively as the earthly and the celestial paradise.[16] The emperor's responsibility for ensuring that humanity attains earthly, philosophical happiness makes him concerned above all with maintaining peace:

Et cum ad hunc portum vel nulli vel pauci [...] pervenire possint, nisi sedatis fluctibus blande cupiditatis genus humanum liberum in pacis tranquillitate quiescat, hoc est illud signum ad quod maxime debet intendere curator orbis, qui dicitur romanus Princeps, ut scilicet in areola ista mortalium libere cum pace vivatur.

(*Mon.* III. xvi. 11)

And since none or few can reach this harbour [i.e. happiness] unless the waves of seductive greed are calmed and the human race rests free in the tranquillity of peace, this is the goal which the protector of the world, who is called the Roman Prince, must strive with all his might to bring about: i.e. that life on this threshing-floor of mortals may be lived freely and in peace.

The emperor is not himself a teacher of philosophy, but he is responsible for maintaining the peace that safeguards humanity's pursuit of secular happiness. In *Convivio* too, although Dante makes it plain that the emperor should take care to promote philosophy and that kings require its support '*per proprio studio*' ('through their own study') or else '*per consiglio*' ('through advice': IV. vi. 19), the proper functions of kingship and of philosophy are kept distinct. While the philosopher is concerned with the discovery and analysis of natural laws and moral truths – and above all, with establishing what is the goal of human life – the emperor is assigned authority over a strictly delimited set of human activities, those which relate to choices dictated by an individual's will and which can be regulated by the rational dictates of legislation.[17] In these matters, his authority is absolute. Exclamatory interpolations underline the urgency of the need for philosophers and rulers to collaborate, with apocalyptic language reminding Dante's readers of the dire consequences of contemporary rulers' neglect of this principle:

Ponetevi mente, nemici di Dio, a' fianchi, voi che le verghe de' reggimenti d'Italia prese avete – e dico a voi, Carlo e Federigo regi, e a voi altri principi e tiranni –; e guardate chi a lato vi siede per consiglio, e

*annumerate quante volte lo die questo fine de l'umana vita per li
vostri consiglieri v'è additato!*

(*Cvo* IV. vi. 20)

Look around you, enemies of God, you who have taken up the
sceptre in the states of Italy – I am speaking to you, King
Charles [of Naples] and King Frederick [of Sicily], and all you
other princes and tyrants – look to see who is sitting beside
you to give you counsel, and tell us how many times a day your
counsellors remind you of this goal of human life!

THE COMMON GOOD: GREED, LAW AND LOVE

In both *Monarchia* I and *Convivio* IV, Dante shows that the chief
obstacle to the imperial peace necessary for achieving happiness is
human greed (*cupiditas, gloria d'acquistare*). Rather than glorying in
economic and territorial expansion, Dante suggests that political
communities should be content with sufficiency (*sufficienza, suffici-
entia*), pursuing a path of moderation equally approved by
Aristotelian philosophy and by Christian tradition. The immoderate
rivalry between powers that threatens the good life of human communities is prompted by greed, the same greed that the *Commedia*
repeatedly diagnoses as having brought about the decline of social
and political *mores* in Florence and throughout Italy in the poet's
own day. Moreover, while humans may be gregarious by nature, as
Aristotle demonstrates, Christianity teaches that since the 'Fall' of
Adam, we are also by nature inevitably inclined towards such sinful
impulses as greed. As we saw in Chapter I, political thinkers from
the contemporary Italian *comuni* such as Brunetto Latini emphasised
a notion of the state as a coercive construct to restrain human violence, rather than a spontaneous, natural form of association. In
adhering to an Aristotelian view of the origin of the state, Dante has
to outline how the ideal political system can both provide a community setting appropriate to the pursuit of happiness, whilst also

restraining sin, especially the primary political sin of cupidity – for Dante does recognise that the state provides a '*remedi[um] contra infirmitatem peccati*' ('remedy against the weakness of sin': *Mon.* III. iv. 14). If the former goal can arguably be served by the city alone, the latter requires the emperor, since, as the *Convivio* remarks, the emperor's unique position – '*tutto possedendo e più desiderare non possendo*' ('possessing everything, and having nothing further to desire': IV. iv. 4) – eliminates him from the pitfalls of human cupidity and so provides a neutral arbitrator in all other cases of disputed political possession and social responsibility. Seeing that no other political agent can be guaranteed to be free from greed, Dante concludes that the emperor, with his moderating authority, is essential to the smooth functioning of all human states – a pro-imperial conclusion which nonetheless is rooted in a strong concern with the political functions of kingdoms and cities.

The emperor's chief weapon in countering cupidity is not military strength – although Dante's Roman convictions allow him to argue that might can sometimes be right[18] – but the mechanism of the law. If law is rightly observed, the emperor's own impartial equity will be transmitted in orderly fashion to all smaller political communities: '*quello che esso dice a tutti è legge, e per tutti dee essere obedito e ogni altro comandamento da quello di costui prendere vigore e autoritade*' ('whatever he says is law for all, and must be obeyed by all, and all other commands must draw their vigour and authority from his': *Cvo* IV. iv. 7). *Monarchia* similarly stresses that the monarch's law provides the common standard for all humanity, being established '*ut humanum genus secundum sua comunia, que omnibus competunt, ab eo regatur et comuni regula gubernetur ad pacem*' ('so that mankind is to be ruled by him in those matters which are common to all men and of relevance to all, and is to be guided towards peace by a common law': I. xiv. 7). The same chapter also amplifies the *Convivio's* brief mention of other governments (*altro comandamento*), specifying that, although the emperor establishes the broad principles of common law, local polities can and should legislate on matters of detail according to the different characteristic needs of the nation, kingdom or city in question.

As in the case Dante made over the importance of peace, so in his discussion of imperial law in *Monarchia* administrative or political arguments are accompanied also by spiritual ones. The jurisdiction of the emperor over humanity is compared to that of Moses over the people of Israel, where some matters could be dealt with by tribal judges, but the prophet's single, central authority prescribed the rules for the whole community. The biblical comparison, evoking the divine Commandments and the law observed by all Israel, gives imperial law a quasi-divine status: rather than viewing the Roman codes as a form of prescriptive *lex positiva*, Dante seems to argue that they conform to natural or providential norms.[19] In *Convivio*, a similar effect is achieved when Dante, discussing imperial authority, translates assertions about law with the term '*ragione scritta*' ('reason written down': IV. ix. 8), juxtaposing a citation from Justinian's *Digest* – "'*la ragione scritta è arte di bene e d'equitade*'" ("'reason written down [i.e. law] is a principle of good and of equity'": IV. ix. 8) – with an Augustinian dictum on law as a *remedium peccati*. Dante pictures the emperor's control over human choices and desires as making him '*lo cavalcatore de la umana volontade*' ('the rider of the human will'); he brings home the urgent necessity for such checks over greed and ambition by extending the metaphor to contemporary realities:

> *Lo quale cavallo come vada sanza lo cavalcatore per lo campo assai è manifesto, e spezialmente ne la misera Italia, che sanza mezzo alcuno a la sua governazione è rimasa!*
>
> (*Cvo* IV. ix. 10)

> How this horse behaves in the field without its rider is clearly evident, especially in wretched Italy, which has been left with no means to support its governance!

Monarchia too uses equestrian imagery to illustrate how imperial law represses humanity's sinful impulse to reject the teachings of reason and of revealed religion: '*has [...] conclusiones et media [...]*

humana cupiditas postergaret nisi homines, tanquam equi, sua bestialitate vagantes "in camo et freno" compescerentur in via' ('human greed would cast these ends and means aside if men, like horses, prompted to wander by their animal natures, were not held in check "with bit and bridle" on their journey': III. xvi. 9).

In Dante's view, the restraint imposed by law over human cupidity is not purely coercive. Being convinced that human beings are naturally gregarious, he is eager to emphasise that in forming political communities, we increase our chances of happiness. Imperial peace, protected by imperial law, is not merely a mechanism for eliminating sin: for Dante, as a convinced Christian, the opposite of sin is love, and so the happiness fostered by the empire goes hand-in-hand with love. *Convivio*, as we saw earlier, emphasised that the emperor's protection against greed allowed city neighbourhoods to enjoy love as well as peace. *Monarchia* comments that the emperor's freedom from greed makes him not only fair but also loving in his commitment to justice, noting that *'cupiditas [...], perseitate hominum spreta, querit alia; karitas vero, spretis aliis omnibus, querit Deum et hominem, et per consequens bonum hominis'* ('greed, scorning the intrinsic nature of man, seeks other things; whereas love, scorning all other things, seeks God and man, and hence the true good of man': I. xi. 14).

With these assertions about the emperor's love for his subjects, Dante moves into a further series of arguments that address questions about how states serve the common good – a concept that, as we have seen, occupied a central place in the traditional political rhetoric of the Italian *comuni*. Having already diverged from his predecessors in his assertions about humanity's inherently political instincts, Dante makes a further break with convention in asserting that empire tends to enhance human freedom: Guelf *comuni* such as Florence typically viewed the Holy Roman Empire as an illiberal and repressive construct. For Dante, the imperial hierarchy is both loving and liberating, because it is held together by a system of law that eliminates the violent consequences of human greed. Each smaller community, with its locally appropriate system of legislation, is thus rendered freer in turn and made to function in a properly state-like way. Using the technical language of academic political philosophy, *Monarchia* asserts that the imperial system alone allows communities to *politizare recte*, that is, to function as proper polities (*politie*).[20] Without empire, states degenerate into the perverted forms that Aristotle labelled democracy (in the sense of mob rule), oligarchy and tyranny (I. xii. 9).[21] Since governors properly exist to serve the law and the people, rather than the people to serve the law, '*politie recte libertatem intendunt, scilicet ut homines propter se sint*' ('just forms of government aim at freedom, i.e. that men should exist for their own sake': I. xii. 10). These just regimes are exercised, under the emperor, by '*reges, aristocratici quos optimates vocant, et populi libertatis zelatores*' ('kings, aristocrats (known as the great and the good), and those zealous for the freedom of the people': I. xii. 9). Whereas per-verted forms of government enslave their subjects by allowing the cupidity or self-interest of the ruling clique to dictate the conduct of affairs, just regimes embrace the principle of the common good, being founded on principles of moderation, love and justice.

Polities are thus distinguished according to the extent to which they serve the common good. Their rulers too are assigned different titles, indicating different constitutional realities – such as tyrant or king, aristocrat or oligarch – accordingly as they occupy themselves with their subjects' wellbeing. The different labels are far from neu-tral in implication: the term 'tyrant' does not, in Dante's usage, simply describe the manner of a state's administration, but passes judgement on it – and a judgement that reflects directly on the individual who occupies the office. Elsewhere in *Monarchia*, Dante is careful to dis-tinguish between the individual and his political office: speaking of pope and emperor, he notes that they are assessed on one scale of judgement as individuals, but on another as officials '*cum suis differen-tialibus*' ('with their differentiating characteristics': III. xii. 10). He also, however, stresses that while official or political position is acci-dental – using Aristotelian terminology once again – human beings are also and always assessed on essentials, as individuals: the different labels assigned in Book I to the leaders of different kinds of polity remind us that official and individual goodness are hard to separate.

In categorising different kinds of polity or official position, moreover, Dante is not only concerned with those who exercise great power. At the heart of his chapter on freedom and constitutional forms, Dante cites an Aristotelian dictum on political and personal virtue that focuses on the ordinary individual:

> *Phylosophus in suis* Politicis *ait quod in politia obliqua bonus homo est malus civis, in recta vero bonus homo et civis bonus convertuntur.*
>
> (Mon. I. xii. 10)

> The Philosopher in the *Politics* says that in bad government the good man is a bad citizen, whereas in good government the good man and the good citizen are one and the same thing.[22]

His citation's ethical terminology allows Dante, as at other times in *Monarchia*, to mix into his constitutional analysis of the administrative benefits of empire, primarily Aristotelian in construction and language, a Christian concern with questions of sin or virtue. The statement concentrates on the basic form of political relationship, that of the *civis*, 'citizen': a position that the average individual can realistically expect to occupy (subject, in medieval Europe, to various conditions such as age, gender, rank and wealth). It reminds us that not only popes and emperors but also ordinary people are called on to undertake political obligations within their own communities, and are judged on the basis of their performance. The next question that we need to investigate, then, is what information Dante gives us about how ordinary people may aspire to become both *boni cives* and *boni homines*, within a local community such as an Italian city-state.

ROLE, RANK, NOBILITY: VIRTUE AND HAPPINESS IN SOCIETY

As was indicated at the beginning of this chapter, *Convivio* provides some quite substantial information on questions about the virtues an individual needs to live a good political life, in the discussion of nobility (*gentilezza*) in its final extant section, Book IV. In the course of the discussion, Dante devotes considerable space to the social impact of noble conduct on fellow members of the political community, and includes enactment of political obligations among the criteria that indicate *gentilezza*. His analysis draws a crucial distinction between 'social' nobility, where an individual is accorded distinction on the basis of genealogy, wealth or rank, and 'personal' nobility, where distinction derives from the person's own words or actions — in fact, from the kind of '*volontarie operazioni*' that fall under imperial or political authority.[23]

Perhaps influenced by the *comuni*'s traditional mistrust of the social nobility as rulers, Dante places considerably more emphasis on nobility as a matter of personal virtue. The *Convivio*'s prose examination of nobility glosses a *canzone* which itself directly addresses the issue '*del valore, | per lo qual veramente omo è gentile*' ('of the merit | by which man truly is noble': ll. 12–13), and argues fiercely against the '*giudicio falso e vile*' ('false and base opinion': l. 15) of those who assign nobility genealogical or financial origins. The lyric, *Le dolci rime d'amor ch'i' solia* (*The sweet rhymes of love that I used to seek out*), opens with the acknowledgement that its subject matter is controversial and even its style unorthodox for an author previously preoccupied with love poetry: it is presented as a formal philosophical investigation and is packed with technical terminology, making it stylistically '*aspr' e sottile*' ('harsh and subtle': l. 14). The accompanying commentary is very full and detailed — about twice as long as the treatise's three preceding books — and it too accommodates polemical material, including the pronouncements on empire that we have reviewed so far. For all kinds of reasons then, the topic of nobility emerges as a highly political one from the very start of *Convivio* IV.

The topic of nobility is also discussed, though in rather different terms, in the third chapter of *Monarchia* II. Here, although personal nobility remains a significant object of interest, Dante also expresses interest in ancestry and rank. Nobility comes under review within an explicitly political context, forming one of the strands in Book II's investigation of the question of whether Rome achieved imperial authority simply by force, or by providential right, 'de iure' (II. ii. 1). Again, Dante's argument proceeds by following the Scholastic syllogistic method, starting out from a statement of first principle:

> Nobilissimo populo convenit omnibus aliis preferri; romanus populus fuit nobilissimus; ergo convenit ei omnibus aliis preferri.
>
> (Mon. II. iii. 2)

> It is appropriate that the noblest race should rule over all the others; the Roman people were the noblest; therefore it was appropriate that they should rule over all the others.

As Dante amplifies his assertion that nobility confers a right to governance, he draws a direct connection between nobility and virtue that suggests his primary interest to lie with personal nobility: 'cum honor sit premium virtutis et omnis prelatio sit honor, omnis prelatio virtutis est premium' ('since honour is the reward for virtue and every position of authority is an honour, every position of authority is the reward of virtue': II. iii. 3).

Dante's next remarks, however, reveal a strong concern with social nobility. An individual can be judged noble, it appears, if his ancestors achieved honour for their display of virtue – a conclusion Convivio IV declares to be erroneous. The outstanding nobility of the whole Roman race is demonstrated on genealogical grounds through an exploration of its single ancestral figure, Aeneas. His nobility is proved in part by his virtuous conduct, which Dante mentions briefly, referring the reader to Virgil and Livy for fuller details. The majority of the chapter on nobility (II. iii) is however dedicated to an exploration of the genealogy and geographical origins of Aeneas himself, and also of his wives, Creusa, Dido and Lavinia, aimed at ascribing them honourable ancestry in turn. The Convivio's passionate assertions (IV. xv) that the creation story disproves all pretensions to social nobility, since all humans share common descent from Adam, seem eclipsed in this exaltation of the noble but exclusive ancestry of the Trojans and the Romans.

Monarchia II does however supply a number of additional *exempla* of virtuous conduct by different individuals, drawn from across the whole of Roman history up to the time of Augustus, that keep the importance of personal, as well as genealogical, nobility in view. Dante emphasises that the Romans, individually and collectively, realised the political *desiderata* of public service, patriotic self-sacrifice, respect for the law, eliminated cupidity and warfare, and created an empire that achieved the conditions that Book I prescribed as essential for human happiness:

> *Omni cupiditate summota que rei publice semper adversa est, et universali pace cum libertate dilecta, populus ille sanctus pius et gloriosus propria commoda neglexisse videtur, ut publica pro salute humani generis procuraret.*
>
> (*Mon.* II. v. 5)

> Having repressed all greed, which is always harmful to the community, and cherishing universal peace and freedom, that holy, dutiful and glorious people can be seen to have disregarded personal advantage in order to promote the public interest for the benefit of mankind.

He goes on to pick out a series of individual heroes who exemplified these ideal political qualities in their own lives: Cincinnatus, Fabritius, Camillus, and especially Cato, along with several others, are all praised for their selflessness and probity. These same names also appear in *Convivio* IV, where the fifth chapter lists examples of Roman heroism and self-sacrifice so outstanding that the individuals in question deserve to be called '*non [...] umani cittadini, ma [...] divini*' ('not human citizens, but divine ones': IV. v. 12).

In *Convivio*, when Dante reverts back to his discussion of the principle of nobility after the imperial parenthesis of the fourth and fifth chapters, the theme of human happiness that came to the fore in those monarchical chapters remains a primary concern.

The prose commentary closely follows the arguments presented in the lyric, *Le dolci rime*. After refuting at some length in stanzas II–IV the assertion that nobility has any but the remotest connection with ancestry or wealth, Dante puts forward his own definition of nobility in stanzas V and VI, which successively connect nobility with the moral virtues (ll.101–102) and with happiness (ll.118–120). Using Aristotelian philosophical terminology and procedure, he tells us that:

> *ogni vertù principalmente*
> *vien da una radice:*
> *vertute, dico, che fa l'uom felice*
> *in sua operazione.*
>
> (*Le dolci rime*, ll.81–84)

every virtue ultimately derives from one root: the virtue, I mean, that makes man happy in his operations.

Since the term nobility always indicates goodness ('*nobiltate [...] importa sempre ben*': ll.89–90), as does moral virtue, Dante enquires which is the broader category, concluding that this is nobility, a general quality of perfection, moral virtues being particular instances of perfection. He is thus able to conclude his examination of nobility by stating that:

> *ad alquanti*
> *ch'è 'l seme di felicità s'accosta,*
> *messo da Dio ne l'anima ben posta.*
>
> (*Le dolci rime*, ll.118–120)

some understand that it [nobility] is the seed of happiness placed by God in a well-disposed soul.

In the commentary this is reiterated emphatically as an inescapable conclusion:

> *Ché se le vertudi sono frutto di nobilitade, e felicitade è dolcezza per quelle comparata,* manifesto è *essa nobilitade essere semente di felicitade, come detto è.*
>
> (*Cvo.* IV. xx. 9, my emphasis)

> For if the virtues are the fruit of nobility, and happiness is a
> sweetness achieved by means of the virtues, then *it is evident*
> that this nobility is the seed of happiness, as the lyric says.

Nobility, virtue and happiness are thus shown to be almost organically interdependent phases in a continuum that Dante's metaphors compare to those of a plant growing from seed to fruit or root to branch. Happiness, as we know from the imperial chapters, is a goal associated with social existence, since satisfaction of an individual's material and intellectual needs requires reciprocal exchanges with members of a wider community. Nobility is properly present only in a soul well-placed in its body (that is, when suffering no defects of '*complessione*' or '*temporale*' – constitution and disposition). It constitutes a gift from God to the individual that enables him to pursue happiness through the exercise of the virtues, both the moral virtues of the active or political life and the intellectual or theological virtues of the contemplative life.[24] Dante specifies that his immediate concern in the *canzone,* and hence in the commentary, is with the former, '*perciò che le vertù morali paiano essere e siano più comuni e più sapute e più richeste che l'altre e abbiano più [...] utilitade ne lo aspetto di fuori*' ('since the moral virtues seem to be, and indeed are, more common and better known and more generally required than the others, and are seen as more useful in their external appearance': IV. xvii. 12). Once again, these remarks stress that his interests in the topic of nobility remain concentrated within a broadly political context.

THE FOUR AGES OF MAN:
NOBLE CONDUCT IN THE ACTIVE LIFE

After establishing that he is primarily interested in the virtues of the active or political life, Dante goes on to define what these are. The seventeenth chapter of Book IV provides a detailed list of eleven moral virtues, corresponding more or less exactly to those Aristotle describes in the *Ethics*: fortitude, temperance, liberality, magnificence, magnanimity, love of honour, patient temper, affability, truthfulness, enjoyment and justice. They are collectively defined in Aristotelian terms as each constituting an '*abito elettivo consistente nel mezzo*' ('a habit of choice that keeps to the mean': IV. xvii. 7).[25] The list heavily emphasises the importance of self-control and restraint, using terms such as *moderare* (to moderate), *ordinare* (to order), *regola* (a rule), and *freno* (a rein) in describing how the virtues guide individuals towards happiness. Dante warns, too, that nobility and its accompanying virtues cannot be maintained in a passive state. Only by training and continual practice can the right, moderate choices be made between excess and lack, or love for appropriate or inappropriate objects, as the noble man grows towards a mature exercise of his powers:

> *Però vuole santo Augustino, e ancora Aristotile [...], che l'uomo s'ausi a ben fare e a rifrenare le sue passioni, acciò che questo tallo [...] per buona consuetudine induri, e rifermisi ne la sua rettitudine, sì che possa fruttificare, e del suo frutto uscire la dolcezza de l'umana felicitade.*
>
> (*Cvo* IV. xxi. 14)

So it is that Saint Augustine, and Aristotle too, desire that men should learn to do good and to rein in their passions, so that this shoot [i.e. the noblest part of the soul] should become sturdy through the habit of good conduct, and grow strong and upright, so that it may bear fruit; and this fruit may produce the sweetness of human happiness.[26]

Finally, Dante turns to the practical matter of how this process of growth and maturation into the virtues should proceed in the career of a single individual and, using organic metaphor once again, describes how different 'fruits' or virtues are appropriate to different stages of life. Both the last stanza of the *canzone* and the closing chapters of commentary provide a detailed breakdown of which virtues – and even what feelings and manners – are appropriate to each stage of a man's life, which is divided into four different 'ages' across the arc of the biblical three-score-and-ten (and beyond). Alongside organic metaphors, Dante begins to introduce topographical and political ones, marking a heightened civic interest in the analysis of what noble conduct implies in practical terms by speaking of the 'straight path' of noble conduct (*'una semplice via'*: IV. xxiv. 8), and of the 'city of the good life' (*'la cittade del bene vivere'*: IV. xxiv. 11). As a further indication of the primarily political concerns of the discussion, women, who in the Middle Ages were rarely permitted political agency, scarcely enter Dante's picture. They are mentioned only briefly in the lyric's sixth stanza and the commentary, where modesty is named as part of the appropriate conduct of a woman or a man in the youngest age (ll. 105–108, IV. xix. 8–10). And to further enhance the political atmosphere of his discussion, Dante chooses a series of predominantly male classical heroes as examples of each age's active qualities and virtues.

The analysis of the first age, *'Adolescenza'* (Adolescence), which lasts from childhood to the age of twenty-five, uses city-based imagery from the start:

> *Questa prima etade è porta e via per la quale s'entra ne la nostra buona vita. [...] Dà adunque la buona natura a questa etade quattro cose, necessarie a lo entrare ne la cittade del bene vivere.*
>
> (*Cvo* IV. xxiv. 9–11)

This first age is the gate and highway by which one enters into the good life. And nature gives this age four gifts, necessary for the entry into the city of the good life.

We are already familiar with the idea that a collective '*bene vivere*' is associated with the city community; now the ethical conduct of the individual, his own good life, is presented as a city. Continuing the metaphor, the youth's moral education is referred to as a kind of guided tour around a city:

> *Sì come quello che mai non fosse stato in una cittade, non saprebbe tenere le vie, sanza insegnamento di colui che l'hae usata; così l'adolescente, che entra ne la selva erronea di questa vita, non saprebbe tenere lo buono cammino, se da li suoi maggiori non li fosse mostrato.*
>
> (*Cvo* IV. xxiv. 12)

> Just as someone who had never been to a city would not be able to find his way around the streets unless guided by someone who knows it well; so the adolescent who enters the tangled woodland of life would not know how to stay on the right path unless it was pointed out to him by his elders.

The image changes unexpectedly half-way through into that of the wilderness, quite the opposite of the city, emphasising the difficulties and dangers that will be encountered when trying to live the good life (the phrase clearly anticipates the opening lines of the *Commedia* itself).[27] Both images emphasise that to acquire virtue an individual requires guidance and training in the ability to distinguish and pursue what is right from amongst a bewildering array of possibilities. *Adolescenza* is, precisely, a period of learning and preparation or, to use the terms of Dante's image, of orientation in the city of ethical conduct. It requires a spirit of obedience ('*Obedienza*') to the teachers who provide this instruction, drawing on the superior understanding and experience of their greater maturity ('*perfetta etade*': IV. xxiv. 2). Quoting the book of *Proverbs*, Dante promises that the adolescent obedient to his teachers will later be accorded glory, winning virtue's reward of public recognition by others:

'Sarà glorioso'; e dice 'sarà', a dare ad intendere che elli parla a lo ado-
lescente, che non puote essere, ne la presente etade.

(*Cvo* IV. xxiv. 16)

'He will win glory'; and [Solomon in *Proverbs*] says 'will' so as
to make it clear that he is addressing the Adolescent, who cannot win it at his present age.

Reciprocity and continuity form an essential element of public
life: one generation learns from its elders and then transmits this
learning onto the next, each in turn becoming worthy of glory
through its deferential apprenticeship in good conduct.

The adolescent must learn to form horizontal as well as vertical
relationships, as part of his social training. Indeed, it is essential that
he should concentrate on forming friendships with his contemporaries, as *'noi non potemo perfetta vita avere sanza amici'* ('our life cannot be considered perfect without having friends': IV. xxv. 1) –
another reminder of humanity's gregarious nature. The reasons
why friendship is valued may relate to an Aristotelian understanding of human nature, but the qualities that Dante prescribes for the
cultivation of friendship are distinctly medieval.[28] *Adolescenza* is a
period particularly appropriate for the cultivation of social graces
('*Soavitade*'), presumably because at this age, one is not yet bur-
dened with many social responsibilities. The adolescent attracts
friendships by his *'soavi reggimenti, che sono dolce e cortesemente parlare,*
dolce e cortesemente servire e operare' ('attractive behaviour, which consists of speaking in a fair and courtly fashion and of acting in a fair
and courtly fashion in person and towards others': xxv. 1). These
qualities, Dante urges, will attract like-minded friends to their possessor. The distinctly chivalric, courtly flavour of ideal adolescent
behaviour – *soave, cortese* and *dolce* – suggests that he may be imagining the formation of some such coterie of friends as he had
known in his own Florentine youth, who were drawn together by
their shared literary taste for the *'dolci rime d'amor'* ('sweet rhymes of
love') mentioned in the *canzone*'s opening line. It is noticeable in

79

fact that none of the qualities associated with the first age of life appear in the original Aristotelian catalogue of the moral virtues that indicate nobility. Instead, they have as much to do with the medieval conception of agreeable social behaviour as with the moral responsibilities of personal choice – the final quality on Dante's list is even physical beauty or fitness ('*Adornezza corporale*'), a pleasant but scarcely a moral trait.

One quality of Adolescence, '*Vergogna*' ('bashfulness': IV. xxv. 3), does however bear a delicate, quasi-ethical sense in Dante's analysis. Although only a passion, its effects seem closely related to the notion of the ethical mean that appeared in the Aristotelian defini-tion of the virtues, teaching the youth to '*essere rifrenato, sì che non transvada*', and '*essere penitente del fallo, sì che non s'ausi a fallare*' ('rein himself in, so that he should not err from the right path', and 'to repent of his faults, so that misconduct should not become a habit': IV. xxv. 4). Dante exclaims enthusiastically:

> *Oh quanti falli rifrena esto pudore! quante disoneste cose e dimande fa tacere! quante disoneste cupiditati raffrena!*
>
> (*Cvo* IV. xxv. 9)

> Oh, how many faults does this honest shame restrain! how many dishonourable remarks and questions does it silence! how much dishonourable greed does it rein in!

While the latent equestrian imagery and the emphasis on honour, keep the medieval, courtly side of Dante's interests in view, the asso-ciation between bashfulness and restraint, with the allusion to greed and the verbal variations on *frenare*, also helps create a linguistic con-nection with the earlier allusion to the role of imperial law as the rein on cupidity (IV. ix. 10), reminding us that Adolescence is a period of training for social and political responsibilities. '*Vergogna*', subdivided into the three qualities of reverence ('*stupore*'), honest shame ('*pudore*'), and fear for reputation ('*verecundia*': IV. xxv. 4), is also the only aspect of noble Adolescence which Dante illustrates with examples, all taken from the classical poet Statius's epic *Thebaid*. The story of Thebes, the city cursed by the gods and destroyed by civil war, might seem a startling source for examples of good conduct: nevertheless, Dante finds in it examples of those heroes who did attempt to observe the gods' will, and to ensure the wellbeing of their polity by their obedience – so that the kings, princes and princesses whom he praises are all shown to have acted in proper awareness of their social, familial and religious responsibilities.

The age of twenty-five is set as the boundary for transition into the next age, '*Giovinezza*' (Youth), which lasts until the age of forty-five. As twenty-five was the legal age of majority in Florence, as in many other medieval Italian *comuni*, it is little surprise to find that Dante sets this age as the point when a noble man is expected to take up public and political responsibilities, and to exercise not just good passions but the virtues themselves.[29] Choice and self-control now lie with the youth himself, who is called on to display two (or three) of the Aristotelian virtues, and three distinctive forms of social or civic conduct, as signs that his spirit is '*temperata e forte,* | *piena d'amore e di cortese lode,* | *e solo in lealtà far si diletta*' ('temperate and strong, full of love and praiseworthy in courtesy, and delighting only in adherence to the law': *Le dolci rime*, ll.129–131). The two Aristotelian virtues, temperance and fortitude (which is elided with magnanimity, a separate virtue on the original list, as '*Fortezza, o vero Magnanimitate*': IV. xxvi. 7), are described with equestrian imagery. Fortitude acts as a spur, temperance as a rein, exercising the control of reason and proper choice over human desires that makes the noble man a '*buono cavalcatore*' ('good rider') or '*buono cavaliere*' ('good knight': IV. xxvi. 6). Once again, the metaphors allow Dante to create a verbal link with his imperial chapters, where the ruler and his laws were portrayed as riders; but they also place the imagery in a distinctly chivalric context, by sandwiching the description of these virtues after the analysis of adolescent bashfulness and beauty, and immediately before the discussion of love and courtesy, as well as by explicitly alluding to knighthood. No longer dependent on the judgment of others, the youth must brace himself

to resist temptation or to face danger: just as Aeneas (the emblematic hero of this phase of life) chose, through temperance, to fulfil his
duty to the Trojans, thus sacrificing his love for Dido, and, through
fortitude, to dare to follow the Sybil into the underworld, to seek
his father's shade and to hear of the destiny of Rome.[30] The explicitly political aims served by these two acts of the epic hero further
highlight Youth as the age when civic responsibilities begin.

Of Youth's other qualities, love and courtesy are both described
in terms that similarly mix the classical with the chivalric. *Amore* is
a central preoccupation of medieval vernacular literature – the dis-
cursive philosophical musings of *Convivio* IV are all prompted by a
lyric in which Dante expresses regret that he has been forced, temporarily, to suspend writing about love. Vernacular tradition portrays love as based on the attraction, sometimes mutual but
sometimes unreciprocated, that a man feels for a woman; though
Italian writers at least – and very notably Dante, in the *Vita Nova*
and elsewhere – often represent love as a desexualised experience,
directed not towards corporeal satisfaction but to achieving social,
psychological and spiritual refinement through the self-denial and
efforts at self-betterment that admiration for another can prompt.[31]
The love felt by the *Convivio*'s noble youth, however, has little to do
with this. Reversing the expectations of any audience mindful of
the *canzone*'s opening line, Dante describes love as a social emotion
shared between men across different generations, dismissing as simply pleasure and enjoyment ('*piacere*' and '*dilettazione*') the attraction between Aeneas and Dido (IV. xxvi. 8). Love is presented
almost as the equivalent in Youth to the obedience of Adolescence,
likewise a quality transmitted between generations in a circular
manner that helps sustain the reciprocal obligations and benefits of
political life:

> *Si conviene guardare diretro e dinanzi, sì come cosa che è nel merid-*
> *ionale cerchio. Conviensi amare li suoi maggiori, da li quali ha rice-*
> *vuto ed essere e nutrimento e dottrina, sì che esso non paia ingrato;*
> *conviensi amare li suoi minori, acciò che, amando quelli, dea loro de li*

suoi benefici, per li quali poi ne la minore prosperitade esso sia da loro sostenuto e onorato.

(*Cvo* IV. xxvi. 10)

He must look behind and ahead, as if in a circle's meridian. He must love his elders, from whom he has received life and sustenance and knowledge, so that he should not appear ungrateful; he must love those younger than him, so that, loving them, he may allow them to benefit from what he possesses, and on this account may later, in less prosperous times, be supported and honoured by them.

Neither private and selfish, nor too selfless, this love is public-spirited but aware of its own worth, confident that the generous gestures made in the prime of life will be repaid in due course by a younger generation educated to show gratitude to their elders. Once again, Aeneas demonstrates the right course, sponsoring the young Trojans' martial training and settling the elders at Sicily when the journey to Latium appeared too arduous, thus lovingly serving the generations both too young and too old fully to sustain civic obligations.

'*Cortesia*' – courtesy or courtliness – is likewise a quality primarily associated with vernacular literary culture, but to which the *Convivio* adds a certain classical dignity (though noting that it can be incompatible with the '*gravezza e [...] severitade*', 'gravity and seriousness', of the next age: IV. xxvi. 12). At this point, Dante delivers only a brief discussion of courtesy, but earlier in the treatise it has been analysed at greater length, in terms that distinguish, as in the case of nobility, both a social aspect of courtliness and a moral one:

Cortesia e onestade è tutt'uno: e però che ne le corti anticamente le vertudi e li belli costumi s'usavano, sì come oggi s'usa lo contrario, si tolse quello vocabulo da le corti, e fu tanto a dire cortesia quanto uso di corte. Lo qual vocabulo se oggi si togliesse da le corti, massimamente d'Italia, non sarebbe altro a dire che turpezza.

(*Cvo* II. x. 8)

What is courtly and what is honourable are one and the same: and since in former times virtues and gracious manners used to be practised at court, just as today their opposites are practised, this word was derived from the court, and courtliness meant exactly the same thing as the manners of the court. If this word were to be derived from the courts of today, especially those of Italy, it would mean nothing other than baseness.

The same passage adds that courtliness is an appropriate accompaniment to '*la grandezza temporale*' ('secular greatness': II. x. 9), and also that it is no mere equivalent to '*larghezza*' ('liberality'), but a wider principle of which liberality is a single manifestation (just as the virtues are a manifestation of nobility). By bringing virtue, as well as good manners, into the picture of courtesy at this first discussion, Dante establishes what Robin Kirkpatrick has called an 'ethics of courtesy', reminding his readers of courtly literature's frequent insistence that *cortesia* and *amore* refine and elevate their possessor in moral as well as social terms.[32] In Book IV, Dante illustrates Aeneas's courtliness by telling how he helped cut wood for the funeral pyre of Misenus, an action of classical *pietas* that shows courtesy, like love, to cement social bonds and draw the community closer together.

'*Lealtade*', the final quality of Youth, is also a social quality, and makes its possessor '*seguire e mettere in opera quello che le leggi dicono*' ('follow and act in accordance with what the laws prescribe': IV. xxvi. 14).[33] The habits of obedience acquired in Adolescence appear in modified form in the careful adherence to law and custom prescribed for Youth, exemplified by Aeneas's observance of funeral games and rewards to the participants, in accordance with a national custom that he follows even in exile and after the destruction of Troy. Despite the relative maturity and responsibility of *Giovinezza*, Dante still strictly limits the extent to which a youth may exercise control over others. Temperance, fortitude, love, courtesy and obedience to law are all qualities that govern personal choice and make for smooth relations in society, but despite the many political resonances of the language and the examples chosen to describe Youth, full political agency has not yet been achieved. The discussion of *lealtade*, for instance, stresses that only '*lo vecchio*', the old or older man, can have a fully autonomous relationship to the law, '*per più esperienza*' ('because of his greater experience': IV. xxvi. 14).

When Dante moves into the discussion of '*Senettute*' (Old Age), an age which runs from forty-five to seventy years old, the emphasis immediately falls on this experience, and on political responsibility and public service. He chooses this moment for his second repetition of the Aristotelian maxim on humanity's social nature and instinct to serve others as well as oneself, illustrated metaphorically as making the noble man '*aprire [...] quasi com'una rosa che più chiusa stare non puote, e l'odore che dentro generato è spandere*' ('open up like a rose that can no longer stay closed, and disperse the fragrance that has been generated inside the flower': IV. xxvii. 4). Dante thus returns in this chapter to the language of organic growth and development with which the discussion of the virtues opened. The noble spirit in this age is described as characteristically prudent, just, liberal and affable – all but the first of these qualities appear on the Aristotelian list of moral virtues, while prudence forms one of the traditional Roman quartet of moral virtues outlined by philosophers such as Cicero or Seneca.[34]

All of the characteristics of Old Age are social and educative and the first two are shown to be specifically political as well. Prudence is declared to be synonymous with wisdom, and is exercised in giving '*buoni consigli, li quali conducono sé e altri a buono fine ne le umane cose e operazioni*' ('good counsel, which guides oneself and others towards the right goal in human affairs and activities': IV. xxvii. 6).[35] Dante cites Solomon as exemplifying this kind of wisdom, which he required specifically in order to exercise his political duties as king. Although it can be seen as a kind of political expertise, Dante warns that prudence is a natural attribute, to be freely shared with one's fellow-citizens, unlike the specialist advice bought from a lawyer or doctor. Indeed, switching from description to apostrophe, he issues a direct, second-person warning to '*messer lo legista*' ('you, sir lawyer': IV. xxvii. 9) against any attempt to profit from natural prudence rather than from technical juristic expertise. The warning echoes his denunciation, earlier in the treatise, of the debased motives of scholars who pursue Latin learning for gain, and who can be clearly distinguished from the vernacular *Convivio*'s chosen audience of the truly noble (I. ix. 5).

Public service is also prominently associated with justice, the virtue that allows the noble man to exercise his discrimination and authority ('*li suoi giudici e la sua autoritade*': IV. xxvii. 10) for the public good. Although justice is discussed only briefly, being intended to form the subject of a separate book in the original plan for the treatise, Dante's comments carry a heartfelt urgency in their analysis of the political necessity of justice:[36]

> *E perché questa singulare vertù, cioè giustizia, fue veduta per li antichi filosofi apparire perfetta in questa etade, lo reggimento de le cittadi commisero in quelli che in questa etade erano; e però lo collegio de li rettori fu detto Senato. Oh misera, misera patria mia! quanta pietà mi stringe per te, qual volta leggo, qual volta scrivo, cosa che a reggimento civile abbia rispetto!*
>
> (Cvo IV. xxvii. 10–11)

> And because this outstanding virtue, that is justice, was seen by the ancient philosophers to reach perfection in this age, they entrusted the government of cities to those who had attained this age; so it was that the college of governors was called the Senate. Oh my wretched, wretched country! I am gripped with such pity for you whenever I have to speak, or to write, anything that touches on civil governance!

Theory and etymology give way to the lament of the political exile who sees himself as a victim of injustice, and the shining example of Rome gives way to the chaos of Florence, giving poignancy to the brief analysis of justice. The tone is still harsher than in the warnings that concluded the analysis of prudence; together, these rebukes inserted into the commentary suggest that Dante feels that Old Age, potentially the most generous and public-spirited phase of life, also runs the greatest risk of corruption, because of the explicitly political obligations that it carries.

From the virtues of prudence and justice, Dante moves into less political, though still social, concerns with the discussion of liberality and affability. Liberality ('*larghezza*') must be exercised in conjunction with prudence and justice, which regulate how we enact its generous gestures. Dante states that this trio of virtues cannot be fully realised before the age of *Senettute*, although in Book II he treated liberality as an aspect of courtesy, which has now been identified as a characteristic of *Giovinezza*. While there seems to be some confusion of categories here, Dante is consistent at any rate in his vehement denunciation of those who fail to practise liberality correctly. Book II scorns as *turpezza* any failing in courtesy (and hence liberality); in Book IV, he offers a still longer condemnation of those '*tiranni*' ('tyrants') whose generosity is displayed almost sacrilegiously at the expense of the poor and vulnerable, '*vedove e pupilli, [...] li men possenti*' ('widows and orphans, the powerless': IV. xxvii. 13), presumably through high taxation and other administrative abuses. Clearly, Dante is here envisioning misconduct among the élite. As with his warning to lawyers, he directly cautions this part of his audience against feigning liberality when '*corredate conviti, donate cavalli e arme, robe e denari, portate le mirabili vestimenta, edificate le mirabili edifici*' ('you serve up banquets, make gifts of horses, weapons, goods and money, wear splendid clothes, build magnificent buildings': IV. xvii. 13) at the expense of the poor. In a colourful simile, he compares such conduct to that of a thief who uses a stolen altar-cloth as a table-cloth, and hopes that his dinner guests will not notice. The simile reminds us that private acts of generosity are nonetheless publicly judged; given Dante's insistence that prudence and justice inform liberality, it would appear that this too is a quality with political implications and requires a similar exhortation against abuse.

The only virtue of Old Age not accompanied by vehement injunctions against improper practice, indeed, is affability ('*essere affabile*') – even though in Dante's definition it has a connection with the arts of speech that would seem to leave every possibility for misuse, and misuse with political consequences, too. Instead of issuing any warning over potential *peccata linguae*, however, as might be justified by both the theory and the practice of *comune* regimes, Dante makes affability a purely positive and essentially private – though educational – quality, involving the tranquil give and take of '*ragionare lo bene, e quello udire volontieri*' ('willingness to talk about, and to hear of, what is good': IV. xxvii. 16). This seems to indicate a gentler, more contemplative side to Old Age than has yet been envisioned: although in the illustrative examples – which appear clustered together at the end of the chapter – affability is demonstrated by a king's instructive historical discourse, suggesting that it is closely allied to the more political virtue of prudence (which involves memory as well as judgement and foresight). All of the examples are taken from the same Ovidian narrative of a king – Aeacus of Aegina – who scrupulously protected the interests of his subjects and his allies.[37] Aeacus is portrayed by Dante as a calmly authoritative figure, who took proper care to nurture the different relationships that linked him to his own people and to his neighbours, and who remained privately approachable (*affabile*) as well as publicly honourable. His good behaviour is the more striking, in that his state was virtually destroyed by a plague, and only saved when the gods metamorphosed ants into humans to repopulate the island: Aeacus thus weathered the collapse of his state, and saw his people reborn. The example both offers an object lesson to Dante's own *misera patria* about the importance of seeking political renewal, and allows him to conclude the analysis of the moral virtues and the active life on a hopeful note.

After Old Age, the final phase of human life is labelled '*Senio*' (Extreme Old Age), which runs from the age of seventy until death (ideally at the age of eighty-one). It is a phase of withdrawal from public life into contemplation, as the noble man prepares himself for death by turning towards religion and pondering his past career. Dante himself died in the chronological age of *Senettute*, at fifty-six, but the evidence of the *Paradiso* suggests that he had already morally entered the age of *Senio* – his initial discussion of the ages' duration acknowledges that the boundaries are not hard and fast but vary according to individual constitution (IV. xxiv. 7). There are no moral virtues assigned to this age, since the political pursuits of the active life have come to an end. The description of proper conduct in Extreme Old Age shifts from the analytical to a more lyrical key, as Dante elaborates a series of images that describe its spiritual preoccupation with preparing for death and for the new life that he faithfully believes to lie beyond existence on earth. He compares the approach to death conventionally to a sea-journey's end in landfall, or a traveller's return to his own city:

> La nobile anima [...] attende lo fine di questa vita con molto deside-rio e uscir le pare de l'albergo e ritornare ne la propria mansione, uscir le pare di cammino e tornare in cittade, uscir le pare di mare e tornare a porto.
>
> (*Cvo* IV. xxviii. 7)

> The noble soul awaits the end of this earthly life with great longing, and seems to be leaving the inn and returning to its own dwelling, to be leaving the road and returning into the city, to be leaving the sea and returning to port.

The images not only draw on traditional Christian discourse, but also aptly counterbalance the description of Adolescence as a jour-ney or as entry into a city, making the active life and the contempla-tive life follow similar phases. Dante finds various examples of noble conduct in *Senio*. Both the Arthurian hero Lancelot and the con-temporary Italian statesman Guido da Montefeltro are praised for their withdrawals from high politics into monastic life in Extreme Old Age. The classical example of Marcia, the wife of Cato, provides an extended example of successful conduct in decrepitude, follow-ing appropriate action in earlier ages: her two marriages and their children signify Youth and Old Age with their specific virtues; her life before marriage, Adolescence; her final remarriage to Cato becomes a sign of the discernment of higher values appropriate to Extreme Old Age (IV. xxviii. 14–15).[38] Dante's admiration for Cato as a statesman and as a man of principle was earlier expressed in his chapter on Roman leadership, and is reiterated here (IV. v. 16, xxviii. 15). That *Senio* is an apolitical age, however, is signified by Dante's reversion to a female example, after the exclusively masculine models of behaviour proposed for Youth and Old Age.

With *Senio*, Dante reaches the end of his discussion of the moral virtues that produce actions which aid us in recognising those who are taking their social responsibilities seriously. His analysis and choice of examples help to substantiate his theoretical assertions – in *Convivio* IV. iv–v, and also in *Monarchia* – about the importance of life in society to individual happiness, by showing how all the phases of active life are shaped by dependence on, or responsibilities towards, fellow members of the community. By bringing into clearer focus the role and responsibilities of the individual, this enhances the conclusions of his theoretical analysis of polities as collectives. At a practical level, Dante's analysis of nobility provides guidance on how to become both a good man and a good citizen. It is in his choice of examples, perhaps, that Dante draws the connections between individual and collective activity most tellingly and most imaginatively. Not only do the examples offer a breakdown of the separate virtues and passions to be cultivated by those noble individuals who truly deserve political responsibilities, they also demonstrate how they can be implemented in particular historical circumstances. The narrative method of the *Commedia* is directly anticipated, as Dante's detailed readings of the stories of Aeneas, Aeacus and the others discovers the relevance of individual action and example, as well as of theory and philosophy, to a proper understanding of human political life. The flurry of direct apostrophes addressed to the contemporary élite in his analysis of Old Age makes it clear that his statements of broad principle and his analysis of individual examples are both intended to have direct, practical relevance to the states of contemporary Italy. The structure of

Convivio IV moves from imperial theory to discussion of moral virtue, and supports both with detailed historical examples drawn from Roman history and poetry. Dante thus reveals his interest in political theory to be firmly rooted in history and in experience; while his apostrophes to the Italian élites stress his concern with the microcosm of individual states and societies, as well as with the macrocosm of empire.

3

RHETORIC, POLITICS AND EXILE

DE VULGARI ELOQUENTIA
AND *TRE DONNE*

Writers on government from the Italian *comuni* of Dante's age closely associated the arts of rhetoric and of government, as we have seen. Dante, too, was very much alert to the political aspects of language, both at a theoretical level and in relation to the affairs of contemporary Italian cities. His passionate commitment to the use of the vernacular for serious literary and philosophical purposes had distinctly political implications. The *Convivio* – which the previous chapter has already found to carry rich political and ethical reflections – makes explicit Dante's conviction that it is vitally important to develop the vernacular in order to open philosophical learning to an audience endowed with nobility and active in the political life.[1] He therefore invites to his 'banquet' of knowledge:

> *coloro che per malvagia disusanza del mondo hanno lasciata la litter-*
> *atura a coloro che l'hanno fatta di donna meretrice; e questi nobili sono*
> *principi, baroni, cavalieri, e molt'altra nobile gente, non solamente*
> *maschi ma femmine, [...] volgari e non litterati.*
>
> (*Cvo* I. ix. 5)

those who through the erroneous neglect of the world have left letters to those who have turned such learning from a lady to a whore; and these nobles are princes, barons, knights, and many other noble people, not only men but also women, who know the vernacular but not Latin.

The treatise still, though, sets limits to its audience, carefully defining the qualifications necessary for access to its semi-exclusive message (I. i. 1). The *Commedia*, by contrast, seems open to all comers, drawing its audience into a narrative that flows irresistibly forwards in the interlocking rhythms of its vernacular verse in *terza rima*.[2] (Only in *Paradiso* does the poet set some limits to his audience: *Par.* II. 1–15.) Dante consciously makes a political choice in using the vernacular for his most serious work, the poem that probes the deepest spiritual and secular truths across its epic, 100-*canto* narrative. Equally political is his decision to abandon the elegant, Latinate vernacular of the *Convivio* for a more mixed, 'comic' form accessible to a popular, as well as a noble, audience.[3] The poem thus invites an audience far broader than the *Convivio*'s to engage with the text – and to act on its urgent messages of political and religious reform within the local, Italian communities where they encounter it.

The decision to use vernacular language and comic style for the poem was by no means casual. That Dante was aware of the political implications of his linguistic choice whenever composing in the vernacular is evident from other early works besides the *Convivio*. Quite shortly after his exile from Florence, Dante began work on a formal treatise on language issues, *De vulgari eloquentia*.[4] This text does not follow the dictaminal pattern so popular with contemporaries, where political rhetoric often occupied a primary position. Instead, as in *Convivio* and *Monarchia*, he declares at the outset his intention to fill a gap in existing thought on his topic, vernacular language:

> *Cum neminem ante nos de vulgaris eloquentie doctrina quicquam inveniamus tractasse, [...] Verbo aspirante de celis locutioni vulgarium gentium prodesse temptabimus.*
>
> (*DVE* I. i. 1)

> Since I find that no-one, before myself, has dealt in any way
> with the theory of eloquence in the vernacular, I shall try,
> inspired by the Word that comes from above, to say something
> useful about the language of people who speak the vulgar
> tongue.

The treatise treats vernacular language with all seriousness, and urges the importance of developing the expressive capacities of Italian. However, its programme for such development is based on refinement and exclusion, rather than on comic inclusion. As this chapter will show, the *De vulgari*'s linguistic conclusions are closer to those of the *Convivio* than of the *Commedia*. At the same time, the treatise's interest in connecting ideas about language and politics provides an element of comparability with the poem, despite the two texts' differences over the form and style appropriate to serious poetry.

Dante's concern with the vernacular in the treatise is closely based on his career as a lyric poet, and he devotes much of his text to aesthetic considerations. Many aspects of the work suggest that it constitutes a formal *ars poetica*: Book II, indeed, is largely dedicated to questions about the form, style, subject matter and vocabulary appropriate to the composition of vernacular lyric verse, or in the later chapters (iv–xiv) to a still more specialised topic, the art of the *canzone* form alone.[5] However, it is at the point when the treatise has moved onto these technical questions that the investigation peters out, midway through a sentence. Critics generally associate this disruption – still more abrupt than that of the contemporaneous *Convivio* – with Dante's embarkation on the project of the *Commedia*. As Steven Botterill remarks in his recent edition of the treatise, it probably marks 'a growing realisation that his views on poetic language were best expounded not in theory but in practice', that is by *using* the vernacular, rather than by analysing it in a learned, Latin treatise.[6] But it is also striking that Dante abandoned his project at the point when an underlying *political* dimension to his linguistic discussion had effectively evaporated – suggesting that he realised that civic, as well as poetic, aims were best served through the far more ambitious project of the *Commedia*.

Almost half of the first book of *De vulgari* is dedicated to a close linguistic scrutiny of contemporary Italy's cities and regions. Dante maintains a lively and often polemical tone of passionate interest in this subject matter, with frequent exclamations of praise and blame. His investigation of the Italian linguistic scene purports to pursue a primarily aesthetic goal, that of identifying the '*decentiorem atque illustrem Ytalie [...] loquelam*' ('most respectable and illustrious vernacular in Italy': I. xi. 1) from among the fourteen major languages, or the thousands of local variant forms, used in the peninsula.[7] Having identified the best form of language, he will go on in the *poetria* of Book II to analyse its employment. In fact, the discussion of the languages of the states and cities of contemporary Italy repeatedly carries political overtones.[8] The exiled Florentine treats the fragmented linguistic situation in the peninsula with a close concern that mirrors his anxiety over Italian political fragmentation. His most enthusiastic comments in the course of the survey are often charged with moral and political significance, lending to the first part of the treatise an urgency that is not sustained by the more neutral and narrowly literary matter of Book II.

Dante's analysis of the languages of Italy is based on an understanding of nuances of local difference that appears firmly rooted in personal experience. He distinguishes very acutely between the vernaculars used in different Tuscan cities, and is familiar enough with Bolognese to know that within this single city different idioms are used in different urban neighbourhoods, but he offers little detail on the languages of southern Italy or the islands, regions that he never visited.[9] But although *De vulgari* presents a probing enquiry into linguistic difference, its overriding interests lie with linguistic unity. In matters of language, just as in the political issues addressed in *Convivio* and *Monarchia*, Dante shows his readiness to challenge the *status quo* in urban Italy. Even when he has identified the most agreeable of the existing vernaculars – Bolognese (I. xv. 6) – he does not propose its adoption throughout the peninsula.

Rather, in a radical and non-partisan vision of Italian linguistic cohesion, he embarks on the project of identifying a single, non-municipal or 'illustrious' vernacular that could be shared through-out Italy without favouring any single region. His quest for linguistic unity recalls in some measure his quest for political unity through the medium of empire. In the case of language, he works on an Italian, rather than a global scale, since Latin, which the trea-tise takes to be an artificial language or *gramatica* (I. ix. II), already provides wider cross-cultural communication in perpetuity.

In *De vulgari*, however, Dante prescribes that the unifying Italian language be used only in rather limited circumstances and prima-rily, at least under contemporary political conditions, for poetic composition. The limitation recalls the common conceit in the lyric poetry of Dante and his contemporaries, that their lofty con-ceptions render the essence of the verse inaccessible to all but a happy few.[10] However, Dante himself was also powerfully drawn towards exegesis and inclusion. His *Vita Nova* and *Convivio* are presented to their readers precisely as collections of sophisticated verse accompanied by prose explanations, which reveal to a wider public meanings that were formerly accessible only to an exclusive inner circle, or perhaps only to their composer. Later in this chap-ter, we will consider another *canzone* from the period of the *Convivio*, the political lyric *Tre donne intorno al cor mi son venute* (*Three ladies have come round my heart*), where an inclusive coda reverses previous claims of impenetrability, inviting first a narrow and then a wide audience to decipher its true significance. In the *Commedia*, Dante goes even further, breaking down the rigid medieval system of styles and genres, mixing elevated language with lower registers, and embracing a wide audience from the outset.[11] Although in *De vulgari* and *Tre donne* he has not yet embraced the linguistic inclusivity shown in the *Commedia*, both, though in different ways, explore the proposition that cohesion in the use of language can heal wider social and political divisions. In both, too, Dante adds a strongly personal dimension to the quest for such unity, by reference to his own exile.

NATURAL LANGUAGE:
EDENIC UNITY AND BABELIC DIVERSITY

As with his political enquiry in *Monarchia*, Dante opens the linguistic enterprise of *De vulgari* by going back to first principles. Not
only does he establish what the term *'vulgare'* ('vernacular language')
means, and how vernaculars differ from artificial languages (*'gramaticae'*: *DVE* I. i. 2–4),[12] but he also sets out to investigate why humans
use language at all. His answers reveal that the need for language is as
innate to humanity as the need for society that he took to be fundamental in his political investigation in the *Monarchia*.

Dante's description of the orders of creation stresses that the
capacity for language is unique to human beings:

> *Eorum que sunt omnium soli homini datum est loqui, cum solum sibi*
> *necessarium fuerit. Non angelis, non inferioribus animalibus necessar-*
> *ium fuit loqui, sed nequicquam datum fuisset eis: quod nempe facere*
> *natura aborret.*
>
> (*DVE* I. ii. 1–2)

> Of all creatures that exist, only human beings were given the
> power of speech, because only to them was it necessary. It was
> not necessary that either angels or the lower animals should be
> able to speak; rather, this power would have been wasted on
> them, and nature, of course, hates to do anything superfluous.

The immortal angels can understand one another by pure intellection and animals by natural instinct; humans, with their compound
existence as mortal beings who also possess intellect, cannot achieve
similarly spontaneous inter-communication.[13] Since humans decide
on their most important actions through the use of reason rather
than purely by animal instinct, they need to be able explain these
decisions to one another, using *'aliquod rationale signum et sensuale'*
('some signal based on reason and perception': I. iii. 2). Language
combines the perceptible (sound) with the rational, through the

conventional meanings assigned to different sounds, and so enables effective communication between individuals.[14] The ability to achieve proper mutual comprehension is especially important given Dante's views on humanity's gregarious nature. Solitude may not require language, but social existence does. Even in the Ciceronian account of political origins that Dante rejects, which was explored in Chapter I, speech was fundamental to the formation of human societies, since humans only grouped together when prompted by the speech of a wise man. To Dante, with his Aristotelian view of humanity's associative instincts, social existence naturally brings with it with the necessity for speech and ordered language.

In Dante's account, indeed, speech even preceded social existence – the first action of the newly created Adam, he asserts, was immediately to utter the name of God.[15] There is no scriptural authority for this claim, but Dante shows it to be a logical necessity that the innocent first man, prompted by his loving creator, should have immediately employed one of his highest and most distinctive faculties in speaking aloud the word '*El*', which Dante identifies as Adam's name for the deity (I. iv. 4). Moreover Adam, in his still incorrupt state, used an idiom naturally shaped by divine grace (a '*lingua [...] gratie*', I. vi. 6).[16] Even after the 'Fall', Dante asserts that this same language was preserved by Adam and transmitted to his descendants, remaining the universal vernacular of early humanity. It survived a second collective calamity or 'Fall', when Noah and his family preserved this language intact after the Flood that drowned the rest of humanity. A third 'Fall' however, with the attempt to build the Tower of Babel, brought about the fragmentation of linguistic unity and, hence, social and political division also (I. vii. 2).

Babel is presented as an absolute '*opus iniquitatis*' ('work of evil': I. vii. 6), a perverted enterprise whose conception and construction fatally misused many of humanity's intellectual and mechanical talents, and so is aptly punished through the rational-sensory medium of language. Only a tiny minority recognised the project's sinfulness and abstained; like Noah, they were exempted from the rest of humanity's punishment, so retaining Adam's Edenic '*sacratum ydioma*' ('holy language': I. vii. 8). Dante identifies this language as Hebrew, asserting that it was preserved from destruction in order that Christ, when born as a human, should speak a language originating in pre-Lapsarian Eden rather than in punishment for sin. He goes on, however, to specify that this language remained in use only until the dispersal of the Jews ('*usque ad suam* [i.e. the Israelites'] *dispersionem*': I. vii. 8): that is, until after Titus's conquest of Jerusalem. The Jewish refusal to accept Christ constitutes in Dante's eyes another 'Fall', punished (as was Babel) by the destruction of their most treasured building, the Temple, and by a diaspora that finally extinguished the language of Eden.[17]

This account follows a clear sequence of cause and effect that creates an orderly pattern; in the longer run, however, Dante did not find it satisfactory. In *Paradiso* XXVI, the question of Edenic language resurfaces, and the soul of Adam himself is made to tell Dante-character a less neat story in which all languages, including his own, are shown inevitably to change and die out over time. Other details that differ from the *De vulgari*'s narrative include Adam's name for God ('*I*' not '*El*': l.133), and the assertion that his language had perished before Babel, revisions that underline the truth that Dante by this time found more persuasive, that, in Adam's words:

> *nullo effetto mai razionabile,*
> *per lo piacere uman che rinnovella*
> *seguendo il cielo, sempre fu durabile.*
>
> (*Par.* XXVI. 127–129)

no work of reason could ever last forever, for human fancy
renews itself following the changes of the heavens.

The *Paradiso* rejects the notion that any historical language enjoys special grace or special durability. Adam spoke a tongue as arbitrary as any other and linguistic mutation is a natural, not a violent, process.[18] The notoriously contradictory assessments of *Convivio* and

De vulgari over the relative nobility and mutability of Latin and vernacular tongues becomes irrelevant in *Paradiso*; and whereas Dante chose, in *De vulgari*, to demonstrate the superior quality of the vernacular by composing his treatise of defence in the learned idiom of Latin, the *Commedia* valorises the message, rather than the medium. Adam's statement implies that Latin cannot enjoy the immutability attributed to *gramaticae* in *De vulgari*: thus, as Gianfranco Contini observes, the conclusions of *Paradiso* XXVI provide a self-justification for Dante's decision to write the *Commedia* in vernacular rather than Latin, by stressing that even the prestige tongue of the Middle Ages is as arbitrary and transitory as any other.[19]

De vulgari, however, by advancing the notion of a stable Adamic *lingua gratie* draws a striking connection between linguistic mutation and human transgression. After Babel, the inevitability of linguistic diversity and instability becomes a constant reminder of humanity's sinfulness. Dante's version of the Babel story even imagines that the split into different language groups followed a pattern that marked out a hierarchy of culpability. Each professional group working on the Tower came to speak a unique language, incomprehensible to the other occupations:

> *Quot quot autem exercitii varietates tendebant ad opus, tot tot ydiomatibus tunc genus humanum disiungitur; et quanto excellentius exercebant, tanto rudius nunc barbariusque locuntur.*
>
> (*DVE* I. vii. 7)

> As many as were the types of work involved in the enterprise, so many were the languages by which the human race was fragmented; and the more skill required for the type of work, the more rudimentary and barbaric the language they now spoke.

As Robert Durling has shown, this statement implies that members of the élite professions – architects, for instance – by exercising more ingenuity and more authority in planning the Tower's construction than the labourers whose manual work they directed, came to speak an uglier, more uncouth language that showed they were 'more to blame'.[20] When Dante later comes to his linguistic investigation of contemporary Italy, this Babelic association between ethical and aesthetic judgements is tacitly carried forward to produce markedly political conclusions.

FROM BABEL TO BOLOGNA:
LINGUISTIC CHANGE AND ITALIAN CITIES

The purpose of Babel's linguistic punishment was to prevent any continuing collaboration on the construction of the Tower to heaven. The destruction of humanity's common language also destroyed the social order that had allowed the sinful project to evolve, and its consequence was a vast diaspora of the different lan-guage groups across the globe. Each group settled in a different region, to form the nucleus of a new society: linguistic diversity thus brought social and political diversity in its wake, due to the scattering of the peoples. Dante's account of the migrations stresses the vast scale of the changes inaugurated by Babel. Where before he was able to discuss collective history because all human beings lived together and spoke the same language, now he has to subdivide his subject matter and can follow the evolutions of only a few lan-guages among the post-Babelic multiplicity of tongues. This allows him to move rapidly from the remote era of *Genesis* to concentrate on contemporary Italy, and on his survey of the peninsula's local languages.

The transition from the global to the local is traced through a series of intermediate stages. The treatise describes the arrival in Europe of speakers of an '*ydioma tripharium*' ('tripartite language': I. viii. 2), who settled variously in the south, the north and the east according to the three broad divisions in this original idiom. With time, each language subdivided again into numerous regional or tribal tongues, as differ-ent nations emerged within each area – such as the northern European '*Sclavones, Ungar[i], Teutonic[i], Saxones, Anglic[i]*' ('Slavs,

Hungarians, Teutons, Saxons, English'), and others, whose common linguistic origin is indicated in their common use of the word '*iò*' for 'yes' (I. viii. 3). Within southern Europe, the distinctive form of the tripartite language also mutated, into three broad forms distinguished again by their affirmatives – the *oc* of Provençals and Catalans, the *oïl* of the northern French, and the *sì* of Italians – but retain many words that display a common root (I. viii. 5). The most important of these shared words, for Dante's argument, proves to be '*amor*' ('love': I. ix. 3) – the key concept in the vernacular courtly literature of contemporary Europe: its shared usage is proved by quoting from a love lyric in each tongue.[21] Each of these idioms displays further local variety, too – choosing Italian illustrations, Dante comments that peninsular languages differ along a broad east–west divide, differ again between cities in neighbouring regions, and can even vary within different neighbourhoods of the same city (I. ix. 4). The post-Babelic languages, in short, display almost infinite variation over time and space.

All of this brings him to Italy itself, and to the brink of his investigation into the diversity of contemporary languages and into the possibility of a more united usage within the peninsula. The strong Italian interest of his treatise has in fact been evident ever since the discussion of Adamic language, where Dante commented on his own personal interest in the languages of Italy, Tuscany and Florence, though ingenuously disclaiming any prejudice in their favour:

> *Nos autem, cui mundus est patria velut piscibus equor, quanquam Sarnum biberimus ante dentes et Florentiam adeo diligamus ut, quia dileximus, exilium patiamur iniuste, rationi magis quam sensui spatulas nostri iudicii podiamus. Et quamvis ad [...] nostre sensualitatis quietem in terris amenior locus quam Florentia non existat, revolventes et poetarum et aliorum scriptorum volumina [...], ratiocinantesque in nobis situationes varias mundi locorum [...], multas esse perpendimus firmiterque censemus et magis nobiles et magis delitiosas et regiones et urbes quam Tusciam et Florentiam [...], et plerasque nationes et gentes delectabiliori atque utiliori sermone uti quam Latinos.*
>
> (*DVE* I. vi. 3)

To me, however, the whole world is a homeland, like the sea to a fish – though I drank from the Arno before cutting my teeth, and love Florence so much that, because I loved her, I suffer exile unjustly – and I will weight the balance of my judgement more with reason than with sentiment. And although for the satisfaction of my own desire there is no more agreeable place on earth than Florence, yet when I turn the pages of the volumes of poets and other writers, and when I reflect inwardly on the various locations of places in the world, I am convinced, and firmly maintain, that there are many regions and cities more noble and delightful than Tuscany and Florence, and many nations and peoples who speak a more elegant and practical language than do the Italians.

And indeed, when Dante launches into his survey of Italian local languages, he proves highly critical of the majority, including those of Tuscany. He labels them dissonant in their entirety and brings a range of pejorative terms to each region, speaking of Rome's *tristiloquium* ('vile jargon': I. xi. 2) and Tuscany's *turpiloquia* ('foul jargons': I. xiii. 4), and describing how Istrians *crudeliter accentuando eructuant* ('belch forth with a cruel intonation': I. xi. 6) or Apulians *loquantur obscene* ('speak in a base fashion': I. xii. 8).

The survey covers a broad range of different regions, in many cases supplying a brief citation of local usage – for instance, the vernacular of Rome is exemplified by the phrase '*Messure, quinto dici?*' ('Sir, what do you say?': I. xi. 2).[22] A number of these examples are drawn from verse compositions, as Dante sometimes makes clear – his illustrations of usage in the Marches and in Lombardy are both taken from poetic sources that comically emphasise the distinctive features of local idiom. Pier Vincenzo Mengaldo's critical edition of *De vulgari* identifies parallel sources for a number of the other regional phrases, predominantly satirical in nature, and suggests that Dante's criticisms are directed not so much at regional languages *in se*, but at regional and municipal literatures.[23] Since poetry, as we shall see, plays a principal part in

Dante's programme for linguistic unity, it is natural that he should also focus on poetic evidence in exposing the shortcomings of regionalism.

The close relationship between Dante's interest in city speech and interest in city poetry is illustrated most clearly in his remarks on Tuscany, the Italian region which he naturally knew best. His discussion amply fulfils his earlier promise to exercise detachment in discussing his native vernacular, opening with a stern criticism of the regional delusion that Tuscan corresponds to Italy's 'illustrious' vernacular. Both commoners and more élite Tuscans, particularly local lyricists, are accused of sharing a misplaced pride in languages that have only ever produced '*dicta municipalia*' ('municipal verse': I. xiii. 1), rather than any truly polished or '*curialia*' ('courtly') products. The gravity of the Tuscans' errors is further underlined by the symmetry between Dante's list of five composers from different towns, and five examples of rather foolish dialect phrases from the same centres: Arezzo, Lucca, Pisa, Siena and Florence thus display double linguistic shortcomings, in both their literary and their everyday practice. The few Tuscan poets (including an unnamed Florentine readily identifiable as Dante himself) who are acknowledged to have achieved literary elegance are shown to have avoided writing in the local vernaculars.[24]

Dante's survey of a number of other urban and regional idioms, which occupies five chapters in total, concludes in the city of Bologna, with the cautious judgement that '*forte non male opinantur qui Bononienses asserunt pulcriori locutione loquentes*' ('perhaps those are not wrong who claim that the Bolognese speak a more beautiful language than most': I. xv. 2). The attraction of their idiom lies in the fact that it fuses the most pleasant elements of a number of languages in the region, balancing the softness of Imola against the abruptness of Ferrara and Modena, to achieve '*laudabilem suavitatem*' ('praiseworthy elegance': I. xv. 5). The subtlety of the Bolognese combination of influences is perhaps also apparent in the nuances that, as Dante noted earlier, distinguish the speech of two urban neighbourhoods, the peripheral Borgo San Felice and the central urban *quartiere* of Strada Maggiore (I. ix. 4). But despite the superiority of Bolognese over other urban and regional idioms, the language does not win Dante's full stamp of approval. When he turns to the poetic evidence that tests the aesthetic appeal of a language, he finds that the best Bolognese poets, like the Tuscans, have had to abandon their native vernacular, since '*non [...] est quod aulicum et illustre vocamus*' ('it is not what we could call aulic or illustrious': I. xv. 6). Dante is thus forced to conclude that no current Italian urban vernacular rises above the 'municipal'. His consideration of the cities has however shown that among their variety of languages, a single 'illustrious' tongue can be found in occasional, primarily literary, use. This idiom is recognisably the same in all regions, showing a unity that reverses the pattern of fragmentation in the peninsular Babel of divided languages. The closing chapters of Book I go on to discuss this shared, pan-Italian *vulgare illustre* – and they do so in terms that firmly couple political to aesthetic considerations.

POETRY AND POLITICS IN 'ILLUSTRIOUS' LANGUAGE

Dante's account of the aftermath of Babel stresses the variety of human languages, and shows a close concern with their relative aesthetic appeal. At Babel itself, he outlines an inverse correlation between social authority and linguistic elegance: the élite directors of the project come to speak ugly languages that mark them as more culpable than the artisans. The survey of Italian languages, however, outlines a contrary situation, again noted by Robert Durling, where Dante classifies the multiple languages of the unlearned as uglier than the more unified idiom of the poetic élite.[25] Significantly, whereas at Babel the élite combined social authority with their technical mastery, Dante's modern Italian élite is a purely artistic one, possessing little or no direct power. In *De vulgari*, the ordinary vernacular remains ugly, provincial and divisive, regardless of the user's social or intellectual standing – as was stressed in the scathing comments on 'municipal' Tuscan verse, which named some of the most learned figures of the previous generation, and is also shown in remarks on political leadership that will be examined later. Moreover, although *De vulgari* declares illustrious Italian an élite language, it is a language that Dante claims is shared by *all* the cities, making it more inclusive, and so less Babelic, than any single local tongue. Its accessibility throughout the peninsula makes for polished and pleasing performances in literature; it is also a potential tool for political co-operation throughout Italy, offering a means to overcome the barriers of local linguistic limitation and exclusion.

Evidence of the *vulgare illustre*'s political efficacy, and of the political as well as aesthetic critique of the 'municipal' limitations of Italy's local communities that Dante wants to launch, has been interspersed into the regional survey from the outset. The account of Babel itself – the paradigm of linguistic, moral, and political confusion – was preceded by Dante's statement on the probable limitations of Tuscan and Florentine language that also drew attention, with its reference to exile, to the political limitations of a contemporary state divided against itself and exercising unjust punishment against its own members (I. vi. 3, above). In the census of Italian vernaculars, the opening chapters offer examples with strong political undertones. The survey begins, for instance, with Rome, '*sicut [...] Romani se cunctis preponendos existimant*' ('since the Romans believe they should always receive preferential treatment': I. xi. 2). Roman claims to prestige rest on the city's glorious past of political pre-eminence, but Dante's comments on both the language and manners of the modern city stress that it now stands out only for its exceptionally unpleasant qualities.

Dante notes that a second candidate for linguistic distinction is Sicily, especially because many of the island's poets have achieved true excellence. As in Tuscany and Bologna, however, they prove to have written not in the local dialect but in illustrious Italian (I. xii. 6). Sicily's high reputation – like Rome's, but in more recent times – has in fact been acquired thanks to political circumstances, and provides an instructive example for other contemporary states:

Sed hec fama trinacrie terre, si recte signum ad quod tendit inspicia-
mus, videtur tantum in obproprium ytalorum principum remansisse,
qui non heroico more sed plebeio secuntur superbiam.

(*DVE* I. xii. 3)

But this fame enjoyed by the Trinacrian isle, if we carefully
consider the end to which it leads, seems rather to survive only
as a reproof to the princes of Italy, who are so puffed up with
pride that they live in a plebeian, not a heroic, fashion.

Italy's contemporary leaders are dominated by pride, and display
plebeian rather than élite qualities – they are apt post-Babelic leaders, since the pride of the Tower project was punished, according to
Dante, in part by making the élite speak in a plebeian manner. Sicily,
however, had the good fortune in the mid-Duecento to be ruled by
princes whom Dante here praises for moral probity, and who, by no
coincidence, were also hostile to papal secular ambitions and were
promoters of the Holy Roman Empire, the '*illustres heroes, Fredericus*
Cesar et benegenitus eius Manfredus' ('illustrious heroes, the Emperor
Frederick and his worthy son Manfred': I. xii. 4). Dante's flattering
adjectives and use of the classical form of Frederick II's imperial title
makes his political agenda very clear.[26] The nobility and rectitude of
these leaders, he says, attracted like-minded followers from all over
Italy to the Sicilian court, which became a national centre of moral
and cultural distinction. Among the products of this talented court
can be numbered the vernacular lyrics of the so-called Sicilian poets
– but Dante is careful to stress that their works should be called
Sicilian only because of the location of the court. The linguistic
characteristics of the *canzoni* in question are 'illustrious', not 'municipal', displaying the same polished, pan-Italian excellence as the cos-
mopolitan courtiers themselves.

The Sicilian example is presented explicitly as an instructive
counterpoise to the political and linguistic predilections of Italy's
contemporary leaders. This is stressed not only in the introductory
remarks cited above, but also in a passage of exclamatory invective

similar to those that occur in *Convivio* IV, reviewed in Chapter 2. Dante cannot restrain himself from pointing out the contrast between the promise of unity offered by the Hohenstaufens' leadership, and the competition and violence endemic throughout the peninsula in his own age:

> *Racha, racha! Quid nunc personat tuba novissimi Frederici, quid tintinabulum secundi Karoli, quid cornua Iohannis et Azonis marchionum potentum, quid aliorum magnatum tibie, nisi 'Venite carnifices, venite altriplices, venite avaritie sectatores?'*
>
> (*DVE* I. xii. 5)

Racha, racha [Fools]! What is the noise made now by the trumpet of the latest Frederick [of Sicily], or the bells of the second Charles [of Naples], or the horns of the powerful marquises Giovanni [of Monferrat] and Azzo [of Este], or the pipes of the other warlords? Only 'Come you butchers! Come, you traitors! Come, you devotees of greed!'

The satirical evocation of these cacophonous military fanfares marks the propensity for disunity and provincialism in both the politics and culture of the princes and magnates of Dante's age. His examples span the peninsula, listing names closely associated with the inter-state warfare of the early Trecento, and his political agenda is made clear with the emotive references to the princes' violence, greed and treachery – significantly, we have seen that the contemporary *Convivio* also picks out Kings Frederick and Charles for their political, moral and philosophical failings (IV. vi. 20). Power and patronage in Italy have passed into unworthy hands, and it is scarcely surprising that under such leadership, Italian vernaculars should show Babelic ugliness as well as diversity.

Continuing poetic tradition has however ensured the survival of the pan-Italian illustrious vernacular. By analogy with the example of Sicily, Dante can envisage that its users' resistance to municipal limitation in poetry may be matched by a similar resilience in political and moral matters. Book I of the *De vulgari* closes with a series of chapters in which the '*illustre, cardinale, aulicum et curiale vulgare*' ('illustrious, cardinal, aulic, and curial vernacular': I. xvi. 6) is analysed, defining each of these adjectives one by one in terms that associate aesthetic and political concerns. Dante's remarks point towards the existence of an alternative élite in contemporary Italian society, whose talents fit them for political position, yet who are deprived of political authority. They presently display their abilities in their use of distinguished language in poetic composition. Dante implies, however, that their common cause in language has political potential, creating oases of united understanding in the desert of divisive regionalism that otherwise characterises the Italian political and poetic scene.

In Dante's set of definitions, the first term, 'illustrious', is analysed through two parallel examples, one human and one linguistic:

> *Viros appellamus illustres, vel quia potestate illuminati alios et iusti-*
> *tia et karitate illuminant, vel quia excellenter magistrati excellenter*
> *magistrent, ut Seneca et Numa Pompilius. Et vulgare de quo*
> *loquimur et sublimatum est magistratu et potestate, et suos honore*
> *sublimat et gloria.*
>
> (DVE I. xvii. 2)

> We call men illustrious either because, enlightened by power,
> they shine forth justice and charity upon other people, or
> because, excellently taught, they teach most excellently, like
> Seneca or Numa Pompilius. And this vernacular of which I
> speak is both sublime in learning and power, and capable of
> exalting those who use it in honour and glory.

To label human actions illustrious thus implies that they reveal the combination of justice and charity appropriate to a political leader, or else the learning of a philosopher. Significantly, *Monarchia* similarly associates the power of the emperor's rule with his combination of justice and love, stressing the close link between philosophy and political happiness (*Mon.* I. xi. 8–20, III. xvi. 8).

In the case of human speech, illustriousness is displayed not only in poetic learning and skill, but also in rhetorical persuasion (the mainstay of *comune* politics in theory and in practice), and in the social recognition and honour it wins the speaker, outshining normal social rank and political status:

> *Nonne domestici sui reges, marchiones, comites et magnates quoslibet fama vincunt? [...] Quantum vero suos familiares gloriosos efficiat, nos ipsi novimus, qui huius dulcedine glorie nostrum exilium postergamus.*
>
> (*DVE* I. xvii. 5–6)

> Does not the fame of its devotees exceed that of any king, marquis, count or warlord? I myself have known how greatly it increases the glory of those who serve it, I who, for the sake of that glory's sweetness, have the experience of exile behind me.

Given Dante's previous strictures, the boast of outshining the current political classes is hardly extravagant. But his vision of a new Italian élite formed from the users of illustrious language, whose leadership is based on personal fame, honour and glory, rather than on social rank, is socially and politically, as well as linguistically, appealing. The idea of the élite, too, colours the definition of the Italian vernacular's 'cardinal' qualities. These mark its centrality, making it the '*cardo*' (hinge or pivot) or '*paterfamilias*' of the other vernaculars, regulating their development and setting an authoritative linguistic standard (I. xviii. 1).

The final two terms are strongly political even in their etymologies: the adjective 'aulic' refers to the *aula* or court of a prince; 'curial', to the *curia* or legal apparatus and tribunal of a governing authority. In Dante's analysis, both adjectives retain their primary political sense and are allowed only strictly limited metaphorical extension. We have seen already how in the *Convivio*, Dante deplored the severance between the term *corte* and the adjective *cortese*, given the degeneration of a modern Italian aristocracy whose entourages may still be termed courts, but are far from courtly in manners and values (*Cvo* II. x. 8). 'Aulic' language is suitable for a true court, Dante urges, due to its pan–Italian inclusivity and authority. Since a court gathers together elements from a whole kingdom, being in social and political matters *'totius regni comunis […] domus et omnium regni partium gubernatrix augusta'* ('the shared home of the entire kingdom and the honoured governor of every part of it': *DVE* I. xviii. 2), so the language that is shared and prized by all and sets the peninsula's linguistic standard can truly be labelled 'aulic'. Dante's readers already know that Sicily under the Hohenstaufen provided the ideal conjunction between court, courtiers and courtly language. He laments that in modern Italy there is no equivalent centre of social refinement, so that aulic language *'velut acola peregrinatur et in humilibus hospitatur asilis'* ('wanders around like a homeless stranger, finding hospitality in more humble homes': I. xviii. 3). The exiled poet depicts the language of fine poetry as an exile, highlighting the inappropriate placing of illustrious language in humble surroundings, yet also stressing the resilience of social and linguistic excellence, which survives despite the adverse cultural and political conditions in contemporary Italy.

When he comes to discuss the final term, 'curial', associated with the peninsula's shared language, Dante reaches the climax of his elision between aesthetic and political concepts. *'Curialitas'* (the essence of being 'curial') is defined in terms that stress order and regulation, using the image of the balanced scale traditionally associated with law and justice (I. xviii. 4). The 'curial' qualities of Italian can be proved, Dante says, *'cum istud in excellentissima Ytalorum curia sit libratum'* ('since it has been assessed before the most excellent tribunal in Italy': I.xviii. 4). The assertion immediately raises questions, since in strict legal and administrative fact there is no single *curia* in the fragmented political environment of contemporary Italy. Nonetheless, Dante emphatically defends his assertion that:

> *falsum esset dicere curia carere Ytalos, quanquam Principe careamus, quoniam curiam habemus, licet corporaliter sit dispersa.*
>
> (*DVE* I. xviii. 5)

> it would not be true to say that the Italians lack a tribunal alto-
> gether, even though we lack a monarch, because we do have
> one, but its physical components are scattered.

Although Italy has no single leader, many Italians have 'curial' abilities and hence form in themselves an equivalent to a princely *curia*.
Rather than owing their unity to the orderly political rule of a
king, as in contemporary Germany, Dante argues that 'curial'
Italians are unified simply through their common rational and
intellectual abilities: '*gratioso lumine rationis unita sunt*' ('they are
brought together by the gracious light of reason': I. xviii. 5).
Reason early in the treatise was declared to be the distinctive faculty of humanity and speech the medium by which we manifest
our rational capacities to others (I. ii. 3, I. iii. 1–3), so it is appropriate that excellence in language and outstanding rational abilities
should be associated in this manner. And since a *curia* is primarily a
legal and administrative centre, it is also relevant here to remember
that in *Convivio*, law is referred to as '*ragione scritta*' ('reason written
down': *Cvo* IV. ix. 8). Dante's imagined *curia* unified by reason thus
embodies the essence of legality and political order. In declaring
the existence of an Italian *curia* based on individual Italians' possession of superior rational capacities, Dante extends the implications
of his political interjections in the discussion of illustriousness,
stressing that despite the deficiencies in Italy's actual ruling classes,
an alternative political model is offered by the discerning few
whose language manifests their genuinely 'illustrious', 'cardinal',
'aulic' and 'curial' qualities.

The tendency of Dante's arguments in Book I of the *De vulgari*,
given the kind of material that he includes and the way in which it
is presented, extends his ostensibly aesthetic concerns into the
moral and political arena. The story of Babel provides him with a
striking parable of how the abuse of intellectual abilities and of
socio-political authority leads to confusion and division, and is
accompanied by linguistic cacophony. His description of the
cacophony of languages in contemporary Italy, and the aspersions

he periodically casts on Italian political leaders, if read within a Babelic framework, use harsh linguistic conclusions to point towards the moral and political shortcomings of the peninsula's divided condition. Yet his picture is not entirely negative. Alongside the blinkered municipal leadership in letters and in politics of a certain local tradition, Italy also possesses a moral and intellectual élite, whose activities – primarily through the medium of poetic composition – offer alternative examples of leadership to the peninsula's inhabitants. Members of Italy's moral *curia*, possessing honour and authority, form potential nuclei of social and linguistic perfection scattered throughout the peninsula.

Interestingly, Dante at no point calls for the complete abandonment of municipal variety in languages and literatures. In the *Commedia*, he will include 'municipal' alongside 'illustrious' language, and override the divisions of genre and style laid out in *De vulgari*, especially in its second book (as will be seen later). The poem realises the kind of linguistic diversity that *De vulgari* imagines for an Italian city, incorporating a diversity of registers into the fabric of the poem rather as the treatise envisages local and illustrious idioms to co-exist within urban communities: as Zygmunt Barański has noted, Dante's poem presents a rhetorical unity that is based on harmonious multiplicity or plurilingualism, rather than on conventional stylistic divisions.[27] *De vulgari* however maintains a more rigidly divided linguistic system than the poem. The genuinely Italian qualities of the illustrious vernacular are demonstrated by the fact that 'omnis *latie civitatis est et nullius esse videtur*' ('it belongs to *every* Italian city yet seems to belong to none: I. xvi. 6, emphasis mine); but it remains an exclusive medium, not to be mixed with the 'municipal'. Illustrious Italian does, however, admit the reversal of the Babelic trend of division and diaspora to move towards greater mutual comprehension and collaboration – and its greater aesthetic appeal represents, on Babelic analogy, a move away from moral degeneration. Since this language, Dante tells us, is present in all Italian cities, we can assume that each local community carries the potential for its own linguistic and political regeneration, provided that it can manage to abandon what is divisive about municipal language and values in favour of 'curial' unity.

THE POETRY OF RECTITUDE AND ITS ITALIAN AUDIENCES

The second book of *De vulgari* takes Dante's investigation of Italian language a step further: having identified the qualities of the best form of language, he moves on to specify how it should be used. Its elevated qualities prove to require similar elevation not only in its users – as the remarks on Sicily, for instance, have already suggested – but also in its subject matter. Dante states firmly that even fine poets should only use the illustrious vernacular on appropriate occasions, limiting the occasions for its use in poetry to those when the composer intends to speak of the most worthy of subjects (II. ii. 5). Dante declares that these worthy topics must represent humanity's highest concerns; since human beings, according to good Aristotelian thinking, possess a three-fold soul, there are three essential concerns that motivate all human actions.[28] The vegetable, animal and rational capacities that humanity shares with the other orders of creation motivate us to seek, respectively, what is useful, pleasurable, or morally good (*'utile, […] delectabile, […] honestum'*: II. ii. 6). This gives three great topics (*'magnalia'*) for verse written in the illustrious vernacular: *'salus […], venus et virtus'* ('wellbeing, love and virtue'), or more specifically, *'armorum probitas, amoris accensio et directio voluntatis'* ('prowess in arms, ardour in love and control of one's will': II. ii. 7). Dante offers the names of three Occitan poets each particularly associated with one of these major themes; in Italy, he declares that *salus* has not found any exponent, but Cino da Pistoia is cited as the poet of love, and *'amicu[s] eius'* ('his friend': II. ii. 8) – in other words, Dante himself – as the poet of moral probity.

In the following chapters, as Dante goes on to discuss the finer details of poetic technique, he frequently cites individual compositions that illustrate his various points, and increasingly draws on his own verse for examples, citing several of his long moral *canzoni* by *incipit*, as well as several of his love poems. The *De vulgari* omits any mention of one of the most famous of his lyrics about virtue, *Tre donne intorno al cor mi son venute* (*Three ladies have come round my heart*). This however is the *canzone* that we turn to next, finding it to deal with questions about exclusivity, audience, and poetic and political worth that we have seen play a prominent part in the treatise. The lyric is commonly dated to a similar period in Dante's career, and it may have been intended for inclusion in the *Convivio*, so it is unsurprising that it should share some concerns with the two prose treatises.[29] The *canzone*'s main subject is justice, represented in the poem through the three ladies of the title, each personifying a different aspect of the virtue. Its five main stanzas present an allegorical encounter between the poet and these ladies, all represented as exiles suffering persecution in a society given over to vice; there is also clear reference to Dante's historical experience of exile from Florence. The poem closes with two short *congedi*. The first dedicates the lyric to a small and exclusive audience, whose members must match the composer in virtue, but the second *congedo* urges the poem to seek an opposite audience, addressing itself to the poet's faction enemies and overturning previous moral restrictions, to seek a broad political public for the lyric. Following a pattern also outlined in *De vulgari*, Dante in *Tre donne* laments the signs of fragmentation in the social fabric. He seeks to use the language of his moral *canzone* to launch an appeal for greater unity within the political community – though here he appears concerned primarily with Florence, rather than with other Italian cities.

The *canzone* opens by describing how three ladies have come to the poet's heart:

> *Tre donne intorno al cor mi son venute,*
> *e seggonsi di fore:*
> *ché dentro siede Amore,*
> *lo quale è in segnoria de la mia vita.*
>
> (*Tre donne*, ll. 1–4)

Three ladies have come round my heart, and sit outside it, for
within sits Love, who is lord over my life.

The women present a pathetic appearance, being dressed in rags,
sorrowful and weary, and show clear signs of being exiles – each
appears *'come persona discacciata [...], cui tutta gente manca'* ('like a person driven out of home, abandoned by all': ll. 10–11). In this lonely
state, they have been drawn to the poet's heart as to a *'casa d'amico'*
('friend's house': l. 17), through their close relationship to Love. The
lyric 'I' is thus made the literal embodiment of an alliance between
Love and Justice – a conjunction that in *De vulgari* was associated
with illustriousness and in *Monarchia* will prove fundamental to the
proper exercise of political authority.[30] The image also matches *De
vulgari*'s personification of the 'aulic' vernacular as an exile seeking
shelter in humble refuges (I. xviii. 3). The ladies lament a drastic
change in their fortunes, and prompt Love later to reveal that he
too, along with a host of other virtues, has lost his former prestige
with humanity; promising, however, a future regeneration when
their enduring worth will be rediscovered.[31]

Dante outlines a complex series of relationships between the
various allegorical figures in the poem. The main speaker of the
three ladies identifies herself as 'Drittura', and the two others as her
daughter and grand-daughter, each generated by her mother's contemplation of her own image reflected in the waters of the source
of the Nile (ll. 45–54). These further derivations of justice are not
named, leaving the reader to puzzle out their identities; Dante's
son, Pietro, identified them as the *ius gentium* and the prescriptive
lex that govern human societies, both deriving from Drittura or *ius
divinum*, the divine norm of justice. Medieval tradition located the
source of the Nile in the Garden of Eden, so the story of the three
ladies' origins firmly associates all three categories of justice with
the period of human innocence before the 'Fall'.[32] Drittura also
reveals that she is sister to Love's mother. Venus's sisters, according
to Ovid, include Astrea, the virgin figure of pure justice who dwelt
among mankind in the Golden Age, but was finally compelled to

leave the earth by the cruelty and violence of the Age of Iron. In *Purgatorio*, Dante associates the classical myth of humanity's Golden Age with the brief pre-Lapsarian age of the Garden of Eden.[33] The *canzone*'s sketch of the relationships between Love and Justice, and of the ladies' Edenic origins, thus underscores their crucial place in re-imposing elements of primary order onto the post-Lapsarian world, in a manner similar to the way that the *vulgare illustre* is imagined in *De vulgari* to help re-impose moral, as well as linguistic, order in the fragmented Italian peninsula.

Dante modifies classical myth in *Tre donne*, where the immortals have not abandoned the earth, but have been dispossessed of their earthly authority. Justice, as Giuseppe Mazzotta notes, appears here stripped of her normal attributes of crown, sword and sceptre, while Love laments that his arrows, intended to instil proper love in mankind, are rusting through disuse (ll.61–62).[34] When, in the fifth stanza, Dante starts to introduce explicitly autobiographical material, he draws compelling parallels between the plight of the exiled virtues and his own personal situation:[35]

> *E io, che ascolto nel parlar divino*
> *consolarsi e dolersi*
> *così alti dispersi,*
> *l'essilio che m'è dato, onor mi tegno:*
> *ché, se giudizio o forza di destino*
> *vuol pur che il mondo versi*
> *i bianchi fiori in persi,*
> *cader co' buoni è pur di lode degno.*
>
> (*Tre donne*, ll.73–80)

And I, who listen to the divine speech in which such noble exiles express their consolation and their sorrow, hold my sentence of exile an honour; for if judgement or force of destiny indeed wishes that the world turn the white flowers into dark, it is yet praiseworthy to fall with the good.

The lyric protagonist may have been stripped of social and political status by his expulsion from Florence, but as the chosen companion of the virtues, he can confidently assert that he remains worthy of honour and praise. As in *De vulgari*, his remarks outline an alternative social order in which the poet proves more worthy than those who hold political power and authority.

The similarities identified between the poet and the virtues add specificity to the generalised laments presented by the latter in the first four stanzas. These opening stanzas outline a broad panorama of moral sterility in which Justice and Love appear to be shunned by all humanity; the fifth stanza concretises this by showing that justice and love are specifically absent from Trecento Florence. In expelling Dante, the embodiment of these virtues, the polity has revealed its own moral shortcomings. Some critics read the reference to white flowers (l.79) as carrying still more political specificity, alluding to the Black Guelfs' expulsion of the Whites; but equally the change of colour may, while probably carrying some factional significance, simply refer to the dimming of virtue, as in Love's reference to the darkening of his brilliant arrows in stanza IV. This latter explanation fits better with the sense of the fifth stanza's last lines (88–90), in which Dante represents himself as having repented of some fault – if read politically, this must be the fault of factionalism, referring to Dante's initial adherence to organised White politics in exile. To condemn this as a fault would scarcely follow comfortably from a previous expression of White partisanship, nor sit well with the obviously political use of the terms 'black' and 'white' in the second *congedo*, as we shall see.[36] The professed hatred of factionalism that is so characteristic a feature of the *Commedia* seems foreshadowed in this declaration of the poet's repentance from fault.

The intervening lines have expressed a desire on the poet's part for Florence, lamenting that '*de gli occhi miei 'l bel segno | per lontananza m'è tolto dal viso*' ('the fair sign desired by my eyes has been removed from my sight by distance': ll.81–82), and stressing that this desire has so consumed him that '*Morte al petto m'ha posto la chiave*' ('Death has put its key to my chest': l.87). The poet admits that

Florence is more an emotional than a moral object of desire, asserting that his honourable companionship with the virtues ought to make his exile bearable, whereas he actually experiences it as burdensome (l.84); there is thus moral ambiguity in the almost self-destructive strength of his desire for return. More positively, though, the poem has so closely interwoven its allegorical and autobiographical material that the historical return of the poet implies the return also of love and justice to the political life of his city. At a meta-historical level, his imagined homecoming would inaugurate the time of regeneration foretold by Love in stanza IV, and restore both political and moral integrity to the fragmented universe of the opening stanzas.

The main body of the *canzone* concludes with the poet's cryptic half-acknowledgement of political or moral fault: '*s'io ebbi colpa*' ('if I have been to blame': l.88). The lyric has presented its readers with a number of puzzles: asking them to extrapolate the identity of two of the three ladies from the first;[37] playing on the paradoxes of honour and disgrace, or praise and blame; and making symbolic allusions to flowers, signs and colours. Other elements in the poem appear fairly transparent: the personification allegory is highly conventional, and Love's prophecy about a future renewal of virtue seems clear enough. The first *congedo* however stresses the elements of impenetrability in the *canzone* and reserves it to an exclusive audience, warning the personified lyric:

> *Canzone, a' panni tuoi non ponga uom mano,*
> *per veder quel che bella donna chiude:*
> *bastin le parti nude;*
> *lo dolce pome a tutta gente niega,*
> *per cui ciascun man piega.*
>
> (*Tre donne*, ll.91–95)

Song, let no man touch your clothes to see what a beautiful woman covers: let the uncovered parts suffice; deny to all the sweet fruit for which everyone reaches out their hands.

Earlier in the *canzone*, Dante described '*la rotta gonna*' ('the torn robe': l.27) of Justice, that revealed to Love's gaze what should normally be covered; now his personified *Canzone* is warned against encountering the same fate. In expressing the hope that his *canzone* about virtue may receive better treatment than the virtues themselves, he highlights the harshness with which both he and they are treated in historical reality – and so mitigates his allusion to possible personal failing in the preceding lines. The only audience to which he can safely entrust the full meaning of the poem is one that already shares his moral worth, and so the poet who provided a '*casa d'amico*' ('friend's house': l.17) to the virtue of Justice dedicates his poem to an '*amico di virtù*' ('friend of virtue': l.97). The *Canzone* is warned to reveal herself fully only to a sympathetic audience, which can be trusted to seek the inner truths hidden – in a common rhetorical conceit – beneath the attractive language of the poem, as the body beneath clothing. Given the personified virtues' earlier lamentations, an audience composed exclusively of *amici di virtù* must indeed be a small one, and seems unlikely to include many Florentines.

The second *congedo*, however, reverses these qualifications, and sets out specifically to seek a Florentine, political audience – precisely the kind of readership that the lyric's opening stanzas have depicted as actively hostile to virtue. The *Canzone* is now personified not as a modestly retiring lady, but as a bold, energetic hunter:

> *Canzone, uccella con le bianche penne;*
> *canzone, caccia con li neri veltri,*
> *che fuggir mi convenne,*
> *ma far mi poterian di pace dono.*
> *Però nol fan che non san quel che sono:*
> *camera di perdon savio uom non serra,*
> *ché 'l perdonare è bel vincer di guerra.*
>
> (*Tre donne*, ll. 101–107)

Song, go hawking with the white wings; song, go hunting with the black hounds, that I have had to flee, but who could give me the gift of peace. But they do not do so, for they do not know what I am: the wise man does not lock the chamber of forgiveness, for to forgive is a fine way to win a war.

The 'black' and 'white' references here clearly allude to the Florentine political factions, but in inviting the poem to accompany both groups the author declares his own neutral position between them. Totally reversing the categories of the first *congedo*, his main target here is in fact that part of the audience most likely to feel hostility, not friendship, towards the poet and consequently to his companions, the virtues: the Blacks who have hunted him out of Florence. As in stanza V, Dante does not necessarily admit the justice of their hostility (to do so would undermine the whole sense of the *tre donne* allegory), but he does acknowledge their power to grant him the political pardon that would repatriate him peacefully to Florence. The *congedo* thus engages explicitly with the problems of *realpolitik*: factionalism, warfare, the legal processes of exclusion and its repeal. It also, however, echoes the kind of idealistic assumptions about poetic language set out in *De vulgari*. The personified *Canzone* is invited to present its message about *directio voluntatis* to an audience obsessed by factional divisions and by the Black and White markers of difference, and to bring them towards unity. The moral *sententia* of the closing lines conveys both a historical and a personal plea for the re-admission to Black-held Florence of a Dante labelled as White, and at a broader level, urges the abandonment of the intractability and violence associated with faction-politics in general. The Florentines are invited to act like wise men – that is, to act in the rational and virtuous manner that both *Tre donne* and *De vulgari* associate with moral and political regeneration in Florence, Italy, and the wider world.

Both *De vulgari* and *Tre donne* – at least in its second *congedo* – explore the possibility that poetic language, when used with discernment to address essential human matters, may transform its audience, awakening a recognition of shared characteristics that unifies and elevates an otherwise divided public. Both present their quests for regeneration, moral and linguistic, as a return to incorrupt Edenic origins and a recuperation of humanity's natural talents for effective communication and for harmonious social existence. While *Tre donne* focuses primarily on Florence, *De vulgari* embraces the whole Italian peninsula in its reforming concerns. Both texts, however, present similar proposals for local or individual change that may bring wider communities together, *Tre donne* pleading for the unlocking of faction barriers, *De vulgari* urging the scattered members of a *curia* to act in unison. The significance that these texts ascribe to local decisions in the Italian cities about unity or disunity, in both cases gives a central place to the interests in reason, justice and communication in human society that are also typical of the *Commedia*.

The *Commedia*, however, presents its concerns more urgently, abandoning academic Latin prose or self-consciously literary personification allegory, to speak through the examples of real, historical individuals and the dramatic details of their personal and political lives. Its vernacular language uses the uncensored vitality of local and municipal idiom, as well as the elevated, lyrical forms that *De vulgari* prescribed for the literary representation of the most serious and most 'human' of topics: the mixed, 'comic' language of its narrative consequently ensures that the poem can reach the widest of audiences. The *Commedia*'s form and idiom thus ensure the dissemination of Dante's ideas not only to *amici di virtù* but also to the popular, vernacular audience who make up the rival factions and states of Italy, and who are urgently summoned to act upon its message of spiritual and political reform.

4

MUNICIPAL LIMITATIONS

INFERNO

Dante's *Commedia* concentrates on and extends many of the concerns about the happiness of individuals, and of the societies in which they live, that we have already encountered in a selection of his shorter prose and lyric works. Its reflections are presented not through allegory or philosophical analysis, but by depicting a series of personal engagements between Dante-protagonist, with all his Florentine reality, and a huge cast of named individuals. The poem is thus rooted in history and in social and secular realities: the *Commedia*'s reflections about salvation and eternal life always stress the fundamental connections between human life on earth and life beyond the grave. The poem constantly reminds its readers that the personal choices on which salvation depends have social consequences. Humans are viewed as political animals no less in the *Commedia* than in the *Convivio* – and while our ultimate goal is to gain entry to the society of heaven, the poem urges that a precondition for this is to act with due regard for social obligations on earth.

At the beginning of Dante's narrative, the *Inferno* provides a series of horrifying reminders of the personal and the social consequences of human decisions to ignore such obligations. Critics often liken Dante's hell itself to a city: like the walled towns of medieval Italy, it is entered by a gate crowned by an arresting inscription, within which lie further walls, gates and towers, with a dense population of sinners and their demonic guardians. Hell's inhabitants include numerous sinners with urban Italian origins, including many from Florence, Lucca, Bologna, and other cities very familiar to Dante.[1] Joan Ferrante has suggested that hell presents the image of a corrupt society – a conclusion that few readers of the *Inferno* would deny – and has argued from this that, given the strongly urban flavour of so much in this first *cantica*, it represents Dante's disillusionment with the city as an independent political entity. In her interpretation of the political framework of the *Commedia*, she concludes that 'Hell is a city, Purgatory a kingdom; only Paradise is city, kingdom, and empire [...] containing all the smaller units within the single, unified whole'.[2] This broad political reading of the *Commedia* rings true in many ways: Dante does use imperial analogies for paradise, and his vision of the fruitful co-operation of the blessed under God does recall the outline of political happiness under the guidance of an emperor that we have seen in *Convivio* and *Monarchia*. Hell, populated by those disobedient to God's rule, is as turbulent and faction-ridden as Dante declares human societies to become when they lack or reject imperial guidance.

Yet the analogy outlined by Ferrante and others does not fully accommodate the political thinking of the *Commedia*. Any political paradigm derived from hell must be negative, as any from paradise must be positive. The poem's comments on earthly society make clear Dante's conviction that the best chance for achieving order in the contemporary age lies in accepting the authority of the Holy Roman Empire, and strongly condemn those princes, citizens and churchmen who neglect or oppose it. Ferrante is thus substantially correct in arguing that Dante advocates a political paradigm of empire, 'containing all the smaller units within the single, unified whole'. It is, however, the smaller units that urgently concern the poet, as he investigates the personal and public implications of human beings' earthly existence as political animals. When it comes to earthly society, Dante is clear that wrong and right choices can be made in any form of community: the story of Babel shows that even the most unified human society can be corrupt; yet even within the most divided societies elements of good can be found, so that the cities of contemporary Italy are strongly represented in purgatory and in paradise as well as in hell. The poem's concentration on individual example means that, time and again, attention is focused onto local communities, investigating how the actions of a single person's life have affected the moral and social wellbeing of the surrounding city or court. Dante concentrates primarily on the microcosm, rather than the macrocosm; the poem itself is structured episodically around the *canto*, building its impressively symmetrical and orderly structure around single narrative units; similarly, his political concerns remain centred on individual localities, those core social units that compose kingdoms and empires. Dante's own experience of life in a city informs the social and political thinking of the whole *Commedia*, making the city a primary image throughout all three *cantiche*, of the society where relationships between individual and community are most naturally exercised, and judged. In *Inferno*, Dante's strictures on the failed leadership of hell's urban politicians provide powerful arguments against civic corruption; they also stress the justice and order that lie beneath both terrestrial and infernal chaos, allowing positive as well as negative political lessons to be drawn from this stage of the *Commedia*'s journey.

PRELUDES TO DISORDER:
THE OPENING *CANTI* OF *INFERNO*

The *Commedia* opens not in a city but in a wasteland, as Dante-protagonist stumbles into the poem through the pathless '*selva oscura*' ('dark wood': *Inf.* I. 2). The allegorical implications of this landscape are evident: in Dante's age, woodland and wilderness were associated symbolically with doubt, sin and sterility of the human soul.[3] Dante-character has lost his way, morally and spiritually, and the journey that he presently embarks upon has its goal in the Christian, otherworldly City of God rather than any human, earthly city. Although the narrative is intensely personal, Charles Singleton has demonstrated that Dante-protagonist is also an Everyman or Wanderer figure, his journey allegorically representing the Christian's ideal movement from sin, through repentance, to salvation, and offering an empathetically instructive example to its audience.[4] In the 'polysemous' *Commedia*, however, the reality of one level of meaning does not cancel another: Dante-character undoubtedly also represents some of the biographical reality of Dante the man.[5] In a further allegorical reading, the dark wood may be interpreted politically as representing the confusion of Florence in 1300, the fictional date of the *Commedia*,[6] with the journey through the afterlife reminding a protagonist still embroiled in civic politics of the need to act according to conviction, not circumstance – and so providing the apology for the actions that led to Dante's exile. The conversion effected by the journey educates the pilgrim to reflect on relationships between human beings in society, as well as on the relationship of humanity to God.

Although *Inferno* opens in confusion, its first few *canti* provide a prelude to hell-proper, during which some of the uncertainties of the dark wood are quelled. The abrupt opening, '*nel mezzo del cammin*' ('midway along the path': *Inf.* I. 1), moves towards equilibrium as the protagonist begins to make an escape from the chaos of his initial internal and external situation – this in spite of the fact that he prepares to enter the greater chaos of hell. He is steadied in part by religious reassurances, but also by reminders of past human achievements that help him to recover a moral balance. In the first two *canti*, the encounter with Virgil sketches out the full reach of the coming journey with its happy goal in paradise and makes explicit its divine sanction under the sponsorship of a female trinity of saints, Lucy, Rachel and Beatrice. But Virgil reassures Dante-character also by his reference to the earthly and political past and future of '*quella umile Italia [...] | per cui morì la vergine Cammilla, | Eurialo e Turno e Niso di ferute*' ('that low Italy for whom the virgin

Camilla, Euryalus, Turnus and Nisus died of their wounds': I. 106–108). He brings into the poem some of the reassuring stability of a classical world founded on law, peace, and political and poetic endeavour:

> *Li parenti miei furon lombardi,*
> *mantoani per patrïa ambedui.*
> *Nacqui sub Iulio, ancor che fosse tardi,*
> *e vissi a Roma sotto 'l buono Augusto*
> *nel tempo de li dèi falsi e bugiardi.*
> *Poeta fui, e cantai di quel giusto*
> *figliuol d'Anchise che venne di Troia,*
> *poi che 'l superbo Ilïón fu combusto.*
>
> (*Inf.* I. 68–75)

My parents were Lombards, both of them Mantuan by birth. I was born under Julius Caesar, though late in his reign, and I lived at Rome under good Augustus, in the time of the false and lying gods. I was a poet, and I sang of that just son of Anchises who came from Troy, after proud Ilium was burned.

The Roman poet's self-presentation securely locates him in history, referring to his own origins in town and region, and framing this information with further reference to the origins of Rome's empire under Caesars Julius and Augustus and to the origins of Rome itself with Trojan Aeneas.

Virgil's statements about his political and poetic identity encourage Dante-character, in turn, to regain a sense of his own origins and achievements. The speech reminds him of his own poetic *métier*, and he recalls that his Virgilian discipleship has brought him a high reputation: '*tu se' solo colui da cu' io tolsi | lo bello stilo che m'ha fatto onore*' ('you alone are the one from whom I have taken the fair style that has brought me honour': I. 86–87). The protagonist's second crisis of doubt leads Virgil to name Beatrice as the sponsor for the otherworldly journey (II. 51–72), and this again brings Dante back to his own personal and poetic past. The *Vita Nova* not only hailed Beatrice as Dante's muse, and as the source of his spiritual enlightenment, but also located her firmly in the historical setting of a city with well-known monuments, festivities and traditions. Reminders of Beatrice's Florentine reality and of the intensely personal relationship that links her to him in death as well as in life allow Dante-character to regain a sense of purpose about his own historical and moral choices, so that he commits himself to the perils of his otherworldly journey with renewed confidence in his poetic and Florentine identity.

The journey-proper begins as the two poets enter the gate of hell. The inscription on the gate firmly identifies the underworld with an earthly political form, calling it the '*città dolente*' ('city of woe': III. 1).[7] Inhabitants of the city are promised eternal grief and hopelessness: yet the gate also tells them that this city is ruled by justice, love and wisdom, and boasts a noble founder:

> *Giustizia mosse il mio alto fattore;*
> *fecemi la divina podestate,*
> *la somma sapïenza e 'l primo amore.*
>
> (*Inf.* III. 4–6)

Justice moved my high maker; I was made by divine power, supreme wisdom and primal love.

Although the narrative of *Inferno* plunges Dante-character into apparent chaos, hellgate tells him that this part of the afterworld is as orderly as purgatory and paradise will prove to be. It is governed by the loving justice of a supreme authority, who holds its disorderly parts in a definite pattern that permits full self-expression to its citizens, just as *Convivio* or *Monarchia* assert imperial rule to do on earth – with the qualification that self-expression in a *città dolente* populated by sinners is inevitably negative. As the narrative progresses, Dante-poet sketches out the political and moral character of the infernal city and of its inhabitants in terms that cast a sharp scrutiny on the mainsprings of disorder on earth.

Hellgate's reference to the infernal city's '*alto fattore*' allows Dante to remind us that, like Florence or Rome, this community boasts a foundation myth. This provides the modern world of the poem's earthly audience with an emblematic image of the town's origins and values and, as in the case of Florence and Rome, the image has a double meaning. Rome is both the descendant of '*superbo Ilïón*'and the model of imperial order; Florence is the daughter, both of rebellious Fiesole and of orderly Rome; this city is rooted in the pride, disobedience and rebellion that brought about the falls of Lucifer and of Adam, yet also in the love and wisdom of the city's *fattore*, which continue to order the post-Lapsarian universes of earth and of eternity. Allusions to the divine order that regulates hell occur periodically in the narrative, although negative images, unsurprisingly, predominate. Earthly cities provide Dante with constant analogies for hell, drawing on both the biblical narratives of the destruction of Babel, Sodom and Jerusalem and the classical myths of the downfall of Troy or Thebes.[8] Not only hell, but also modern societies are shown to resemble these self-destroying communities: Pisa is labelled a '*novella Tebe*' ('new Thebes': XXXIII. 89), and a Pistoian outdoes a Theban sinner in blasphemous pride (XXV. 10–15); while in *Purgatorio* Rome is compared to the widowed Jerusalem of *Lamentations* (*Purg*.VI. 112–113). Florence is several times compared to the destructive city of hell itself – in parody of the city's own boast to rule land and sea, emblazoned on its government palace, Dante adds that '*per lo 'nferno [s]uo nome si spande*' ('its name is spread throughout hell': *Inf*. XXVI. 3); he rewrites its myth of origins in making Satan, not Caesar, Florence's founder:'*di colui è pianta | che pria volse le spalle al suo fattore*' ('it is planted by he who first turned his back on his maker': *Par*. IX. 127–128).

Jerusalem, Rome and Florence, however, also play prominent parts in the poem as symbols of virtue and harmony in earthly society.[9] As Dante-character enters hellgate, he is accompanied by Virgil, the poet whose epic revealed order within the apparent disorder of civic destruction, the downfall of Troy bringing about the birth of Rome. The first stopping-place on the poets' journey is in Limbo, where Dante-character encounters heroes, poets and philosophers from the non-Christian world, whose achievements in contributing to the moral and political wellbeing of their own orderly societies merit freedom from the physical punishments suffered in all other areas of hell.[10] As Virgil will later reveal (*Purg.*VII. 34–36), the leaders of Limbo cultivated the moral virtues to the fullest possible extent; they make up an orderly and dignified mini-community within hell, in which the virtues of human nature are celebrated even as the community is also punished for closure to God's grace. Limbo's inhabitants, who cannot hope for the joys of paradise, show an emotionless solemnity of speech and conduct: '*sembianz'avevan né trista né lieta*' ('their faces were neither sad nor happy': *Inf.* IV. 84). Their expressionless calm demonstrates something of the limitations of the human spirit when deprived of grace, but also underlines the authority that humans can achieve through the exercise of their moral and philosophical powers alone. The experience of Limbo and the companionship of Virgil fortify Dante-character for his gruelling passage through the underworld-proper, showing him that even without divine help humanity can achieve an enduring command of power, knowledge and eloquence, and so build and serve stable communities. The negative visions of the city that predominate in lower hell are mitigated by the memories of Limbo, with its historical examples of illustrious commitment to the virtues of the political life.

ORDER AND STRUCTURE WITHIN HELL

The first *canti* of *Inferno* thus maintain a careful balance between elements of confusion, uncertainty and outright error; and those of order, confidence and self-awareness. As the travellers enter the regions of physical punishment, signs of chaos increasingly predominate. Images of the city, for instance, are not only negative in kind, but run counter to many of the primary connotations of the term. After entering the *città dolente* through hellgate, the poets encounter not buildings, but the River Acheron and the plain of Limbo, before entering the castle and garden reserved in Limbo for the most heroic. On leaving Limbo, they press on through mud, streams and swamps towards a second set of city walls, guarding an inner city *'c'ha nome Dite'* ('which is named Dis': VIII. 68). Inside these walls, however, they encounter a graveyard (which by classical and medieval tradition should lie outside a city's walls), and a river, a wood and a sandy desert, before arriving at a rocky precipice separating the upper and lower areas of hell. Apart from the castle of Limbo, in upper hell at least the features of the infernal city are the antithesis of urban, bearing indeed the same connotations of disorder and alienation as the *selva oscura* of the opening scene. To a medieval Italian citizen, accustomed to assume that city walls provide a barrier excluding untamed nature, this topography makes symbolically evident the political and spiritual perversion of the *città dolente*.[11]

The conduct of the citizens, too, runs against the established norms of civic order – although to a Florentine they may bear disturbingly familiar overtones. The brawling of the angry and the avaricious, or the determined separation of the violent into distinct groups and sub-groups that refuse to mingle with one another, recalls the factional mistrust and violence of contemporary Italian cities. Above all, the words of the sinners reveal their disorderly, anti-civic characteristics, often offering disturbing echoes of the faction rhetoric of the *comuni*, as we saw in the survey in Chapter 1 of the Florentine politicians who appear in hell.[12] Abuse of political rhetoric is not only a Florentine or urban fault, moreover: Pier della Vigna, the chancellor of Frederick II's imperial *curia*, presents Dante-protagonist with an insidiously elegant, self-exculpatory account of the political intrigues that led to his disgrace, that can almost dazzle an audience into ignoring the moral self-accusation in his account of a suicide that *'ingiusto fece me contra me giusto'* ('unjust made me against my just self': XIII.

72).[13] The historical Pier, a southerner by birth, in life possessed the literary and political talents of the 'Sicilians' admired in the *De vulgari*, showing outstanding linguistic skills both as a vernacular poet and an expert in the Latin *ars dictaminis*, but in the *Commedia* Dante makes his spirit employ this skill to defend the abuse of reason and morality, in his suicide. Although historically a leader in the imperial *curia*, he is shown to have betrayed the commitment to reason that *De vulgari* identified as the marker of Italy's true *curia* in the post-Frederician age. In the terms of Dante's linguistic treatise, indeed, even the most accomplished of the speakers of upper hell fall into linguistic errors that reveal equivalent moral errors: Francesca da Rimini composes an elegant speech that appears to represent the *magnalia* topic of love, but is based around adulterous lust; Farinata's review of Florentine warfare subverts *salus* to factionalism; Brunetto, Pier and others protest a comprehension of *virtus* that is undermined by the fatal flaws revealed in their most important moral choices.

The journey through much of upper hell is thus surrounded by highly prominent markers of visual and linguistic confusion, which threaten to overwhelm the precarious equilibrium achieved by the protagonist in the opening *canti*. The chaos is kept in check, however, by a series of reminders that hell's *alto fattore* has structured the city on orderly foundations. Visual order is maintained by the strict division of sinners into different areas according to the nature of their sin and by the subdivision of some of these groups so that different aspects of a fault are individually punished. Dante-poet also ensures that the narrative is punctuated by doctrinal sequences that reveal other orderly patterns in the physical, and hence the moral, structure of hell. In *canto* XI, for instance, Virgil provides his charge with an outline of the hierarchy of sin in hell. He distinguishes the major categories of errors caused by force and fraud, or by '*incontenenza, malizia e la matta | bestialitade*' ('incontinence, malice and mad bestiality': XI. 82–83), which are punished in descending order of gravity, and he carefully enumerates the different sub-categories of each kind of sin, so that the protagonist may understand the spiritual significance of hell's topographical divisions.

In *canto* XIV, Virgil enhances his charge's comprehension of infernal order by describing how the Old Man of Crete forms a physical and symbolic link between the worlds of history and of eternity. Crete, and later Italy, was the seat of Saturn's just rule during the Golden Age of classical legend (and of *Tre donne*'s political allegory). Virgil's brief description of how the fertile island has become a desert recalls the Ovidian story's emphasis on temporal decline as humans became addicted to violence and justice, personified in Astrea, vanished from the earth.[14] Virgil goes on to describe the statue hidden on the island of an old man, whose golden head is perfect, but whose silver bust, brass loins, iron legs and clay foot leak tears that drain away to form the rivers of hell. The variety of metals echoes those of Ovid's different Ages, but the statue also corresponds to that of Nebuchadnezzar's dream, also signifying human decline and discord through a series of sinful chronologies.[15] The image, with its composite classical and biblical antecedents, provides a powerful reminder of the intimate interconnection between the earth and the afterlife, and of the social and political consequences of sin. The tears that flow from the temporal world into the underworld draw attention to the symmetry that links misconduct on earth to its punishment in hell; humanity may have lost the companionship of Justice in its Age of Iron, but in hell receives the perfect justice of God in the punishment carefully apportioned to each different kind of sin.[16]

In the lower regions of hell in particular, the divine punishment accorded to different sins often echoes the rituals of human punitive justice, allowing Dante to emphasise further the connections between the temporal and the eternal worlds. This is particularly the case in the densely crowded section of lower hell called 'Malebolge' ('evil pouches': XVIII. 1). By contrast with upper hell's bewildering wildernesses, in this area of the *città dolente* recognisably urban physical characteristics finally appear. Malebolge consists of a concentric series of ten circular ditches (*bolge*) resembling city streets, and both

the features of the different sections and the activities of their occu-
pants often echo those of an urban community on earth, some relatively innocuous, but others borrowed from penal practice.

In echoing the mechanisms of human justice within the convincingly urban environment of Malebolge, Dante-poet invites further reflection on the politics of the city, and on the challenges of
regulating the social bonds that humans are naturally drawn to
form, but prove almost equally ready to abuse. In Malebolge, as in
the areas of upper hell reviewed in Chapter 1, much attention is
devoted to contemporary Italian politics, and especially to affairs in
the regions of Tuscany and Romagna, areas Dante knew well.
There is a sense of claustrophobia in the way that the narrow chan-
nels of Malebolge are crammed with sinners from the same
restricted social and geographical circles; members of the same family clans and alliances are found in different *bolge*, as are political
opponents who fought to control single cities for family and factional motives, or moved between different cities in party-dictated
appointments to office, or in exile.[17] Dante's close examination of
the institutions and individuals that controlled a representative
selection of familiar cities places political concerns under the
microscope. The Malebolge sequence, overall, reveals a concern
with questions about language and justice that shows some continuity with the ideas of the secular philosophical treatises on which
Dante had been engaged before starting the *Inferno*. The minute
analysis of precise historical examples that he undertakes in the
poem allows him to endow these issues with a sense of personal and
social urgency that makes direct emotional claims on his audience.
In the following pages, analysis of a selection of episodes will, I
hope, reveal something of the subtlety and the flexibility with
which the political morality of the Italian cities and institutions is
exposed to searching appraisal in the Malebolge sequence. A selection of episodes will function as 'case studies' of the *Inferno*'s
approach to political concerns, and above all, to questions about
how, and how not, to conduct personal and public life in an urban
community.

POLITICAL TRADING OF WORDS AND DEEDS: PIMPING, FLATTERY AND SIMONY

Dante-poet opens his description of this new area of hell with an apparently reliable, formal statement: '*luogo è in inferno detto Malebolge*' ('there is a place in hell called Malebolge': *Inf.* XVIII. 1). After the protagonist's terrifying descent on the back of Gerione across the precipice separating upper and lower hell, the pronouncement of place and name seems reassuringly confident but, as Robin Kirkpatrick notes, it also carries strong traces of ambiguity.[18] The very conviction with which the name of this fictional infernal location is uttered is self-undermining, bringing a weight of rhetorical elevation to what is evidently unverifiable. The section of the poem devoted to Malebolge is often obsessively concrete and physical in its descriptions and imagery, and returns repeatedly to the issue of words, names and identity. This opening line, at once confident and unbelievable, affirmative and parodical, tacitly alerts the reader to the insecurity of claims and appearances in an area that, according to Virgil's sketch of infernal topography, is devoted to sins of fraud.

The sins first encountered in Malebolge are based on material gratification, both sexual – with the panders, seducers and flatterers of *canto* XVIII – and financial, with the simoniacs of *canto* XIX. In all these forms of sin, bonds between human beings that are usually considered especially sacrosanct are exploited for personal advancement. Panders and seducers defraud human love; flatterers devalue language by disjoining words and meaning; simoniacs treat what should be pre-eminently reliable, ecclesiastical authority and the transmission of the word of God, as material merchandise. City-like features in the three *bolge* draw attention immediately to the social and political aspect of these sins. The sinners of the first *bolgia* push against each other as in a busy city street:

> *Come i Roman per l'essercito molto,*
> *l'anno del giubileo, su per lo ponte*

hanno a passar la gente modo colto,
che da l'un lato tutti hanno la fronte
verso 'l castello e vanno a Santo Pietro,
da l'altra sponda vanno verso 'l monte.

(*Inf.* XVIII. 28–33)

Just as the Romans in the Jubilee year, because of the crowds up on the bridge have found a way to let the people pass across, so that on one side all have their faces towards the Castel [Sant'Angelo] and are going to St Peter's, and on the other side all are heading towards Monte [Giordano].

These pimps and seducers appear to be imitating a sophisticatedly urban form of traffic regulation that ensures an orderly conduct unexpected in hell. The next *bolgia*'s representation as a sewage ditch is more conventionally infernal, recalling less attractive aspects of medieval city life, in which emptying the town privies was an even more practical and orderly concern than traffic direction. Dante evokes in gross detail the *bolgia*'s resemblance to the ditches outside the city walls into which the waste was emptied for use as manure in the fields (thus recycling it for ultimate communal benefit):[19]

Quindi sentimmo gente che si nicchia
ne l'altra bolgia e che col muso scuffa,
e sé medesma con le palme picchia.
Le ripe eran grommate d'una muffa,
per l'alito di giù che vi s'appasta,
che con li occhi e col naso facea zuffa.
[…] Quivi venimmo; e quindi giù nel fosso
vidi gente attuffata in uno sterco
che da li uman privadi parea mosso.

(*Inf.* XVIII. 103–108, 112–114)

From here we heard people groaning in the next ditch and snorting through their nostrils, and slapping themselves with their own hands. The banks were crusted with mould that sticks there from the rising vapours that battled with the eyes and nose. We came up there; and from here I could see people down in the ditch pitched into filth that looked as if it came from human privies.

Likewise, the *bolgia* of the simoniacs strikes an urban note, displaying distinctive architectural features that recall familiar Florentine scenes to the protagonist. The bottom of the ditch is '*piena [...] di fóri*' ('full of hollows': XIX. 14), corresponding exactly in size and shape to the basins of the baptismal font in Florence's Baptistery, ('*nel mio bel San Giovanni*': l.17).[20] Throughout Malebolge Dante-poet describes topographical features of a strongly urban stamp, marking a distinct change from the parodic natural landscapes that predominated in upper hell.

Malebolge's mimicry of city topographies or occupations often carries distinctly pejorative significance, reproducing forms of castigation applied under contemporary criminal law. Dante signals the socially as well as morally transgressive nature of the sins by according them retributions exacted by earthly society. This is the case with both the simoniacs and the panderers and seducers. Thus the single-file progress of the latter recalls criminal exposure and humiliation as much as it does the orderly pilgrims of the opening Jubilee image. Dante shows the souls following '*cerchie etterne*' ('eternal circles': XVIII. 72), tormented by devils who '*li battien crudelmente di retro*' ('cruelly whipped them from behind': l.36), so mimicking the public flagellation of criminals in Italian cities, which often took place along specifically designated routes called *cerchie*.[21] The position of the simoniacs, who occupy their 'fonts' head downwards, recalls judicial execution by *propagginazione*, in which murderers were suffocated by being buried head downwards in a hole in the ground; in his dialogue with one of the sinners, Dante-protagonist has to lean down '*come 'l frate che confessa | lo perfido assessin*' ('like the friar confessing a wicked assassin': XIX. 49–51). In the Malebolge *canti*, moreover, the souls behave for the first time like earthly criminals, attempting to conceal their identities. They can no longer be appeased, as Pier della Vigna, Brunetto Latini, or the Florentines of *canto* XVI were, with a promise of mention among the living; while a sign of the sinners' increasing malice is their readiness to identify their companions exactly in order to dishonour them. Nonetheless, Dante makes sure that the names and the civic, familial and personal identities of the majority of Malebolge's sinners are revealed in sufficient detail to relate their faults to the context of a real community against which their frauds have offended. Such detail is central to the work of personal and political reflection and reassessment to which the *Inferno* is directed.

Attempts by the first soul encountered in Malebolge to conceal his identity are defeated when the protagonist recognises and names him. Venedico Caccianemico reveals himself only '*mal volontier*' ('unwillingly': XVIII. 52), but the subsequent encounter centres on his pronouncement of city and family names. After Venedico has been identified, he reveals the names not only of his accomplice in crime – the '*marchese*' (l. 56) can be identified easily by an interlocutor aware of his earthly career[22] – but also of his victim, his own sister Ghisolabella (l. 55); he also identifies his city of origin, Bologna (l. 58). Although Dante-poet makes Venedico claim to be correcting '*la sconcia novella*' ('the infamous story': l. 57) regarding his manipulation of these intimate ties by selling his sister's sexual favours to the marquis, this crude affirmation of the facts actually confirms and propagates the scandal. Gossip about Caccianemico's activities is apparently in wide circulation, something that is particularly scandalous given that, historically, he occupied important political positions. Venedico was a leader of the Bolognese Guelfs, he frequently held office as *podestà* outside Bologna, and he finally joined the Ferrarese court of the marquises of Este as a close associate of its rulers. As Dante's comments on nobility and on courtliness in the *Convivio* emphasise, such social and political prominence should be matched by high standards of personal behaviour, but in fact, Caccianemico's conduct has abused even the closest of familial and political relationships.

Venedico is forced into his self-revelation by Dante-character's '*chiara favella*' ('clear speech': l. 53). As the encounter progresses, this clarity is revealed as all too direct, even crude, in its stripping away of pretence – it even bears traces of what the *De vulgari* terms 'municipal' local terminology. When Dante-protagonist puts the question, '*che ti mena a sì pungenti salse?*' ('what has brought you to such pungent sauces?': l. 51), his choice of expression seems almost gratuitously pejorative – it is the next *bolgia*, not this one, that is filled with slops and stench. His words however carry a specifically Bolognese reference all too suitable here: the Trecento commentator Benvenuto da Imola, who knew Bologna well, reports that *Le Salse* was the name given to a grave pit beyond the Bolognese walls, unconsecrated ground into which the corpses of criminals were thrown, and so closely matching the conditions of the infernal *bolge* of perpetual, not merely human, damnation.[23] Dante-protagonist's use of local jargon compels engagement from the reluctant sinner and in his reply, Caccianemico too uses language as the means of defining his Bolognese identity and also the characteristically Bolognese nature of his sin:

> *Non pur io qui piango bolognese;*
> *anzi n'è questo loco tanto pieno,*
> *che tante lingue non son ora apprese*
> *a dicer 'sipa' tra Sàvena e Reno;*
> *e se di ciò vuoi fede o testimonio,*
> *rècati a mente il nostro avaro seno.*
>
> (*Inf.* XVIII. 58–63)

I am not the only Bolognese weeping here; indeed, this place is so full of them that so many tongues do not know how to say 'yes' now between the Savena and Reno rivers; if you want corroboration or testimony of this, just recall to mind our avaricious nature.

Venedico's reference to the local affirmative recalls *De vulgari*'s division of European languages into the idioms of *oc*, *oïl* and *sì*: but whereas these languages were the chosen mediums of the most elevated vernacular literature, these words cast Bolognese as a far from illustrious language that serves only to facilitate its users' transmission of sinful and duplicitous civic values, showing none of the sweetness praised in *De vulgari*. The appearance of local idiom and allusions within the text helps Dante-poet underline the political aspects of even this apparently private sin. Venedico's faction-based loyalties to his patron are the immediate cause of his offence, and the location of his crime within an urban court setting highlights the wide impact of misconduct by persons holding political authority. The deeper roots of the sin lie in a Bolognese commitment to avarice, which the *Convivio* identified as the primary cause of political conflict in kingdoms, cities, neighbourhoods and families. Venedico's remarks thus definitively conjoin his own abuse of familial ties with acquisitive and self-serving politics, and with an apparently all-pervasive climate of civic sin in his home town.

'Municipal' language and the principles of linguistic practice remain prominent concerns in the next *bolgia*. The sin itself here is linguistic flattery and usually employs an elevated idiom that falsifies the mediocrity of underlying facts. Dante-poet counters the normal procedures of flattery by employing direct colloquial, even grossly vulgar language throughout this section – starting, as we saw, with the description of the *bolgia*'s repulsive physical features. Once again, exposure of the sin is accompanied by the forcible naming of an exemplary sinner against his own will. 'Alessio Interminei da Lucca' (l.122) is identified with full details of patronymic and citizenship; as with Venedico, the use of city-specific references underlines the social nature of his sin, which disseminates insincerity and false values within the community. Interminei is described as almost unrecognisably covered with filth, with sewage even covering '*la zucca*' (l.124): by employing the Lucchese term 'pumpkin' for 'head', Dante-poet increases the satirical tone of the episode, emphasising his 'municipal' usage by its prominent position in rhyme with the city name itself, '*Lucca*'.[24] The grotesque choice of vegetable-metaphor is further highlighted by Alessio's accusation that Dante-character looks at him greedily (*'perché se' tu sì gordo | di riguardar [...] me?'*: ll. 118–119), and by describing flattery as forming a sticky coating over the tongue, making Alessio, too, a metaphorical glutton (*'le lusinghe | ond' io non ebbi mai la lingua stucca'*: ll. 125–126). With the setting of the whole encounter in a sewage-dump, Dante demonstrates symbolically that the end product of this linguistic gluttony is excrement, filth that has to be laboriously removed from the city, and so reminds his readers that linguistic malpractice is deeply damaging to social health and wellbeing.

The following *canto* brings Dante-character into the *bolgia* of the simonists: clerics who sell appointments to Church positions. It introduces Dante-author's first open attack in the *Commedia* on the Church as an institution, rather than on individual sinners who happen to be clerics, because the sin is specifically ecclesiastical. Dante himself, as a layman under accusation of the abuse of official position (barratry) and of hostility to the Church (White Guelfism), is dangerously exposed as he embarks on a denunciation of clerical corruption. The poet therefore adopts various strategies to assume authority to himself and to the words of his poem. The *canto* opens with a severe, personal attack on the individual, '*Simon Mago*' ('Simon Magus': XIX. 1), after whom the sin of simony is named, addressing Simon and his followers in the second person with exclamatory vocatives and using images of gluttony and adultery to describe their abuse of ecclesiastical authority (ll. 2–4). This is followed by another exclamatory passage, directed in prayer to the deity in praise of his orderly government of the universe. The founding principles of the city of hell, as described on hellgate, are recalled in the invocation:

> *O somma sapïenza, quanta è l'arte*
> *che mostri in cielo, in terra e nel mal mondo,*
> *e quanto giusto tua virtù comparte!*

> (*Inf.* XIX. 7–9)

> O supreme wisdom, how great is the art that you display in
> heaven, on earth, and in the realm of evil, and how justly your
> power rules over them!

The rhetorical emphasis of the two contrasting passages of con-
demnatory and laudatory exclamation makes it evident that
Dante-poet understands his God better than the deity's professed
servants; while the self-conscious repetition of key terms from hellgate ('wisdom' and 'justice') recalls the providential blessing of
Dante-character's mission.

Dante-protagonist's position in this *canto* is also aggrandised, so
as to increase narrative authority via the autobiographical identification between the virtuous pilgrim and the writer who relates the
events in the first person. A variety of devices attribute quasi-reli-
gious authority to Dante-character, highlighting the contrasting
failures of the *bolgia*'s clerical sinners. As we have seen, the protagonist is compared to a minister of the Church taking a criminal's last
confession (ll.49–51), a simile that associates him with the sacral
language of confession and absolution, but associates the papal sinners with violent crime against humanity. The parodic baptismal
immersion of the simoniac popes in 'fonts' filled with fire rather
than water, likewise casts Dante-character, as he stands over the
basins, into the role of a priest performing a sacramental ritual.
When Pope Nicholas III misidentifies Dante-character in a kind of
anti-baptism as Pope Boniface VIII (l.53), he is corrected with the
words '*non son colui*' ('I am not he': l.62), recalling the Baptist's
denial of Messianic status.[25] The words of the protagonist are
described as '*gravi*' ('weighty': l.103) and as '*vere*' ('true': l.123), giving a semi-sacred resonance to the *canto*'s denunciation of clerical
misconduct.

Nicholas's attempts to speak authoritatively are undermined by
equivalent devices that stress his inability to perform clerical ritual. Not only does he wrongly 'baptise' the protagonist by calling
him Boniface, but the soles of his feet are licked by flames, in a
satirical re-interpretation of a familiar symbol of clerical author-

ity: the Church's claims to possess and transmit authority, especially in the high ecclesiastical offices that are the object of simony, rest partly on the Pentecostal manifestation of the grace of the Holy Spirit to the Apostles in the sign of tongues of fire.[26] Nicholas and the other simonists have forgotten the concerns with individuality and identity that should regulate human, and above all Christian, life and that are symbolised in the sacrament of baptism. Dante-protagonist accuses them of forgetting their relationship with the God whose incarnation in Christ has shown the importance of human individuality, by worshipping not the Trinity but coined money:

> Fatto v'avete dio d'oro e d'argento;
> e che altro è da voi a l'idolatre,
> se non ch'elli uno, e voi ne orate cento?
>
> (*Inf.* XIX. 112–114)[27]

You have made of gold and silver a god for yourselves; how does the idolater differ from you, except that he prays to one god and you to hundreds?

And, in a further subversion of priestly roles and of the link between individual naming and salvation affirmed in baptism, the money that the popes worship is, as the *Commedia* later reveals, the florin marked with the Baptist's image (*Par.* XVIII. 133–136).[27]

The scenes of the third *bolgia* thus impress on the reader Dante's identity as a 'true' Florentine and as a speaker of *parole vere*, both as poet and protagonist. His authority is substantiated by the security of his civic identity, as he names the patronal church symbolic of Florence, displaying awareness of his civic and political, as well as religious, origins in this single reference. The authority of his language is ratified by a direct use of scriptural images and words (including the citation of Christ himself, '*Viemmi retro*', 'Follow me', l.93).[28] Nicholas, by contrast, openly admits to having abused the sacred authority of the papacy to promote the interests not of the Church but of his own family. He places himself in a context of unremitting corruption in his references to his predecessors, and to his successors, Boniface VIII and Clement V, whose careers trace not an apostolic but a simoniac succession. Nicholas's use of language reveals marked contrasts with the protagonist's solemn, scriptural idiom in this *canto*. The pope's speech is ironic and rich in word-play, punning on the etymology of his family name, Orsini (ll.70–71), and on the similar shape of money bags to the basins of this *bolgia*: '*sù l'avere e qui me misi in borsa*' ('in life I put goods, and here myself, into the purse': l.72). When he uses scriptural language, drawing on *Revelations* to accuse the supposed Boniface of seducing and raping the Church (ll.56–57), he seems more mocking than authoritative, in contrast to the similar imagery employed very seriously by Dante-author and -protagonist at the beginning and end of the *canto*. However well-founded Nicholas's denunciations of Clement and Boniface may be, they carry little authority when uttered apparently by a pair of waving feet and by a sinner guilty of an identical crime. Dante-protagonist underlines the incongruities of the situation with heavy sarcasm: he is only restrained from harsher speech, he claims, by his own better understanding of the social and spiritual identity that Nicholas once possessed which permits him to temper his recrimination against a man whose person deserves contempt but his office respect:

> *E se non fosse ch'ancor lo mi vieta*
> *la reverenza de le somme chiavi*
> *che tu tenesti ne la vita lieta,*
> *io userei parole ancor più gravi.*
>
> (*Inf.* XIX. 100–103)

And if I were not still held back by my reverence for the great keys that you possessed in the happy life, I would use still more weighty words.

CORRUPTION AND CONCEALMENT WITHIN THE CITY:
BARRATRY AND HYPOCRISY

The *bolgia* of simony serves to bolster the position of both poet and protagonist considerably, emphasising the protagonist's virtues as a Christian and as a Florentine, at the same time as stressing the identification between the poem's *actor* and its *auctor*. In the next *bolgia*, where soothsayers are punished, Dante-poet gives a further demonstration of his authority, making Virgil-character offer an explanation of the origins of his native town, Mantua, that differs from the historical Virgil's account in the *Aeneid*.[29] When the travellers enter the fifth *bolgia*, however, this increasing authority is rapidly undercut. The new *bolgia* is dedicated to the punishment of barratry, the buying and selling of public office, and this was one of the crimes of which Dante was historically accused in his exile from Florence. Critics have often suggested that the protagonist's profound unease throughout the sequence marks a covert allusion by the author to the circumstances of his banishment.[30] This is not to say, however, that the *canto* allows its readers to infer an admission of guilt on Dante's part: rather, it offers an examination of the ambiguities surrounding any accusation of this intensely political crime.

The first description of the *bolgia* compares the boiling pitch that fills the ditch to the tar used for ship-repair in the Venetian Arsenal, with a detailed evocation of the purposeful activity of the shipyard that once again gives the episode a distinctively urban flavour (XXI. 7–15).[31] The *bolgia* too is a site of considerable activity, with a squad of demons – the 'Malebranche' or 'evil claws' (XXII. 100) – supervising the punishment of the barrators. When a group of demons is allocated to accompany Dante-character and Virgil to the bridge leading to the next *bolgia*, new imagery compares them to a military cavalcade performing the orderly manoeuvres of warfare or tournament (XXII. 1–12). The devils occupy a position of some authority in the *canto*, acting as custodians of the sinners and as guides to the travellers; but Dante-poet's descriptions carry a burlesque element, with their weapons compared to kitchen forks (XXI. 55–57); their military trumpet-blast being sounded from a devil's anus (l.139); and their fantastical names being Dantean inventions rather than borrowed from biblical or classical sources.

As custodians of their circle, the devils give Virgil information about its topography, telling him that the bridges connecting this *bolgia* to the next were damaged centuries ago, on a date corresponding to Good Friday – presumably by the earthquake that the Bible records as occurring at the moment of Christ's death[32] – but that one crossing-point was preserved; they offer to lead the poets to it (ll.106–114). During the uneasy journey through the *bolgia* accompanied by these demons, Dante-character learns that a high proportion of the barrators are his close peninsular compatriots: several hail from Lucca, from the Sardinian regions controlled by Genoa and Pisa, and from elsewhere in Tuscany and Lombardy. As in the *bolge* of the pimps and the flatterers, regional allusions help identify their urban origins, with sarcastic references to Lucca's sacred icon of the '*Santo Volto*' ('Holy Face': XXI. 48) and to the local Lucchese St Zita (l.38), and also to the Sardinian dialect form '*donno*' of the title *dominus* ('lord': XXII. 83, 88). The most prominent speaker in the sequence actually comes from the kingdom of Navarre, but the clusters of Italian references reveal barratry as a crime characteristic of the peninsula's urban polities; even discounting Dante's historical exile, the protagonist's unease among the Malebranche is thus very natural, given his Tuscan regional origins. Virgil's reactions also seem to indicate that this is a crime especially relevant to an Italian; speaking on behalf of the frightened Dante-character, he questions the Navarrese about peninsular cases of barratry, asking: '*conosci tu alcun che sia latino | sotto la pece?*' ('do you know any under the pitch who are Italian?': XXII. 65–66).

The Navarrese capitalises on this question to escape from the Malebranche: promising to call Tuscans and Lombards to join them, he plunges back into the pitch, and the enraged Malebranche abandon Dante and Virgil in their desire to punish this trick. The two poets are thus enabled to flee the devils themselves, sliding down into the *bolgia* below with an undignified haste that is compared to the escape from a house on fire (XXIII. 37–42). They arrive in the sixth *bolgia* as fugitives from hell's appointed custodians – and further ambiguity about Dante-character's position is created by their arrival in the region dedicated to hypocrisy, since the condemnation of barratry by a convicted barrator could easily be seen as hypocritical. However, although under the laws governing hell the devils of the fifth *bolgia* exercise due authority in their punishment of the barrators, their grotesque appearance and behaviour marks them too as criminals rightly placed in hell because of their resistance to God's order.[33] By making it clear that barratry is being punished by a 'kangaroo court', Dante draws attention to the politicised nature of the sin itself. Corruption in office is vicious indeed, but it is commonly judged by factional, prejudiced courts; and although Virgil and Dante may seem like fugitives from justice when fleeing the demons, they are escaping persecution by a system as locally malicious and unjust as the historical Dante claims his banishment from Florence to be.

The chaos of the barratry sequence contrasts immediately with the relative calm and order that appear to govern the activities of the sixth *bolgia*. The hypocrites, dressed in gilded pseudo-monastic habits, pace along slowly as if taking part in a solemn religious procession, and the first sinner to speak in the *canto* attempts to maintain this quasi-religious impression by describing the group as the '*collegio | de l'ipocriti tristi*' ('the college of the sad hypocrites': ll.91–92), as if they were a penitential order.[34] In fact, the robes are made of lead, and with this detail, Dante once again subverts the innocuous familiarity of first appearances by drawing a link between the ritual of punishment in hell and an earthly device for criminal correction, when the robes are compared to those used by the Emperor Frederick II to punish crimes of *lèse-majesté* (XXIII. 65–66).[35] This second comparison reminds the reader that this *bolgia*'s congregation of pseudo-monks is guilty, like all hell's inhabitants, of grave crimes against the majesty of God himself. Their main fault, however, will be revealed as political – or rather, as based on the attempt to use spiritual authority for political ends that Dante sees as endemic in the contemporary Church, and as deeply disruptive of both religious and secular order.

The weight of their habits forces the hypocrites to move so slowly that Virgil and Dante speed past them, even at walking pace. Dante-character therefore requests his guide to find him an inter-locutor, preferably someone famous: *'alcun ch'al fatto o al nome si conosca'* ('someone who may be known by deed or by name': l.74). But the request draws attention to Dante himself, when a sinner recognises his Tuscan manner of speaking (l.76), and engages him in conversation. As they speak, Dante-traveller realises that he does indeed know something about the individual addressing him, although his fame is a restricted and local one. He proves to be a Bolognese politician and cleric from the generation before Dante's own, Catalano di Guido di Madonna Ostia, and he is accompanied in hell by his close earthly associate in civic and religious matters, Loderingo degli Andalò, another Bolognese. Catalano in turn pro-vides the travellers with information about the place and its occu-pants, but his apparently authoritative words often prove on examination to be incomplete or inaccurate, matching the nature of a sin that is based on appearances.

The encounter begins with an apparently straightforward exchange of personal information. The protagonist identifies him-self proudly as a citizen of the *'gran villa'* ('great town': l.95) of Florence, and explains the privilege of his *ante mortem* journey. The two sinners in reply offer considerable concrete information about their earthly careers:

> *Frati godenti fummo, e bolognesi;*
> *io Catalano e questi Loderingo*
> *nomati, e da tua terra insieme presi*
> *come suole esser tolto un uom solingo,*
> *per conservar sua pace; e fummo tali,*
> *ch'ancor si pare intorno dal Gardingo.*
>
> (*Inf.* XXIII. 103–108)

> We were Joyful Friars, and Bolognese; I was called Catalano,
> and this one Loderingo, and we were chosen together by your
> city, in the way that normally a single man is picked, to keep its
> peace; and we were such, that it can still be seen around the
> Gardingo.

Not only do these infernal companions look like monks but they were in life members of a religious order, popularly known as the *Frati Gaudenti* or 'Joyful Friars', one of the many local orders that sprang up in Italy during the thirteenth century in imitation of the great reforming movements of the Franciscans and Dominicans.

The *Ordo Militiae Beatae Mariae Virginis Gloriosae* ('Order of Knights of the Blessed and Glorious Virgin Mary') was established at Bologna in 1261, with papal backing, and had a mixed clerical and lay membership: historically, Catalano and Loderingo were among the earliest adherents of the movement (whose most prominent member was probably the poet Guittone d'Arezzo).[36] The order's designated activities very much reflected the natural concerns of an Italian city-state in the 1260s. Its brief was to combat heresy, defend the weak and, especially, to attempt pacification of the civil violence provoked by family feuds and faction-politics.[37] The rule specifically permitted its knightly members to take up arms in defence of religious and civil probity and, under special dispensations, to accept public office in the cause of promoting civic peace. However, the order rapidly acquired a poor reputation: its lay members in particular were often accused of insincerity in profiting from clerical privileges, whilst continuing to enjoy the comforts of domestic and married life. The name *Frati Gaudenti*, probably intended originally to indicate the members' joy in religious vocation, came rapidly to be used in a mockingly pejorative sense.[38]

As Brothers, Catalano and Loderingo proved far from lax, and despite having pursued active factional careers in their secular lives – Catalano as a Guelf and Loderingo as a Ghibelline – they were prominently involved in their order's pacifying activities.[39] In 1266, they were elected as joint *podestà* of the Florentine *comune*, to provide neutral leadership as the Ghibelline government established by Farinata and his allies was dismantled. According to Villani's chronicle, the much-publicised pacifying aims of their order were the cause of the Brothers' election.[40] In the event, their activities as *podestà* favoured the Guelfs – not surprisingly, given their newly founded order's dependence on papal protection. In the eyes of Dante's generation, however, Catalano and Loderingo themselves carried full responsibility for a disastrous term in office, during which faction quarrels flared up into riots and the Guelfs attacked their rivals, looting and destroying property and expelling the Ghibellines from Florence.[41]

Dante's Catalano alludes, indirectly, to these events, in his comment that in office: '*fummo tali, | ch'ancor si pare intorno dal Gardingo*' ('we were such, that it can still be seen around the Gardingo': ll. 107–108). His references to Florence, and his ready response to the protagonist's Tuscan accent, suggest that he wishes rhetorically to create sympathy in his interlocutor, much as a *podestà* would try to do in office. His choice of Florentine allusion is ill-advised for any such attempt. The Gardingo watch-tower, popularly believed to date from the city's Roman foundation era, was a landmark of the strongly Ghibelline Florentine neighbourhood dominated by Farinata's aristocratic Uberti clan.[42] This clan's possessions were singled out for destruction during the Guelf riots; indeed, the space occupied by the Uberti houses was left in ruins for some thirty years, in the spirit of pro-Guelf zeal that came to dominate the city and retrospectively justify such actions, so that what Catalano claims '*ancor si pare*' ('can still be seen': l. 108) is the civic destruction produced by faction-fighting.[43] Dante-poet makes Catalano's reference to the Gardingo hypocritically oblique, but knows that to a contemporary Florentine audience it would be easily deciphered to recall the disastrous consequences of corrupt government.

Dante-traveller's response to the information about the Brothers' earthly careers has provoked conflicting interpretations among commentators. The suspension of his reply, as a new visual phenomenon is encountered, leaves it ambiguous: Dante-traveller gets no further than, '*O frati, i vostri mali...*' (l.109), which could indicate compassion – 'Oh Brothers, your sufferings...' – or equally condemnation, 'Oh Brothers, your evils...'.[44] Dante's Florentine patriotism and his disapprobation of Church intervention in political affairs, make the latter more likely; commentators also note that suspension (*praecisio* or *aposiopesis*) is classified as a figure of disapprobation in medieval rhetoric.[45] The historical Dante, who spent time as a young man in Bologna, Catalano and Loderingo's home city and a leading centre of dictaminal scholarship, was certainly familiar with rhetorical conventions; and both as poet and as protagonist, he could well assume similar familiarity among his audience that would make obvious the intention behind his suspended invocation.

There is, however, room for speculation, not least because the disruption of his speech is attributed to a cause whose significance overrides rhetorical niceties: the sight of a crucified figure lying across the path, so that the hypocrites will have to walk over him. Catalano identifies the sinner as Caiaphas, the high priest who urged the council of Pharisees to agitate for Christ's crucifixion (adding that the council's other members suffer the same punishment). In priestly fashion, he uses a scriptural quotation to recall how the high priest '*consiglià i Farisei che convenia | porre un uom per lo popolo a' martìri*' ('advised the Pharisees that it was necessary to put one man to torture for the people': ll.116–117). In the Gospel, Caiaphas advises his fellow-priests that 'it is expedient for us, that one man should die for the people, and that the whole nation perish not' (*John* 11. 50). This is intended to safeguard their customs and religion from the threat of Roman annihilation: 'if we let him thus alone, all men will believe on him; and the Romans shall come, and take away both our place and nation' (*John* 11. 48). To a believer like Dante, the religious tradition that the Jewish priests were trying to save had in fact already been superseded by the salvation-message of the Messiah whom they failed – or rather, by medieval tradition, hypocritically refused – to recognise.[46] Moreover, Dante's political writing in *Convivio* and *Monarchia* reveals his conviction that the authority of the Roman empire whose encroachment the Jewish leaders feared, is divinely sanctioned. Caiaphas thus attacked two sacred bodies when he urged the policy of double-dealing that led to the execution of the innocent Jesus. The juxtaposition of the example of Caiaphas and his miscomprehension of the authority both of Christ (and in him, the embryo Church) and of the Roman empire, with the example of the Brothers' biased interventions in Florentine affairs, allows Dante to show that modern, local history is susceptible to the same readings as the events of scripture. Factionalism, which causes the fracturing of a community held together by shared history and beliefs, is eternally reprehensible, whether it occurs at the highest symbolic moment of the history of Rome and of Jerusalem, or in a city-state in contemporary Italy.

A final example of the rhetorical, political and spiritual confusion that reigns in the *bolgia* of the hypocrites appears as the travellers attempt to depart. Catalano reveals that the Malebranche misled them about the condition of the bridge to the next *bolgia*, which is in ruins. Catalano is no more capable than the demons of giving complete information about the true cause of the bridge's collapse (the Crucifixion earthquake). His reading of the topography of hell recalls the selectiveness which he earlier applied to the map of Florence: he draws no connection between the bridge's demolition and the actions of Caiaphas and his accomplices, who promoted the internal betrayals in spiritual matters that find their external correlative in the destruction of physical monuments. When Virgil comments that the devils misinformed them, Catalano retorts that:

> *Io udi' già dire a Bologna*
> *del diavol vizi assai, tra' quali udi'*
> *ch'elli è bugiardo e padre di menzogna.*
>
> (*Inf.* XXIII. 142–144)

In Bologna I heard that the devil has many vices, among which I heard that he is a liar and the father of lies.

Catalano is once again quoting the Gospels almost word-for-word, recalling Christ's statement that the devil 'is a liar, and the father of it' (*John* 8. 44). However, his awareness of the source of this final citation seems faulty, when he presents it as a piece of hearsay picked up in his native town, Bologna. Dante appears to be satirising Bolognese scholarship in this ostentatious parade of the university city as Catalano's source for a piece of information that is, in reality, far from arcane.[47] The stress of the rhyme between '*Bologna*' and '*menzogna*' underlines the dubious associations that have accumulated around the city's representatives in this *canto*, and around the clerical and political traditions they have been made to represent – just as the rhyming of '*Lucca*' and '*zucca*' in *canto* XVIII exposed an individual fault corrupting a wider civic society.

Throughout the *canto*, Dante implicitly asks the reader to uncover the hypocrites' own lies by comparing Catalano's words (which are of course invented by Dante-poet) with the external realities of history and scripture. Similarly, Venedico Caccianemico, Alessio Interminei and Pope Nicholas, as well as the devils and barrators of the fifth *bolgia*, all manipulate language and historical or geographic references so as to undermine the stability of social and political structures. The Malebolge episodes that we have reviewed draw attention to the violent consequences of neglecting the duties to society that accompany both civic and religious office. The sinners' misapprehension of their social functions has been revealed in their linguistic malpractices, whether in attempting to assume classical or biblical-sounding authority, to dazzle their interlocutor with witty wordplay, or by the blunt use of unrefined and municipal language in slander, perjury or defiance. Linguistic impropriety is revealed above all in their inability to name themselves properly. Whether attempting concealment or frankly admitting their identity, all fail to understand that true identity is established within a context of social interaction and responsibility. They can speak of being *bolognesi* or *lucchesi*, popes or friars, only in ways that diminish the standing of their towns or their offices. In this way, their own words prove them to be profoundly dysfunctional in moral, political and spiritual terms, since they are unable to recognise their own personal origins, as proper citizens and social beings should.

Similar political themes can be traced through the remaining sections of Malebolge, and in the bottom-most level of hell, dedicated to crimes of treachery. In these *canti*, Dante-character encounters grand figures from the classical and biblical past: the seductive rhetorician Ulysses; Sinon the Greek; Potiphar's wife; and the arch-traitors, Caesar's assassins Brutus and Cassius, and the biblical Judas and Lucifer. But he also continues to encounter contemporary Italians, especially those politically active in Tuscany and Romagna in the past decades. These range from the Florentine Mosca dei Lamberti, whose malicious counsel of 1215 reputedly kick-started the vendetta and faction-rivalry that dominated the city's thirteenth-century political fortunes (see Chapter 1), to the Faentine politician and *Frate Gaudente*, Alberigo dei Manfredi, so close a contemporary to Dante that he was not yet dead in 1300 (XXXIII. 121–135) – Dante's *ante mortem* condemnation of Alberigo to hell is theologically highly unorthodox, emphasising the gravity of the eminently socio-political sin of treachery.[48] The sinners' accounts of the actions that have earned them infernal punishment highlight the significance of what often seem to be petty, local crimes – for even unimportant figures affect their neighbours through their personal and political decisions. When Dante-poet focuses on the details of an individual biography – citing names or nicknames of cities and of people, dialect words, local landmarks – he evokes a social context for their activities, drawing private and public morality together.

The city of hell is joined, as we saw, to the cities of earth and to human historical and political concerns, through the symbolic figure of the Old Man of Crete, as well as by the individual lives and actions of all of its inhabitants. It is also, however, connected to the City of God: infernal justice is also divine justice and the inscription at hell's entrance gate stresses that love and wisdom form its foundations. A counterpoise to the Old Man of Crete, moreover, comes in the figure of Lucifer himself. Like the Old Man, Lucifer is a composite figure, parti-coloured (his three faces are red, yellow and black: XXXIV. 39–45) and dripping moisture (tears and spittle: ll. 53–54), who also occupies a position beneath a mountain conjoining two worlds – but in Lucifer's case, the mountain is the location of purgatory and of the earthly paradise. Paradoxically, therefore, at the heart of the spiritual and political disorder of hell, the travellers rediscover its orderly foundations, and Satan himself provides them with their pathway towards the City of God as they climb down his hairy body towards the path that leads them to the new dawn which greets them in purgatory. The connections between the events of earthly history and the phenomena of the parodic anti-city of hell are strongly drawn throughout the *cantica*, especially in the claustrophobic pseudo-civic circles of Malebolge. At the same time, Dante also stresses that justice and order lie beneath terrestrial and infernal chaos, allowing positive, as well as negative, political lessons to be drawn from this stage of the *Commedia*'s journey.

5

CREATING COMMUNITY

PURGATORIO

As the theological concept of purgatory evolved in the twelfth and thirteenth centuries, it came to be designated a separate topographical space in the medieval cartography of the afterlife, dedicated to the *post mortem* atonement for sin by the truly repentant.[1] In Dante's *Commedia*, the physical separation of purgatory from hell is of primary importance. The poet assigns it a geographical location in the southern hemisphere, on an island mountain crowned with a garden identified as Eden so as to stress purgatory's fundamental theological connection to the stories of humanity's 'Fall' and Redemption as real, historical events. The mountain is rooted in the mortal world of time and change – so concretely that, according to the infernal spirit of Ulysses, sailors may sight it on voyage (*Inf.* XXVI. 133–135), and its lower slopes, at least, are subject to an ordinary cycle of daily and seasonal change. Yet Mount Purgatory is also a world apart, and Dante makes its inhabitants display a carefully moderated attitude towards the temporal world where they committed the errors that cause them still to be debarred from God's '*vera città*' ('true city': *Purg.* XIII. 95). Sandwiched between hell and heaven, and located on the created globe, purgatory is an area both closely connected to, yet clearly distinct from, the world of mortals and of politics.

Political ideas occupy a prominent place in the *Purgatorio* and have been the object of considerable scholarly attention in the past few decades. The spirits of purgatory define their earthly existence as pilgrim-like ('*peregrina*': XIII. 96), putting their own corporeal experiences behind them; they retain, however, strong interests in how mortal pilgrims are guided through life, both spiritually and politically. Critics such as Peter Armour and John Scott point out the strong concern running through this *cantica* with questions about the relationship of the Church to the empire, as well as the vehement language used to denounce failures in imperial leadership, abuses of papal authority and the divisiveness of Italian faction politics. Giuseppe Mazzotta and Lino Pertile have further underlined the scriptural, prophetic tone of Dante's urgent appeals for political renewal.[2] Among the obviously political episodes of *Purgatorio*, several famous sequences are devoted to investigating the problematic relationships between the spiritual and the secular authorities at the level of high European politics: for instance, the valley of the princes in ante-purgatory, the speeches of Marco Lombardo and of Hugh Capet in *canti* XVI and XX, and the second allegorical pageant of the earthly paradise. Others – such as the denunciations of Tuscany and the Romagna in *canto* XIV – have a local, Italian focus; although often concerns of this kind are linked into discussions of a wider political picture, as in the review of Italian politics in *canto* VI. Dante's political interests in the *Purgatorio*, then, are undoubtedly strongly engaged with imperial questions, but they cover a wide geographical and constitutional range that includes an eager concern with city society, as well as with kingdoms, empire and papacy.

Joan Ferrante, approaching the politics of *Purgatorio* from a rather different angle to the critics cited previously, has argued that Dante's purgatory represents the polity of a kingdom, occupying a midway position between the city-like chaos of hell and the imperial perfections of paradise, and representing society in transition, after the infernal journey through political corruption.[3] The proposal fits convincingly into her wider political interpretation of the *Commedia* and she demonstrates that the physical and organisational structures of the mountain show plausible correspondences with those assigned to individual kingdoms in Dante's theoretical writing. This critical scheme, however, like that of the studies mentioned earlier, leaves little room for the consideration of *Purgatorio*'s treatment of questions about the city as a self-contained society. Structural analogies, too, are inconclusive: if purgatory shows some similarities to a kingdom, it also displays physical features that recall a city. Purgatory-proper is entered, city-like, via a well-guarded gate in a set of protective walls, inside which the mountain is divided into separate sections as street-like as the circles of Malebolge and linked by rocky flights of steps. The terrace of pride is ornamented with marble sculptures, while its penitents resemble the caryatids seen on earthly buildings, suggesting the formal architecture of an earthly cityscape. But other features do not fit an urban pattern: some are rural, such as the seashore and valley of ante-purgatory, the tree and stream of the terrace of gluttony, and the forest and garden of Eden; others have no specific topographical character – the terrace of anger is filled with smoke, that of lust with fire. Visual analogies with earthly polities are in fact as partial and imperfect in purgatory as they were in hell.

This *cantica* resembles *Inferno* in its intense concern with the specific historical experiences of contemporary Italian cities and with extrapolating from these examples a notion of how private morality impinges on the public sphere. Dante-poet continues to scrutinise telling municipal details such as minutiae of dress and conduct, or personal and place names and other linguistic clues, which give an insight into the conduct of relationships between the members of a local society. As in *Inferno*, he pays particular attention to the words and actions of close contemporaries who have occupied positions of authority within the cities, courts and parties of Italy, juxtaposing modern situations with reflections on classical and biblical examples of vice and virtue. An innovation in the *Purgatorio* is that the leaders chosen for such scrutiny increasingly include writers as well as politicians. *Inferno*'s main contemporary, vernacular authors were Brunetto Latini, Pier della Vigna and Bertran de Born; but they are outnumbered in purgatory, where Dante locates

Sordello da Goito, Forese Donati, Bonagiunta da Lucca, Guido Guinizelli and Arnaut Daniel, as well as giving a prominent place to the classical author Statius.[4] The poets assist Dante-traveller's understanding of challenging points in the moral structures of both earthly and purgatorial communities, becoming mouthpieces for Dante-author's moral judgements on the ills of contemporary society, including the society of urban Italy.

The prominence that this *cantica* accords to poets as commentators on law, government and peace, puts them on a par with the numerous princes and governors who also appear. Dante-poet appears to be building on the notions expressed in *Convivio* about the joint responsibility of politicians and of philosophers – and the treatise itself shows that philosophy may be treated in poetic form – to guide humanity towards moral happiness. Anticipations of the *Monarchia* may be discerned in the fact that Dante-character's journey up the mountain, helped by the virtuous pagan Virgil and the throng of purgatorial politicians and poets, ends in the Garden of Eden which in the treatise portrays the secular happiness protected by empire (*Mon.* III. xvi. 7).[5] There are certainly links between the ideas, imagery and language of certain political passages from *Purgatorio* and those of *Convivio* and *Monarchia*, and it should not be forgotten that *Purgatorio* was composed, in part, while Dante's imperial enthusiasms were kept at a high pitch by the Emperor Henry VII's Italian campaigning (1310–1313).[6]

The prominence accorded to poets, however, also recalls *De vulgari*, and reminds us that Dante was furthermore passionately concerned about the role of urban centres within the unity of Italy or of the empire itself. The treatise's notion that small societies contain the potential for unified endeavour, facilitated by the use of fitting language, is extended as Dante explores his poets' relationships to city and court, emphasising the notions of service and love that form an important part of his political ethic. In *De vulgari*, Italian vernacular poets are identified as naturally setting the linguistic standards of what is illustrious, aulic and curial, and are said to constitute in themselves the rational *curia* of fragmented Italy; the poets and their compositions provide each and all of the Italian cities with nuclei of authority and reason. The purgatorial poets' commentaries on political and moral issues similarly represent the curial potential within the different Italian cities, and Dante's examination of political issues in *Purgatorio* thereby maintains a close focus on local, urban communities and on the linguistic and moral markers of their wellbeing. Because the encounters with vernacular writers provoke some of the comments with greatest immediate relevance to the city, they provide the primary material for this chapter, which leaves any detailed analysis of the imperial thinking of *Purgatorio* to one side.

CITY LOYALTIES: MANTUA, ROME AND FLORENCE

From the outset, one of the main themes of the *Purgatorio* is defined as freedom: theological freedom from sin, but also the moral freedoms of self-control and self-expression, which we know from the *Convivio* to be fundamental to proper conduct in the active life. At the foot of the mountain, Virgil tells Cato that Dante-traveller is seeking freedom (*'libertà va cercando'*: *Purg.* I. 71); at its summit, he congratulates the protagonist on its achievement: *'libero, dritto e sano è tuo arbitrio'* ('your will is free, upright and whole': XXVII. 140). Political freedom is also an important issue and in the first extended passage of political commentary in *Purgatorio*, in *canto* VI, Dante-poet conducts a probing enquiry into the nature of the liberty claimed by contemporary Italian city-states, which shows their freedom to be excessive. The absence of restraint in their political ambitions has descended into chaos, and Dante begins his survey with the pointed exclamation, *'Ahi* serva *Italia'* ('Alas, *enslaved* Italy': VI. 76, emphasis mine). Later, in *canto* XVI, the same ideas are echoed and expanded when Marco Lombardo tells the protagonist that the disorder of contemporary Italy – he especially focuses on his native Lombardy – results from the wilful rejection of the guidance of the empire in politics, and of the Church in religion (and in religion alone). In both passages, the imperial arguments and imagery of the *Convivio* are clearly echoed; in *canto* VI, generalised laments over regional and national disorder are accompanied also by more specific reflections on the politics of urban Italy and on the histories of individual cities.

Indeed half of *canto* VI is solely occupied by a stern invective against the political ills of Italy addressed directly to the reader by Dante-poet (ll.76–151). Three Italian cities in particular are identified by name to exemplify the nature of contemporary problems, each represented by one of the three participants in the encounter that sparks the political outburst. The cities are Mantua, Rome and Florence, and their representatives, the poets Sordello da Goito, Virgil and Dante himself. Mantua and Florence are historically the trio's native cities; as the sequence develops, Rome comes to represent something of an ideal fatherland for all three, combining the orderliness of both the urban microcosm and the imperial macrocosm.[7] Virgil, the obvious Roman of the sequence, first introduced himself to Dante-character as a Mantuan, and here too mentions Mantua as his city of origin (*Inf.* I. 68–69; *Purg.*VI. 72). Dante-character was in *Inferno* ascribed Romano–Florentine ancestry by Brunetto Latini, but this 'Roman' connection had as much a moral as a genealogical implication (*Inf.* XV. 74–78). Sordello's highly peripatetic career took him to many different parts of Italy and southern France, but he has no historical connection with Rome. 'Roman' qualities shared by all three, however, include their devotion to their place of origin and their appreciation of the virtues of political order: an appreciation reflected in the urgency with which all three wrote about the need for strong leadership and the adverse consequences of political venality – Virgil in the *Aeneid*, Dante in the *Commedia* and Sordello in various strongly worded lyrics.

Dante-poet's examination of the Italian cities is launched via the encounter of the three poets in ante-purgatory, when Virgil approaches the '*altera e disdegnosa*' ('lofty and disdainful': *Purg.* VI. 62) figure of Sordello to ask for directions towards the gate of purgatory-proper. Sordello's initial response is forbidding: '*non rispuose al suo dimando, | ma di nostro paese e de la vita | ci 'nchiese'* ('he did not reply to [Virgil's] question, but asked us about our birthplaces and our lives': ll.69–71). But the name of his and Virgil's common city of origin has an irresistibly *'dolce suon'* ('sweet sound': l.80) that immediately creates a bond between them, causing him to interrupt Virgil's reply with the spontaneous revelation of his own name and origins: *'O Mantoano, io son Sordello | de la tua terra!'* ('O Mantuan, I am Sordello, from your city!': ll.74–75). Encouraged by this expression of civic fellowship, Virgil in turn responds with unusual readiness, naming himself with the same direct simplicity as the other: *'io son Virgilio'* ('I am Virgil': VII. 7). Within the time-frame of the encounter, his response is as quick as Sordello's, although Dante-poet so constructs the narrative that his reply occurs only after the long authorial interjection on the state of Italy, thus contrasting the Mantuan civic fellowship of purgatory with the factionalism of Italy's earthly politics. Dante-author's political lament stresses how civic corruption and disorder prevents living Italians from reproducing the unifying, patriotic sympathy displayed in the *'accoglienze oneste e liete'* ('honourable and joyful welcome': VII. 1) shared between the two Mantuan spirits.

Virgil occupies a contradictory position in the episode centred on the meeting with Sordello. As author of the *Aeneid*, as representative of imperial Rome and as a patriotic native of the city of Mantua, he occupies a position of poetic and political authority. Nonetheless, his status is vulnerable, as his qualifications as guide to the protagonist are undermined by the specifically Christian activity and orientation of the purgatorial realm.[8] In the course of this encounter, Sordello explicitly takes over his role as guide on this stage of the journey (VII. 42, 87) and, to some extent, shares his role as poet and commentator on political probity. Virgil himself, in *canto* VII, draws attention to the ambiguity of his position when he identifies the community to which his soul belongs in eternity – although this information is offered only after his historical citizenship of Mantua and Rome has been firmly established. He uses precise, emotionally restrained language, such as characterised his first encounter with the protagonist in *Inferno* I, to describe Limbo as a stable, orderly society, stressing that he and his fellows are punished '*non per far, ma per non fare*' ('not for what they have done, but what they have not done': *Purg.*VII. 25).[9] Virgil's description of this community emphasises the moral and political perfection attained by its pagan inhabitants in life, but also points to the vacuum at the heart of the social order they created, which was not blessed by the theological virtues of faith, hope and love:

> *Quivi sto io con quei che le tre sante*
> *virtù non si vestiro, e sanza vizio*
> *conobber l'altre e seguir tutte quante.*
>
> (*Purg.*VII. 34–36)

I reside there among those who were not clad in the three holy virtues, and who knew the others and followed them perfectly without any vice.

Virgil's words are particularly poignant, for they follow Dante-author's lengthy description of the ills of modern Italy, where both moral and theological virtues have been rejected, and even partial – 'Limboesque' – equilibrium cannot be maintained.

In *Inferno*, Limbo's decorous and welcoming community of pagan heroes provided a stark contrast to the chaos of subsequent, inner circles, heavily populated by Christian sinners. In *Purgatorio*, Virgil's description of Limbo follows Dante-poet's evocation of earthly communities similarly adrift from both Christian and classical virtues. Dante even adopts pagan terminology to address Christ as '*sommo Giove*' ('mighty Jove': VI. 118), in a prayer for political renewal that pointedly sanctifies the orderly authority of the classical past and stresses the confusion of contemporary Christian conduct. The imperial city of Rome, with its past splendours and present disorder, occupies a prominent position in the long authorial interjection on the woes of contemporary Italy.[10] Dante-poet laments the modern absence of political morality and stability in a peninsula personified as destitute and abandoned: Italy is no longer the '*donna di provincie*' ('mistress of the provinces') described in the Glosses to Justinian's legal code, but a '*bordello*' ('brothel': l.78); the city of Rome, like the Jerusalem of *Lamentations*, '*piagne | vedova e sola*' ('weeps, widowed and alone': ll.112–113).[11] Using animal imagery, the peninsula is also portrayed as the unbridled horse of the *Convivio* (ll.94, 98), when the imperial saddle is empty (ll.89, 92), and the rein (l.88) and spurs (l.95) of Justinian's laws neglected.[12] Disorder at the pinnacle of the political hierarchy has contaminated the lower levels, and Dante comments that justice and freedom have given place, through imperial negligence, to cupidity ('*cupidigia*': l.104), factionalism – he sarcastically employs the specialised verb *parteggiare*, meaning to form a political party – and tyranny:

> Ché le città d'Italia tutte piene
> son di tiranni, e un Marcel diventa
> ogne villan che parteggiando viene.
>
> (*Purg.*VI. 124–126)

For the cities of Italy are all full of tyrants, and every low-born leader who forms a faction becomes a Marcellus.[13]

To underline imperial negligence, Dante characterises the emperor of 1300, Albert of Austria, as '*Alberto tedesco*' ('German Albert': l.97), an epithet with moral rather than national significance, like *De vulgari*'s use of 'Sicilian', or Brunetto Latini's of 'Roman' and 'Fiesolan' in *Inferno* XV. Dante urges that only properly 'Roman' rule, by an emperor responsive to the responsibilities of his position, will restore political stability throughout the peninsula and promote the peace, law and order that are vital to the well-being of its constituent communities, rescuing them from the tyranny of competitive, independent freedoms. In an image that half anticipates the *Monarchia*'s use of the myth of the Garden of Eden to represent secular, political happiness, Dante describes

Italy as the ancient 'garden' of the empire founded by Aeneas and the Caesars ('*giardin de lo 'mperio*'), and shows that it has been rendered a desert ('*diserto*': l.105) by the absence of imperial justice. Virgil, who is both Mantuan and Roman, symbolises the happy conjunction that can be achieved between imperial and civic order, and his presence in the sequence provides the real correlative for Dante-poet's insistence on Roman themes throughout his commentary on Italian political conditions. Virgil and Sordello's purgatorial embrace provides an example of ideal normality both for the Italian cities and for their emperor, whose function is to create the conditions in which such civic fellowship may flourish.

The lament for *serva Italia* opens with Mantua and pays lengthy attention to Rome, but it closes with the city of Florence. The native city of the *Commedia*'s author and protagonist is at first ironically exempted from a political '*digression che non ti tocca*' ('digression which does not affect you': l.128). By the end of the *canto* Florentine disorder has been made evident and she joins the anthropomorphised figures of Italy and Rome in the guise of a weak and restless invalid (ll.149–151). At the start of the lament, the embrace prompted by Mantua's name illustrates what a community of citizens can, and should, be – drawn together by shared language and references.[14] In Italy's degenerate modern cities, however, the mouth is used not for welcome but for division and abuse, portrayed as a form of quasi-cannibalism horrifyingly reminiscent of the infernal encounter with the treacherous Pisan Count Ugolino (*Inf.* XXXII. 122–XXXIII. 78):

> *Ora in te non stanno sanza guerra*
> *li vivi tuoi, e l'un l'altro si rode*
> *di quei ch'un muro e una fossa serra.*
>
> (*Purg.*VI. 82–84)

Now your [i.e. Italy's] living souls cannot remain without war, and those who are encircled by one wall and one moat gnaw at one another.

In Florence, at the end of the passage, attempts at the construction of a meaningful municipal language fail completely. Its citizens react volubly to political crisis, but use the hasty ('*in sommo de la bocca*': l.132) and strident ('*grida*': l.135) language of over-confident public rhetoric that gives only an impression of assurance. The actual insubstantiality of their political ideas and language is illustrated in the spinning metaphors that describe their legislative attempts. Medieval Florence's wealth and international reputation rested largely on the wool trade and the reliable quality of her cloth production, but Dante denounces her linguistic products as faulty, a single month's use wearing out any legal fabric the citizens attempt to create: '*a mezzo novembre | non giugne quel che tu d'ottobre fili*' ('by mid-November what you spin in October doesn't hold': ll.143–144).[15]

Matters of formal political organisation, especially of law, intermingle with more emotive points of criticism in this Florentine passage that concludes the political invective. Dante refers to Florentine attempts to institute the secular happiness of the good life ('*viver bene*': l.141) through consultation and legislation; the defects in her '*sottili | provedimenti*' ('subtle provisions': ll.142–143) contrast poorly with the still-valid legislation of Justinian (l.89), or the codes of Athens and Sparta (l.139) whose value Justinian's law-codes themselves praise (*Institutes* I. ii. 10).[16] Unlike the stable polities of antiquity, or the good modern leaders who have fully committed themselves to justice, Florentines are content with a superficial show of legality alone. Dante's image offers echoes of the allegory of *Tre donne* in contrasting those who have '*giustizia in cuore*' ('justice in their hearts': l.130), with the Florentines who only have justice '*in sommo de la bocca*' ('on the tip of their tongues': l.132). Other symbols of stability and shared identity, too, change as rapidly in Florence as the law:

> *Quante volte, del tempo che rimembre,*
> *legge, moneta, officio e costume*
> *hai tu mutato, e rinovate membre!*
>
> (*Purg.*VI. 145–147)

How many times, in living memory, have you changed laws,
currency, office, and customs, and renewed your members!

Dante associates the continual destruction of all the outward signs
of order and reliability with the continual renewal of the city's
members. The phrase might simply indicate the rapid changeovers
of official personnel specified by the Florentine constitution, but it
applies equally well to the patterns of political restriction (such as
anti-magnate legislation), *coups d'état*, and exile that punctuated
Florentine affairs. It also carries a sinister suggestion of bodily
mutilation: *membre* in the *Commedia* are almost always literally
limbs, not members of the political community. The Florentine
'body politic' is compared in the following lines to a sick woman:
the reference to her members makes her mutilated. Rather than
accepting the imperial authority that a little earlier was urged on
the Italians to '*cura[r] lor magagne*' ('cure their wounds': l. 110), she is
continually dismembered through the inept surgery of municipal
measures of change.[17] If the opening of the authorial interjection
focused on the plight of urban Italy as a whole, Florence has by the
end of *canto* VI emerged as the specific historical fulfilment of
Dante's warnings about the effects of political transgression on
individual urban communities.

POETS AND POLITICIANS IN THE COMMUNITY
OF ANTE-PURGATORY

Dante-poet addresses his readers directly in the '*Ahi serva Italia*'
invective, stressing the magnitude of the issues it raises. The lament,
with its opening and closing concentration on urban and
Florentine issues, highlights the importance Dante accords to the
city as a social and political form. The sequence is otherwise dominated by Sordello and Virgil, the two principal speakers and actors
of *canti* VI and VII. Both bring into the sequence other political
concerns and associations. Virgil represents imperial Rome and the

moral perfection associated with the heroes of Limbo. Sordello, however, is associated historically with precisely the kind of factional activity that Dante's invective denounces and, moreover, with the grand European extension of such struggles. Significantly, in view of his dubious political career, Sordello's initial appearance raises ambiguous associations. With his '*mover de li occhi onesta e tarda*' ('slow and decorous movement of his eyes': *Purg.* VI. 63), he might recall the '*genti [...] con occhi tardi e gravi*' ('people with slow and solemn gaze': *Inf.* IV. 112) of Limbo, perhaps sharing their calm authority; but his position of lofty solitude and his politicised determination to establish the origins of his interlocutors echo equally closely the '*sdegnoso*' ('disdainful': *Inf.* X. 41) Farinata of *Inferno*.[18]

The resemblances are not casual. Like Farinata, the historical Sordello was closely involved in the mid-thirteenth-century clashes between the papacy and the empire, though on the side of the Guelfs. A native of Goito, near Mantua, Sordello was a fiercely partisan supporter of the Angevin cause who spent long periods of his political career in the princely courts of northern Italy and southern France, and in the Angevin kingdom of Naples. His dubious record of faction activity includes his abduction of Cunizza da Romano (who appears in heaven, *Par.* IX. 25–36), wife of one of his patrons and sister of another, which caused social and political repercussions in several of the Italian courts. Sordello's political career, therefore, was one of violence and factionalism, making his appearance in purgatory surprising after the infernal encounters with Farinata, Brunetto, the *Frati Gaudenti* and other contributors to the Italian factional turmoil of the 1260s, whose instincts he would appear to have shared. The Sordello of *Purgatorio*, however, corrects the example of Farinata by seeking inclusivity rather than exclusivity. He focuses on the unifying aspects of citizenship in his warm welcome to Virgil as a still-anonymous Mantuan, rather than demanding the details of his interlocutor's family and faction-loyalties as Farinata did. For Dante, the redeeming feature in this case apparently lies in Sordello's poetic activity as commentator on political negligence.[19]

Dante's admiration for Sordello's verse, in political perhaps as much as artistic terms, overrides the compromising facts of the Mantuan's political career, allowing him to be represented as a figure who, in death if not in life, displays laudable patriotic sympathies. As numerous critics have noted, the main speech attributed to Sordello-character in *Purgatorio* VII carries distinct echoes of the historical Sordello-poet's political lyric, *Planher vuelh en Blacatz* (*I wish to lament Sir Blacatz*), an inter-textual relationship that gives clear evidence of the poetic grounds on which Dante-author probably selected him to figure in this political sequence.[20] The lyric, like Sordello-poet's whole corpus, is composed in Occitan; Dante notes in *De vulgari* that Sordello so acclimatised himself to the language of *oc* that he abandoned his native Mantuan in speech as well as writing (*DVE* I. xv. 2). His linguistic choices thus followed his political choices, given his activities in Provence and in Italy in the service of Charles I of Anjou; but although it may have faction origins, his adherence in art to an idiom associated in *De vulgari* with illustrious topics and writers apparently dignifies his literary activity in Dante's view. As Teodolinda Barolini points out, Sordello's example enables Dante to provide a poetic counterpoise in *Purgatorio* to the *Inferno*'s Occitan poet of political violence and division, Bertran de Born, who is also prominently, but approvingly, mentioned in *De vulgari*.[21] Barolini notes another contradiction that suggests a further allusion to the treatise: that Sordello's words in *canto* VII echo Guittone d'Arezzo's lyric *Magni baroni certo e regi quasi* (*Great barons indeed and almost kings*) as much as Sordello's own *planh* (lament).[22] Guittone was reproved in *De vulgari* for using municipal language, but here Dante extends the concepts and images from one of the Aretine's best-known poems on Italian local politics into a wider European context, and places them in the mouth of a habitual user of the illustrious idiom of Occitan (although Sordello's purgatorial speech uses, of course, the vernacular Italian of the *Commedia*), thus silently transforming Guittone's *dicta municipalia* into something more closely resembling *dicta curialia*.

The atmosphere, both of the purgatorial valley of the princes and of Sordello-poet's original *planh*, is literally courtly and aristocratic – though in both cases tinged with some of that scepticism about courtliness that Dante outlines in the *Convivio* (II. x. 8). The *planh*, under cover of mourning the death of the valiant Blacatz, satirically exposes the lack of valour in Europe's other princes: eight rulers, starting with the Emperor Frederick II, are urged to abandon political and military timidity and imitate the decisive leadership of the deceased. The lyric investigates the question of moral versus social nobility in a similar vein to Dante in the *Convivio*; like Dante, indeed, the author offers his audience an elevating metaphorical feast, inviting the princes to eat the heart ('*cor*': *Planh*, 7) of Blacatz which, with a play on words, will make them '*coratjos*' ('stout-hearted': l.17) rather than '*descorat*' ('faint-hearted': l.8).[23] In *Purgatorio*, Dante conducts a reworking of similar themes: as his fictional Sordello guides Virgil and Dante to a secluded valley where they can spend the night, he presents a speech on the valley's noble inhabitants, in which he names eight principal figures in descending order of status, from emperor down to marquis. All eight are implicated in the charge levelled at the first, '*d'aver negletto ciò che far dovea*' ('of having neglected what he ought to do': *Purg.* VII. 92), in a speech that not only echoes the structure of the *planh* but focuses on the same principalities and (in all but one overlapping case), on the heirs of the figures named in the original *planh*.

In *Purgatorio*, the harsh satirical tone of the lyric is modified and Dante's Sordello, for the most part, employs a melancholy register appropriate to the themes of meditation and reconciliation predominant in ante-purgatory. At times, however, he breaks into highly charged denunciations of the princes' misconduct that echo the language of the preceding *canto*'s political lament for *serva Italia*, or the pungent idiom of Guittone d'Arezzo, as well as that of the *planh*. Thus the first leader, the Emperor Rudolf, has failed to '*sanar le piaghe c'hanno Italia morta*' ('heal the wounds that have killed Italy': VII. 95), an accusation that recalls the earlier plea that Emperor Albert may '*cura le magagne*' ('heal the wounds': VI. 110) of

Italy; the actions of Guglielmo of Monferrat make the city of Alessandria weep (VII. 135–137), as Rome did in the previous *canto*.[24] In a mournful '*ubi sunt?*', Sordello insists that all but one of the princes has been succeeded by unworthy heirs; he is particularly harsh on the new king of France, Philip IV, who is also severely criticised later in *Purgatorio* (XX. 85–93, XXXII. 148–160). Taken in conjunction with the *planh*'s criticisms of the princes' forebears, the speech in *canto* VII sketches out a trajectory of declining political values across several generations that leaves the states of Europe, like the cities of Italy in the previous *canto*, destructively dominated by competition and conflict.

In the valley of ante-purgatory, however, earthly state and dynastic rivalry are left behind, and the princes join collectively in prayer. Instead of competing for primacy, they fit into an orderly hierarchy in which the emperor naturally takes the highest seat (l.91), but where even former enemies mingle as companions and equals, creating a courtly harmony that mirrors the solidarity of Sordello's and Virgil's embrace. The valley of the princes provides a powerful image of political and linguistic concord that also provides reminiscences of *De vulgari*: in this case, of the treatise's evocations of the harmony of a true *curia*, as exemplified in Hohenstaufen Sicily and also in the rational unity that links the best poets of all Italy together. When the travellers enter the valley, they find its noble and curial inhabitants eager, like Sordello, to share their reflections on the political fortunes of the states they knew in life; and these are, once again, Italian states familiar to Dante from personal experience. Both the '*Ahi serva Italia*' passage of *canto* VI and Sordello's speech in *canto* VII emphasise the malfunctioning of the imperial, regal and civic polities of contemporary Europe, with the predominantly Italian concerns of *canto* VI extended by Sordello into an engagement with the political ills of a wider European order, stretching from England to Sicily and from Aragon to Bohemia. In *canto* VIII, as the episode dominated by Sordello draws to a close, Dante brings attention back to Italy, in the personal encounters between the protagonist and two other

political figures. The rival party affiliations of the two princes –
Nino Visconti was a prominent Guelf, Currado Malaspina headed a
traditionally Ghibelline branch of his family – bring Dante back to
the theme of factional division: but like their companions, these
princes now present a picture of harmony and attentive friendship.

Both Nino and Currado are praised for their political conduct
in life, and both are very aware of their earthly reputations and of
meriting honourable remembrance, as individuals and as members
of prominent and upright families. Dante-protagonist encounters
Nino Visconti almost as soon as he enters the valley, and they joy-
fully recognise and greet one another. Dante-author describes him
as '*giudice Nin gentil*' ('noble judge Nino': VIII. 53), giving him his
hereditary title as judge of the Sardinian region of Gallura, but the
reference to his personal friendship with Dante reminds us that
Nino was equally closely associated with Tuscany and urban politics. The biographical realities of Nino's career bring together
many of the concerns raised in the previous two *canti* regarding
political conduct in both the municipal and the feudal arenas of
Italy and Europe. Nino's Sardinian position gave him hereditary
political responsibilities, like those of his fellow princes listed by
Sordello in *canto* VII. Shortcomings in his performance of these
duties are suggested by the fact that in *Inferno*, Dante-protagonist
learned that Nino's Sardinian deputy *in absentia*, Fra Gomita, was
one of the barrators punished for political corruption in
Malebolge (*Inf.* XXII. 81). Visconti's absence from Gallura was
occasioned by his involvement in the affairs of Pisa, where he
served in the Guelf regime headed by his grandfather, Ugolino
della Gherardesca. The latter's faction-driven manipulation of the
city's affairs forced Nino to flee to Florence (where presumably he
formed the friendship with Dante referred to here) – a painful
series of events in which personal ambition and factional ferocity
overrode city and family unity, earning Ugolino punishment in the
lowest circles of hell (*Inf.* XXXII. 124–XXXIII. 78). Ugolino and
Nino were the joint dedicatees of Guittone d'Arezzo's lyric, *Magni
baroni*, whose inter-textual echoes Barolini has identified in

canti VI and VII, a poem that exposed the pair to a critical political scrutiny that this purgatorial episode continues but also revises.
Dante's use of Nino's title of judge stresses that he has at least
attempted to act righteously towards his political allies; his political
record may show negligence, but it avoids the direct abuse pursued
by the associates, Ugolino and Gomita, whose actions he came,
however tardily, to repudiate.

Nino's references to family show an understanding of the deli-
cacy of relationships between individuals that counterbalances the
sinister anti-paternal example of his grandfather, Ugolino. Nino
expresses tender affection for his young daughter (l.71), and though
he speaks with measured disapproval of his widow's remarriage, he
focuses more on its negative consequences for her than on the
slight to himself, which is passed over with a brief, conventionally
misogynistic judgement on female inconstancy (ll.76–78).[25] Nino's
comments have a primarily political thrust, reflecting on the politi-
cisation of family relationships among the Italian nobility in tracing
his widow Beatrice d'Este's matrimonial career, which proves
emblematic of the discontinuity and unreliability of private and
public life in the Italian city-states.[26] The widow's remarriage has
made her abandon significant symbols of status and identity: when
she changed husband, she abandoned her mourning clothes (l.74)
and changed her family crest (from a cockerel to a sinister snake,
ll.80–81), marking the disruption of family unity with outward and
public signs that draw attention to its political implications.[27]
Marrying into another family surnamed Visconti (the rulers of
Milan), her named identity maintains an illusion of stability, but in
fact she has made a complete domestic, social and political volte-
face – and one that Nino prophesies will lead to misfortune when
the dynastic and factional fortunes of the Milanese Visconti collapse (l.75). Beatrice d'Este's fate parallels the upheavals and factional reversals that *canto* VI showed to pattern the affairs of the
Italian cities and, in the example of Florence, to undermine the stability of such symbols of social order as laws, currency and social
custom. Dante emphasises elsewhere in the *Commedia*, notably in

the central *canti* of *Paradiso*, that women and family relationships have more than merely domestic significance. As the long political sequence dominated by Sordello draws to a close, the example of Beatrice d'Este's matrimonial and political fortunes forcefully demonstrates that the conduct of even the private individual (and women, with marginal political status, are emphatically such) reflects the values held within the political sphere: Nino's reflections on his wife's career expose all three of the urban states of Ferrara (seat of the Este family), Pisa and Milan, as venal, factional and self-destructive.

Nino's purgatorial redemption from such corruption is demonstrated when he spontaneously calls Currado Malaspina, in life a Ghibelline, to meet the protagonist. Currado's speech shows that he shares Nino's fine understanding of family and social relationships. He greets Dante-character courteously, and his double loyalty to birthplace and family emerge in his request for news of his home region, Val di Magra, and in his emphasis that, in life, '*a' miei portai l'amor che qui raffina*' ('I felt for my people the love that I am refining here': l.120). The expression '*a' miei*' embraces family, but also the dependants and allies towards whom his political position gave him responsibilities. Dante's reply, using the honorific *voi* and filled with enthusiastic praise, asserts that the traditional virtues of Currado's well-governed territory and of its dynastic rulers have been maintained since Currado's death, and are famous '*per tutta Europa*' ('throughout Europe': l.123). The Malaspina thus provide a notable contrast to *canto* VII's list of defective European rulers and their degenerate heirs, allowing the Sordello sequence to close on a more optimistic political note.[28]

The Malaspina house is praised for the courtly qualities of liberality and valour ('*pregio de la borsa e de la spada*': l.129), nurtured by both '*uso e natura*' ('habit and nature': l.130), making it the only contemporary political centre that '*va dritta e 'l mal cammin dispregia*' ('goes straight ahead and despises the wrong path': l.132). Dante-character's comment clearly echoes the opening of the *Commedia* itself, where his personal misdirection from virtue is represented as a deviation from the '*diritta via*' ('straight path': *Inf.* I. 3) and also the topographical metaphors of *Convivio* IV's discussion of moral education (XXIV. 9–12). In a prophetic allusion to Dante's exile, Currado assures the protagonist of his future direct experience of the comforts of the Malaspina court; he thus becomes associated with the political probity of this local state, and its traditions of patronage and chivalric valour. By looking towards the future, Currado's prophecy provides the assurance that the pattern of degeneration outlined by Sordello and Dante-author in the preceding *canti* does not become too oppressive: although Florence, Italy and Europe may collectively tend towards the worst, pockets of resistance survive in which political probity will be maintained.

In their future patronage of Dante, the Malaspina will fulfil some of the hopes for unity expressed in the *De vulgari*, by founding an association between political leaders and poets drawn together by their shared values. The association, Dante seems to suggest, may echo the concord of the valley of the princes, where courtly collaboration replaces the rivalry of earthly politics and where the mutual mistrust of the Italian cities and factions is overcome by the fellowship that draws together the poets Virgil and Sordello or the Princes Nino and Currado. Both opening and closing with personal, Italian encounters, the Sordello sequence thus highlights the importance Dante accords to local communities and to personal relationships in his political thinking. It is by local endeavour within the family, the city, or the princely court that the pattern of progressive political decline can be halted or reversed. Within the scheme of Dante's purgatory, the valley of the princes in itself provides a microcosmic illustration of how the rebirth of political values can occur within a restricted, local space, counterbalancing the disquieting earthly examples raised in *canti* VI and VII that show how discord may corrupt close political associations.

TUSCAN SOCIETY AND MUNICIPAL POETRY:
FORESE AND BONAGIUNTA

The meeting with Sordello in ante-purgatory brings together three poets – Sordello, Virgil and Dante – whose interest in politics is unsurprising, since all three had historically written on political matters outside the *Commedia*. After the travellers enter the gates of purgatory-proper, the majority of political commentary is for some time provided not by poets but by politicians. In *canto* XIV, Dante-protagonist listens to a denunciation of factionalism and corruption in the cities of Tuscany and Romagna by Guido del Duca and Rinieri da Calboli, noblemen who, like Nino Visconti and Currado Malaspina, express sympathy and share political anxieties in purgatory but were respectively Ghibelline and Guelf faction-leaders in life. Marco Lombardo, who in *canto* XVI denounces the intervention of the papacy in secular affairs and the negligence of the contemporary empire, has not been securely identified by the commentators, but his remarks make evident his politically active background. In *canto* XX, Hugh Capet, the first Capetian king of France, himself condemns the increasing degeneracy of his heirs. In the final stages of the journey through purgatory-proper, however, political commentary is once again attributed to poets.

Dante's final selection of vernacular writers in *Purgatorio* for the most part had no historical reputation as political poets. Forese Donati, Bonagiunta da Lucca, Guido Guinizelli and Arnaut Daniel appear on the final two terraces of Mount Purgatory; while the latter two are praised in *De vulgari* as outstanding love poets, Bonagiunta is dismissed as a typically limited 'municipal' Tuscan, and Forese, who exchanged comic verses with Dante in his youth, receives no mention at all. In returning political commentary to poets, but here to an unexpected selection, Dante once again revisits the notion of curiality, outlined in *De vulgari*, which he began to rework in the Sordello sequence. The concept is now refined once again, as he further scrutinises the role of poets within their own local societies and beyond, revealing the deeply political implications of poetic commitment to the cultivation of art and reason, which now is seen to extend even outside the bounds of curiality prescribed in *De vulgari* and to include municipal and comic, as well as illustrious, composers.

Dante-character's encounters with this selection of modern, vernacular poets take place in the company of not one but two classical, epic poets, since he and Virgil have now been joined by the spirit of Statius, author of the *Thebaid*. Statius's presence alongside that of the author of the *Aeneid* provides Dante with a pair of lofty examples of the elevated levels that political poetry can reach. The *Aeneid* and *Thebaid* each take the theme of a city and a people with an appointed moral destiny, whose leaders' ethical choices definitively affect the safety and stability of the lives of a whole people, though reaching opposite outcomes.[29] In intentional paradox, Dante stresses that Virgil, the poet who celebrated the foundation of Rome and the origins of empire, has been excluded from Christian salvation; while Statius, poet of the rivalry and violence that wiped out Thebes, has been saved – largely thanks, ironically, to his Messianic interpretation of Virgil's fourth *Eclogue* (*Purg.* XXII. 64–73). The contrast stresses once again the attainability of moral and political order by humanity even without divine grace, and so further emphasises the culpability of political disorder within contemporary Christendom. The two classical poets are responsible for works that carry important and unmistakable messages about the political order, and about the ways in which poetry can represent that order's values and achievements. In the series of encounters with vernacular writers that dominates the upper terraces of purgatory, the presence of these representatives from the classical past helps remind us that Dante's poetry in the *Commedia* differs from both modern and ancient models, focusing our attention onto the implications of such difference, and onto the nature of writing, as a later political passage asserts, '*in pro del mondo che mal vive*' ('for the benefit of the world that lives badly': *Purg.* XXXII. 103).

The first poetic encounter of the upper terraces is with the least famous of the vernacular writers, Forese Donati. Like the earlier encounter with Sordello, this meeting carries distinct echoes of an infernal episode, one that also focused on questions about politics and use of language – the meeting with Brunetto Latini in *Inferno* XV. As in the Sordello episode, too, initial infernal similarities are rapidly reversed. Forese, like Brunetto, greets the protagonist with an abrupt, astonished exclamation: in purgatory, though, the presence of the divinely privileged traveller is understood not as a bizarre *'maraviglia'* ('marvel': *Inf.* XV. 24) but as a providential *'grazia'* ('grace': *Purg.* XXIII. 42). Forese, like Brunetto, is a Florentine and a close acquaintance of Dante's, yet – again, like Brunetto – he is initially unrecognisable thanks to a harsh punishment that has drastically altered his facial appearance. Forese's appearance, however, is less destructively changed than Brunetto's. The word *'omo'* ('man': l.32) that can be read in the gaunt faces of the gluttonous has a positive meaning, indicating that they are regaining true humanity as their excesses are purified through self-denial.

The punishment of the gluttonous marks them with *'la piaga | de la giustizia'* ('the wound of justice': XXIV. 38–39). Dante-character, too, was marked by epigraphic wounds (*'piaghe'*: IX. 114) on his entry to purgatory-proper, when the angel guarding the gate traced seven 'Ps' on his forehead, standing for the sins (*peccati*) refined by purgation. In *Convivio*, Dante-author lamented that Florentine injustice had marked him with *'la piaga de la fortuna'* ('the wound dealt by fortune': I. iii. 4); the *Purgatorio* transforms this symbolic scar of human error from a marker of personal and contingent misfortune into a universal sign, where humanity's attraction to sin (*omo*'s to *peccato*) disfigures individuals and societies, but can be redeemed through commitment to reason and order, whether in life or after death.[30] Moreover, in one of the six satirical poems that Dante and Forese historically exchanged in the 1290s, Dante accused Forese of gluttony and remarked on his scarred face – *'questi che ha la faccia fessa'* ('this man with his face split open': *Bicci novel, figliuol di non so cui* [*Bicci novello, son of I don't know who*]: 7).[31] Here, the mockery of the *tenzone* lyric is reformulated. The scars

that mark Forese's face in purgatory are not disfiguring but meaningful, and the physical wounds and pangs of appetite marking
Forese's spirit-body turn into signs of redemption and true understanding. In speaking of the punishment which he and his companions undergo, Forese explains that their hunger 'rifà santa' ('makes
them holy again': *Purg.* XXIII. 66), restoring them to humanity and
to wholeness after their sinful deviation from '*misura*' ('due measure': l.65), that is, from the proper use of their faculties of choice
and self-restraint.

Forese's restored humanity is demonstrated clearly through his
allusions to his wife, Nella. He speaks of her to Dante-character
with a tone of affectionate trust and respect that contrasts strongly
with Nella's other poetic citation between the two friends, in the
tenzone. The comic and aggressive vulgarity of the *tenzone* poems,
in one of which Dante refers to '*la mal fatata | moglie di Bicci vocato
Forese*' ('the unfortunate wife of Bicci, called Forese': *Chi udisse
tossir la mal fatata* [*Whoever heard coughing the unfortunate*]: 1–2), is
here counterbalanced by a quasi-stilnovistic praise for her virtue,
love and religious sincerity. Forese refers to her affectionately as
'*Nella mia*' ('my Nella': *Purg.* XXIII. 87) and states his feeling for
her simply: '*la vedovella mia, che molto amai*' ('my dear widow, whom
I greatly loved': l.92). The diminutives and endearments he
employs could be said to atone for the harsh language of the *tenzone* poems, where she was denied proper personal standing by
becoming a counter in a witty, masculine exchange of literary
insults. Nella Donati is now offered the kind of attentive valuation
that Dante's youthful praise-lyrics showed to Beatrice in the *Vita
Nova*, making her an example of female excellence; like Beatrice,
too, she is '*a Dio [...] cara e [...] diletta*' ('dear and beloved to God':
l.91). Her conduct merits every expression of esteem – and contrasts strikingly with the fickleness of Nino Visconti's widow – for
Forese tells Dante that she is personally responsible for the rapidity
of his salvation. Her commitment to him, expressed in inarticulate
'*pianger dirotto*' ('broken weeping': l.87), or in the language of
'*prieghi devoti*' ('devoted prayers': l.88), has almost physically

dragged him ('*tratto*': 1.89) from ante-purgatory and from the lower terraces to the penultimate ledge of the mountain in less than four years (Statius, by contrast, has spent over a millennium on the mountain, and four centuries on the terrace of sloth alone: XXII. 92–93).[32] Nella's Christian piety is matched also by the virtue of Forese's other female relative, his sister, Piccarda; Dante-protagonist learns from his friend that she has already won a place in paradise, where indeed he will meet her later on his journey (XXIV. 13–15, *Par.* III. 4).

Forese may in purgatory speak appreciatively of his widow and sister, but his remarks on other women display something of the harsh, satirical spirit of the *tenzone*. Nella's conduct is praiseworthy in itself, but still more because it runs counter to the Florentine feminine norm, which makes her '*in bene operare [...] soletta*' ('solitary in acting well': XXIII. 93). Instead of behaving like elevated lyric '*donne*' ('ladies': l.101), her Florentine peers have become less virtuous than the most uncivilised '*femmine*' ('women' l.95) of the mountains. Forese ironically contrasts feminine conduct in the notoriously remote and savage Sardinian region of Barbagia and that of the 'Barbagia' of the ultra-civilised city (ll.94–96). As was suggested in the case of Nino Visconti's wife, female conduct and dress are important indicators of the moral wellbeing of the community, and Florence is shown to have abandoned the standards not only of civilisation, but of nature itself. As Forese comments, even the least enlightened '*barbare*' and '*saracine*' (women 'barbarians' and 'infidels': l.103) draw the line at baring the breast when displaying their figures ('*l'andar mostrando con le poppe il petto*':l.102), unlike the Florentine 'ladies' who have to be re-taught modesty from the pulpit (ll.98–105). The inappropriate dress of Florentine women indicates a loss of discipline in society as a whole, a conclusion that becomes evident as Forese's criticisms of the citizen-body broaden into a scripturally inspired prophecy of impending downfall (ll.106–111). By avoiding for the moment any mention of Florence's male leaders or any precise political reference, Forese emphasises the far-reaching implications of many sorts of social irresponsibility; the powerful image of the bare-breasted Florentine woman carries a similar symbolic charge as the anthropomorphised image of the city as a sick woman in the '*Ahi serva Italia*' passage earlier in *Purgatorio*.

The revisions of the *tenzone* achieved by Forese's purgatorial attitude to Nella also matches his attitude to Dante, with whom in the lyrics he exchanged a series of gross insults – Forese accused Dante of poverty and inherited cowardice, while Dante made Forese illegitimate, gluttonous, thieving and poorly married. Here, Forese calls Dante his '*dolce frate*' ('sweet brother': l.97); Dante-character in turn evokes the memory of '*qual fosti meco, e qual io teco fui*' ('what you were to me, and I to you': l.116), with no trace of the *tenzone*'s jocularity. By naming both Beatrice (l.128) and Virgil (l.130) directly, the protagonist provides a clear indication of the new literary and moral understanding to which the journey is bringing him. His youth, which was characterised by light-hearted male friendships and by satirical literary exercises such as the *tenzone*, as well as by the elevated love experience chronicled in the *Vita Nova*, was also without sufficient poetic or civic self-discipline. In the earthly paradise, Beatrice will upbraid him for his easy distraction by '*le cose fallaci*' ('fallacious matters': XXXI. 56) away from the enlightened and responsible course of conduct that her example indicated to him.

In the following *canto*, both Forese's and Dante's attention turns to specifically political matters, when the latter speaks of the deep depression that he feels over Florentine affairs:

> 'L loco u' fui a viver posto,
> di giorno in giorno più di ben si spolpa,
> e a trista ruina par disposto.
>
> (*Purg.* XXIV. 79–81)

The place where I was set to live from day to day strips itself more of good, and seems directed towards dismal ruin.

The ambivalence of Dante's civic feelings is expressed in his circumlocution about *''l loco u' fui a viver posto'*, stressing his problematic relationship with a community that deliberately rids itself of all the qualities that made it home to him. Forese, taking up the same political concerns, once again prophesies impending retribution for Florentine misconduct, in this case focusing in horrifyingly concrete terms on his own brother, Corso Donati, leader of the Black faction and of the coup that exiled Dante. Forese imagines Corso, the prime mover in the city's degeneration, being dragged down into the subterranean valley of hell, his body *'vilmente disfatto'* ('ignobly broken': l.87) and pulled at a horse's tail like that of a criminal condemned to earthly execution.[33] The moral and physical divisions that factional confrontations bring about in the Florentine body politic are mirrored in the image of Corso's own torn body, destined to suffer forever the torments that Dante-character has witnessed in hell. The destructive laceration of Corso's corpse, moreover, contrasts markedly with the meaningful mutilation of Forese's and Dante's scarred faces, which spell out the same kind of reconciliatory, reflective messages as are expressed in this exchange, creating moral and social community between the two virtuous Florentines.

In between Forese's two speeches on the future of Florence, and of its male and female citizens, Dante-character – encouraged by Forese – speaks to another of the terrace's spirits, Bonagiunta da Lucca. Forese stresses that since their emaciation makes his companions unrecognisable, it is appropriate for him to name them; the souls themselves *'del nomar parean tutti contenti'* ('all appeared pleased at being named': l.26), unlike the sinners of hell who attempted to conceal their identities and hence their guilt. In his positive eagerness to attract the protagonist's attention, the Lucchese spirit provides a clear contrast to his compatriots in *Inferno*, in the *bolge* of flattery and barratry. Dante's prominent placing of the city name in rhyme position (l.35), with the consequent chain of harsh rhyme endings, makes a stylistic parallel with *Inferno* XVIII's encounter with Alessio Interminei. Like Alessio, Bonagiunta accuses himself of linguistic shortcomings in his earthly life. His failings however were not, like Alessio's, due to a self-serving desire for social advancement but to defects in his poetic activity; poetic and political matters dominate his exchanges with Dante-character.

Bonagiunta identifies the protagonist as author of the *canzone*, *Donne ch'avete intelletto d'amore* (*Ladies with understanding of love*), the lyric that in the *Vita Nova* inaugurated Dante's new presentation of a relationship with Beatrice that was satisfied simply by composing in praise of the beloved (*VN* XVIII. 6–9, XIX). The resulting verse is here famously hailed as constituting a '*dolce stil novo*' ('sweet new style': l.57), which Bonagiunta acknowledges to have surpassed his own achievements and those of Giacomo da Lentini of Sicily and of Guittone d'Arezzo.[34] Both Bonagiunta and Guittone were listed in the *De vulgari* among the defective, 'municipal' poets of Tuscany (I. xiii. 1); but Giacomo was named as one of the illustrious writers drawn to the virtuous court of the Hohenstaufen and the first line of his *canzone*, *Madonna dir vi voglio* (*Lady, I wish to tell you*), approvingly quoted (I. xiii. 8). Since the lyric admired by Bonagiunta, *Donne ch'avete*, is also cited in *De vulgari* as illustrious (twice: II. viii. 8, xii. 3), the comment might simply indicate that Dante has artistically outstripped not only lesser poets, but also accomplished ones; but in the purgatorial context of the framing encounter with Forese, we are reminded that Dante's past poetic record includes the composition of 'comic' as well as of 'illustrious' verse and that he, too, therefore has a literary past that may require correction.[35] Dante-character's reply to Bonagiunta suggests that the *dolce stil novo* is distinguished by more than stylistic difference from previous vernacular practice – it is the sincerity of poetry directly inspired by love that marks it out from both 'municipal' and 'illustrious' precedent:

> *E io a lui: 'I' mi son un che, quando*
> *Amor mi spira, noto, e a quel modo*
> *ch'e' ditta dentro vo significando.'*
>
> (*Purg.* XXIV. 52–54)

> And I to him: 'I am one who, when Love breathes in me, take
> note, and in the way that he dictates within I set it forth.'

Dante hallmarks his poetic difference by citing a poem associated
in the *Vita Nova* with stylistic but also emotional conversion, and
with a shift from stylised, somewhat derivative laments over love's
pains to a generous celebration of the noble and ennobling virtues
of the beloved.[36] Forese has expressed for Nella the same kind of
generous, celebratory love, in the purgatorial revision of a satire for
which Dante shares linguistic and conceptual responsibility.
Bonagiunta, too, in purgatory attains some of the same elevation of
language and idea, in a prophecy about Dante's future experiences
at Lucca, which moves the former closer towards 'curial' and away
from restrictedly 'municipal' attainments.

Bonagiunta's comments on his native city parallel those of
Forese on Florence: he highlights the town's generally negative
reputation, but accords praise to a single, virtuous Lucchese
woman. He promises Dante that Lucca will become dear to him
in future – presumably a reference to Dante's residence there in
exile – '*come ch'om la riprenda*' ('however much people reprove her
[i.e. Lucca]': l.45). The cause for Dante's reversal of popular opin-
ion on the city will be his relationship with a Lucchese '*femmina*'
('woman': l.43). Some of the early commentators identify this
woman, a friend or patron of the exiled Florentine, as bearing the
name '*Gentucca*', the first word Bonagiunta utters (l.37), or as the
dedicatee of Dante's '*pargoletta*' lyrics.[37] The 'Ottimo' commentary
even proposes an allegorical reading that casts the whole of the
speech's opening in a highly political key: it takes *gentucca* as a dis-
approbatory comment on the Florentines who will banish the
poet and sees the *femmina* as the White faction, for adherence to
which Dante suffered the exile that would later bring him to
Lucca. No such complex interpretation is necessary, however, to
find a strongly political significance in Bonagiunta's comments.
His choice of term in referring to the woman who embodies the
value of his earthly community, *femmina* instead of the courtlier

donna, conforms to his 'municipal' reputation in the *De vulgari*. However, it also reinforces Forese's usage in the previous *canto*, where the Sardinian *femmine* showed greater virtue and belonged to a healthier community than the perversely sophisticated, '*sfacciate* donne *fiorentine*' ('brazen Florentine *ladies*': XXIII. 101, emphasis mine). Similarly, Bonagiunta points to a feature of feminine dress that marks his female compatriot as virtuously compliant with social norms. In 1300, the woman who will welcome Dante to Lucca '*non porta ancor benda*' ('does not yet wear a wimple': l.43), the modest headdress worn by married women and widows – she will presumably be married and virtuously veiled by the time of Dante's visit to Lucca. Thus social decorum is better preserved in Lucca than in Florence, or in the aristocratic courts where Beatrice Visconti made unseemly haste to abandon the '*bianche bende*' of mourning (*Purg.* VIII. 74), despite the poor civic reputation that Bonagiunta acknowledges, and the widespread political corruption of Lucca identified in *Inferno* – '*ogn'uom v'è barattier*' ('every man there is a barrator': *Inf.* XXI. 41), accuse the demons. Moreover, in welcoming Dante and his polished, authentic poetry to their city, the *lucchesi*, like the Malaspina of ante-purgatory, will demonstrate sympathy between their community and a poet of love and rectitude, making Lucca a centre of more than merely municipal values. Bonagiunta may speak in unsophisticated style, calling a woman *femmina* and employing the local term *issa* ('now': l.55), but the germs of *curialitas*, with its political, as well as artistic, implications may be detected within his society, offering the possibility of the city's moral and political regeneration.

POETIC ENDEAVOUR AND THE INSPIRATION OF LOVE:
GUINIZELLI AND ARNAUT

The encounters with Forese and Bonagiunta on the terrace of gluttony provide a measure of re-evaluation of the *De vulgari*'s verdicts on 'municipal' and 'comic' poetry. The sequence draws composers whose *oeuvre* in the treatise's terms was limited and inadequate into the 'curial' circle of rational unity and elevation of purpose, turning them (Forese more conspicuously than Bonagiunta) into poets of rectitude through their interest in politics and society. On the next terrace, the last in purgatory-proper, Dante-character encounters two of the most celebrated vernacular lyricists of the *De vulgari*: Guido Guinizelli and Arnaut Daniel, love poets now purging themselves of the final traces of lust. These are poets whom Dante has always known to be curial and whom he praises in the treatise for their use of the illustrious forms of their native tongues. In representing them in purgatory, he stresses their poetic integrity to the point of composing Arnaut's speech in the Occitan native to the historical poet (although in a different style to Arnaut's own). At the end of the *Purgatorio*, he chooses poets as the final representatives of the mountain community of change and conversion; without touching directly on politics, their speeches show a generous, measured self-awareness that creates an impressive picture of humanity on the verge of true perfection, and of the earthly paradise of moral wholeness.

The terrace is filled with the flames of the '*ultima tortura*' ('final torture': XXV. 109), which Dante calls the cure for the wound of sin ('*con tal cura conviene [...] | che la piaga [...] si ricuscia*', 'with such a cure must the wound heal over': ll. 138–139). The spirits are shown to adhere with painful care to the discipline of their particular community, '*sempre con riguardo | di non uscir dove non fosser arsi*' ('always taking care not to move to a place where they might not be burned': XXVI. 14–15), even when partially distracted by curiosity about the protagonist. They refuse to be distracted, too, from greeting their companions with '*accoglienza amica*' ('friendly welcome': l. 37), for the words and gestures exchanged between them assist the progress of their communal movement towards a shared goal. The generous courtesy that has been attained by this stage of the purgatorial process means that Dante-character answers their questions before turning to his own curiosity about their identities, and Guinizelli's swift response, explaining the organisation of their punishment, shows answering courtesy. The ready match between protagonist and spirit is appropriate in a poet famous for his insight into the noble heart. Dante's youthful admiration for Guido's *canzone, Al cor gentil rempaira sempre amore* (*Love always seeks the noble heart*), which is cited in *De vulgari* (II. v. 4), led him to compose a sonnet directly inspired by this *dictum* of the authority on love, *Amor e 'l cor gentil sono una cosa* (*Love and the noble heart are one and the same*: *VN* XX. 3).[38] In purgatory too, Guido's '*alto cuor*' ('lofty heart': l.72) retains its sensitivity and is quick to understand and to react, recovering swiftly from the astonishment of encountering a living man to explain that the terrace purges two forms of lust, homosexual and heterosexual, and to identify himself and his companion, Arnaut, as love poets.

Nonetheless, Guinizelli does briefly display surprise at the protagonist's privilege and Dante chooses a striking image to describe the reaction of this sophisticated and truly noble poet:

> *Non altrimenti stupido si turba*
> *lo montanaro, e rimirando ammuta,*
> *quando rozzo e salvatico s'inurba.*
>
> (*Purg.* XXVI. 67–69)

Not otherwise does the mountain-dweller display his stupefied confusion, and keep silent while staring round when, coarse and wild, he enters a town.

The image is incongruous for a writer praised in *De vulgari* for his adherence to illustrious language in preference even to the attractive vernacular of his native Bologna, adopting an idiom categorically opposite to any crude '*montaninas et rusticanas loquelas*' ('languages of the mountains or the countryside': *DVE* I. xi. 6). Guido is, of course, literally a *montanaro* on Mount Purgatory. The image, moreover, anticipates Beatrice's description to the protagonist of the respective conditions of the earthly and of the celestial paradise, or in the *Monarchia*'s terms, of the happiness of the political and of the spiritual life. She tells Dante in Eden that:

> *qui sarai tu poco tempo silvano;*
> *e sarai meco sanza fine cive*
> *di quella Roma onde Cristo è romano.*
>
> (*Purg.* XXXII. 100–102)

here for a short time you will be a forest dweller; and without end you will be with me a citizen of that Rome of which Christ is a Roman.

Beatrice's words characterise the moral perfection of humanity's natural state in the active life as rustic, compared to the citizenly state of beatification; it is in fact paradoxically appropriate, then, that Guinizelli should be described as a backwoodsman, as he shows his mastery of intellectual and political virtues by straining after understanding of his fellow-being's condition and by welcoming him, however temporarily, into his own *post mortem* community ('*le nostre marche*': XXVI. 73).

Guinizelli's retrospective over his own life concentrates first not on his achievements but on his failings, stressing that he and his companions have transgressed against '*umana legge*' ('the laws of humanity': l.83). Guinizelli appears to have been in life an expert in law, a notary trained in the famous faculty of his native city, but here Dante makes him show an understanding of law that stretches beyond the forensic. The lustful have on earth lived '*seguendo come bestie l'appetito*' ('following their appetites like beasts': l.84), thus deserting humanity's natural rationality and discernment of morality – law at its most fundamental. Spoken at the summit of the mountain, the words recall the speech of Ulysses in *Inferno*, urging his companions that '*fatti non foste a viver come bruti*' ('you were not made to live like brutes': *Inf.* XXVI. 119), and embarking on a journey towards Mount Purgatory. Ulysses, too, transgressed the laws of nature, by deliberately passing outside the limits set for humanity

(*Inf.* XXVI. 109), and never attained even the base of the mountain that Guinizelli has nearly scaled. Where the classical sailor attempted a forced landing on the mountain, Guinizelli chose the only practicable route: that of repentance (*Purg.* XXVI. 93) – an embarkation on the spiritual journey that will lead him both to Eden and to the heavenly Rome beyond.

Guido displays the quality of his conversion and renewed commitment to *umana legge* by concentrating all his initial energies on analysis of his fault. It is only at the end of his speech that he reveals his name and not until prompted by Dante-character does he turn to poetry – but the admiring reaction accorded him by the protagonist shows us that his poetic artistry provides the grounds for the redemption accorded him by Dante-author. Echoes of the encounter in *Inferno* with Brunetto Latini underline this further: the protagonist calls Guido the 'father' ('*padre*': l.97) of himself and of his fellow vernacular love poets, recalling Brunetto's '*cara e buona imagine paterna*' ('dear and good paternal image': *Inf.* XV. 83), from whom the protagonist was held back, as he is here, from approaching physically by the flames of punishment. Dante-character's reverent response to Guinizelli's name, using the honorific *voi* to acclaim the lasting fame of '*li dolci detti vostri*' ('your sweet sayings': l.112) recalls Brunetto's claim to '*vivere ancora*' ('still be alive': *Inf.* XV. 120) in his literary work. Here, though, it is the protagonist who mentions reputation; Guinizelli, a poet with greater linguistic awareness and greater fidelity to his native language than Brunetto (whose major work, the *Tresor*, was written in French), in fact defers to another individual whom he recognises as '*miglior fabbro del parlar materno*' ('a better workman in the mother tongue': l.117).[39]

Sketching a new hierarchy of poetic achievement, Guinizelli accords higher prestige to the love poet Arnaut Daniel than to the *De vulgari*'s Occitan poet of rectitude, Giraut de Bornelh (*DVE* II. ii. 8; *Purg.* XXVI. 119–120). He leaves open the question of Italian vernacular superiority, by similarly decrying Guittone d'Arezzo's exaggerated reputation (ll.124–126). Comparison with the reordered Occitan hierarchy implies, however, that Italian supremacy belongs either to himself as the acknowledged father of Dante and other composers of '*rime d'amor [...] dolci e leggiadre*' ('sweet and gracious rhymes of love': l.99), or to Dante, who has just been established in the dialogue with Bonagiunta as the poet most faithful to the inspiration of love.[40] The specialised skills that poets bring to communication, shaping and extending the possibilities of human expression, are acknowledged in the term *fabbro* that Guido applies to Arnaut, comparing his craftsmanship with language to a metalworker's skilled shaping of tools or ornaments.

In the encounter with Arnaut, the dynamics of the meeting with Guinizelli are reversed, for Arnaut sinks any curiosity about the protagonist's identity in order to reply '*liberamente*' ('freely': l.139) to his '*cortes deman*' ('courteous question': l.140), and offers an implicit homage to Dante's own moral and poetic stature in using the respectful *vos*, equivalent to the Italian *voi* with which Dante-character addressed Guinizelli. The protagonist stresses his wish to reserve a '*grazïoso loco*' ('gracious place': l.138) for the poet's name, a promise self-fulfilled by its prominence in the *Commedia*. The formulation also echoes the *De vulgari*'s notion that poets may unite to form a *curia* founded on the gracious light of reason ('*gratioso ratione luminis*': *DVE* II. xviii. 5) – here, two poets linked by *cortesia*, the vernacular translation of *curialitas*, create a microcosmic community in which the virtues of a wholesome society are exercised. Mutual respect and esteem make each act generously towards the other, with a freedom tempered by attention to the laws of their respective conditions (one remaining within the flames, the other shrinking from them). Each also shows loyalty to his birthplace and authenticity of personal expression, in their adherence to their own native and poetic tongues.[41]

By composing Arnaut's speech in Occitan, Dante-author demonstrates his own ability as a linguistic *fabbro* in using the language and vocabulary of the poetic tradition of *fin'amors*, working into a brief eight lines clear allusions to both Arnaut's and other troubadours' poetry and adapting the troubadour's distinctive poetic signature in the declaration '*ieu sui Arnaut*' ('I am Arnaut': l.142).[42] But it is also a gesture of generous *cortesia* towards a poet he admired to make this final purgatorial encounter take place in the authentic language of the individual speaker (although admittedly, using a style closer to the *dolce stil* admired by Bonagiunta than to Arnaut's characteristically opaque *trobar clus*).[43] Within the narrative, the protagonist's courteous speech makes Arnaut not only willing but eager to reveal his identity: '*ieu no me puesc ni voill a vos cobrire*' ('I cannot and I wish not to conceal myself from you':l.141). The earthly paradise, summit of philosophical perfection in the *Monarchia*, lies just beyond the circle of flames at the peak of Mount Purgatory, and Arnaut's prompt response to Dante-character shows how near the souls of the last terrace are to this goal, in moral as well as physical terms.

The closing encounters of purgatory-proper offer a wide overview of different kinds of poetry, and of poetic and political identity, showing the latter two to be closely related issues. Guido Guinizelli and Arnaut Daniel do not speak directly about politics: but *canto* XXVI, with its close focus on questions about poetic and linguistic origins, rounds off the more obviously political concerns of encounters with poets earlier in the *Purgatorio*. Arnaut's words review and rework his native tradition, including as they do tags from other Occitan authors, displaying his artistic awareness and demonstrating his commitment to the place and idiom of his birth. In Guinizelli's case, his speech looks back over the origins both of his own and of his companion Arnaut's vernacular literary traditions, outlining a new hierarchy of poetic achievement that gives final supremacy to poets inspired by an interest in love; this interest in love Bonagiunta and Dante have already established as the mark of true authenticity of inspiration and expression. Bonagiunta and Forese's own speeches likewise review the poetic past, Bonagiunta hailing the supremacy of Dante's *dolce stil novo*, and Forese adopting the elegant literary language associated with those new rhymes ('*nove rime*': XXIV. 50) rather than the idiom of his historical, satirical output. Bonagiunta and Forese arrive at formulae that force

them to demote their own real-life poetic practice; but in politics
they remain true to their origins, engaging seriously with questions about the moral, social and factional choices of their compatriots. By making women the symbols of their analysis of the
political wellbeing of Lucca and Florence, they also rework the
idiom of the love-poetry tradition, transposing the amorous
writer's quest for nobility and refinement into the political arena.

In this long sequence of reflections on both poetic and political
origins, Dante prepares his readers for the impending encounter
with Beatrice at the summit of the mountain, within the Garden of
Eden that is the place of origin for all humanity. Within the garden,
the *Monarchia*'s symbol of imperial perfection, Beatrice will show
the protagonist a series of pageants or masques that probe the realities of the political order, examining the relationships between the
spiritual and the secular in human history. Dante's own poetic and
political origins are thus retrieved in the encounter with his youthful muse and her reminders of their shared Florentine past, and in
the meditations on wider political values that are prompted by the
allegorical tableaux he witnesses. The *Purgatorio*'s extended focus
on the interaction of poets and politicians, both in ante-purgatory
and in purgatory-proper, has prepared the reader for the earthly
paradise's insistence on both the general and the local, the poetic
and the political, in the reunion of Dante and Beatrice, which
places the specifics of an urban love story as an essential linking
term between the mountain and forest of Eden's moral perfection,
and the Rome of paradise, the city-empire of spiritual perfection.

6

IDEALS OF CITY LIFE

PARADISO

The *Paradiso* brings the journey of the *Commedia* to its conclusion, narrating the protagonist's effortless, joyful movement through the spheres of the heavens towards unity with the Godhead. Dante-poet surrounds his protagonist with souls who enjoy perfect spiritual happiness and are eager to share their theological insights with a mortal audience. Critics often note the differences in style and in content between this *cantica* and the previous two; in seeking to represent the perfections of the divine, the poet increasingly reveals doubts about his audience's ability to comprehend his rarefied material, and about his own ability to give it due expression.[1] Dante-author draws attention to this change from early on in the *Paradiso*, in his famous warning to unprepared readers:

> *O voi che siete in piccioletta barca,*
> *desiderosi d'ascoltar, seguiti*
> *dietro al mio legno che cantando varca,*
> *tornate a riveder li vostri liti:*
> *non vi mettete in pelago, ché forse,*
> *perdendo me, rimarreste smarriti.*
>
> (*Par.* II. 1–6)

O you who in your little boat, desirous of listening, have followed behind my ship that sails forward singing, turn back to

see your shores again: do not embark on the open seas, for per‐
haps, losing me, you would remain off course.

The narrator who introduced himself to us in *Inferno* as *smarrito*
within the pathless wasteland of the dark wood has recuperated far
enough to be confident of his own readiness for the next stage of
the journey, but its difficulties risk reducing the reader to his own
condition at the start of the *Commedia*, a state he has due cause to
warn against. From the opening *canti* of *Paradiso*, Dante's audience
is thus encouraged to expect a different and more challenging
experience than those offered in *Inferno* or *Purgatorio*. In its discus‐
sion of political matters, however, the *Paradiso* shows strong points
of continuity as well as of change when compared to the other two
cantiche.

Sensory differences between paradise and the other two realms
of the afterlife are evident from the outset. Both in the abyss of hell
and on the mountain of purgatory, Dante-character has his feet
firmly planted on the ground and toils downwards and upwards
through a recognisably terrestrial environment; in heaven he flies
effortlessly through the new medium of celestial aether, and even
when he enters the physical body of a planet, it possesses the elu‐
sive, quasi-intangible quality of a cloud (*Par.* II. 31–33). Political
comparisons of hell and purgatory to a city or a kingdom have a
certain visual plausibility, given their physical features of walls,
gates, stairways, bridges and alleyways, all of which are absent in the
celestial spheres. The souls themselves take on a different appear‐
ance, affecting our ability to envisage them as 'citizens' of heaven,
for the spirit-bodies that populated the other two realms with
forms that were recognisably human, even when mutilated in pun‐
ishment, are visible only in the opening and closing sequences of
the *Paradiso*. During most of this stage of the journey, the souls are
seen only as amorphous sparks of light. They often group together
to form patterns, presenting the protagonist at various points with
the symbols of a cross, an eagle and a ladder; writing a slogan about
justice in governance; or forming simple circle shapes that remind

Dante-character of the intricacies of man-made clockwork or the formal figures of a human dance.

Although the human form is largely lost to view in these patterns, they sustain political comparisons quite as much as the densely populated, city-like physical structures of *Inferno* and *Purgatorio*. The souls' consensual incorporation into these symbolic shapes reveals a different and deeper understanding of the meaning of political community than the physical features of the other realms. States are composed not of buildings but of people: the souls of heaven, in forming living images of the secular and spiritual values that they hold, bring alive the true significance of humanity's natural instinct to seek community and communication. Paradise itself may be seen as an ideal society, the exaltation and perfection of all human polities; the souls of the blessed constantly speak of heaven with the language of earthly communities, likening it both to the secular society of the city, the court, the kingdom and the empire, and also to an ecclesiastical college or convent.[2] Questions about earthly politics, moreover, continue to occupy Dante's attention in the *Paradiso*. Humans are made perfect in heaven and because, in Dante's view, we are naturally and instinctively political beings, the beatified spirits maintain a sense of the importance of social existence. They rejoice in their own celestial fellowship and they turn eager attention to the mortal protagonist and to the questions that his presence in heaven raises, about how fellowship may be attained within earthly communities.

Among the human societies considered in *Paradiso*, Dante-poet offers extended attention to earthly ecclesiastical communities, which offer a natural focus of concern for the large numbers of clerical saints whom he includes in the narrative. The heavenly representatives of the Franciscan and Dominican orders of Friars, and of the Benedictine monastic order, accord serious attention to the moral decline of earthly fortunes of those orders; and the papacy and the secular clergy, familiar objects of censure in hell and in purgatory, are held up for further criticism. The empire and the kingdom are also analysed attentively. The whole of *canto* VI is dedicated to a speech by the Emperor Justinian that outlines the history of Rome and defends its universal political authority, before going on to deplore the destruction of imperial unity and justice by contemporary factionalism. *Canto* XIII praises the kingship of Solomon, one of the souls encountered in the heaven of the sun, and urges the necessity of wisdom and justice to successful governance. *Canti* XIX and XX explore the theme of justice further, in the speech of the single eagle formed from the community of Jupiter's souls, who include not only the Jewish King David and the first Christian Emperor of Rome, Constantine, but also the Trojan Prince Ripheus, in an astonishing choice that places a pagan from Virgil's *Aeneid* in the Christian heaven solely on the basis of his reputed commitment to justice.[3] Even in the Empyrean, political themes are not forgotten, and Beatrice points out to Dante-character the throne reserved for Henry VII, praising his attempt to '*drizzare Italia*' ('make Italy straight': XXX. 137) and condemning the cupidity of the Italians, especially that of Pope Boniface VIII, which will undermine his imperial campaign.[4]

The most extended political commentary of *Paradiso*, however, concentrates on the city and more precisely, on Dante's own native city: *canti* XV, XVI and large parts of XVII are dedicated to a review of the social, economic and political fortunes of Florence, covering past, present and future. The sequence offers a minute analysis of the experiences of a single community, which shows how significant a place urban society occupies in Dante's political thought, for the Florentine examples of these *canti* illustrate questions fundamental to the political life in general. Their examination of the Florentine polity emphasises the importance of political principles already deeply familiar to readers of the *Convivio*, such as justice, fortitude and temperance. A detailed survey of the public and the private conduct both of named individuals and of collective groups – women, merchants, aristocrats – allows Dante to explore the origins of social disorder within an earthly community, tracing its transition from quasi-paradisal order to quasi-infernal

corruption, and using Florentine experiences to exemplify universally applicable patterns of political prosperity and decline.

From the first to the last *canto* of *Paradiso*, Dante emphasises the
orderliness of the God-centred universe and the harmony that,
from paradise, is seen to draw together its different parts (I. 1–3,
XXXIII. 85–87, 145). But he also stresses that humanity has the
freedom to turn against the providential pattern and to create disorder. It is unsurprising then that political questions remain so
prominent within the third *cantica* and that the language of exhortation, denunciation and invective is frequently employed. The
contrast that Dante draws between earthly confusion and the heavenly souls' joyful acceptance of order makes his reflections on
human society very forceful. Paradise offers a vision of harmonious
human co-existence to the protagonist, but equally importantly,
the souls he meets remind him that earthly harmony is also possible, and urge him to examine the realities about human nature and
about human society on which the possibility of such political
renewal depends.

UNITY AND DIVERSITY IN HUMAN SOCIETY:
THE GUIDANCE OF VENUS

The *Paradiso*'s first extended passage of political commentary
occurs in *canto* VI, with the Emperor Justinian's sketch of Rome's
history and of the providentially sanctioned authority of its empire.
Justinian's survey of the high points of Roman history and the
praise that he accords to the heroic actions of both republican and
imperial leaders, in many respects match the lists of outstanding
Roman achievements that appear both in the *Convivio*, which
Dante had composed almost a decade earlier, and in the *Monarchia*,
composed perhaps more or less simultaneously with this section of
Paradiso.[5] Given the correspondences with these two texts, it is
unsurprising that almost immediately afterwards, Dante should
return to another principle fundamental to the political argument

of both prose treatises: that of humanity's inherently social nature, as an Aristotelian 'political animal'.

This material is placed in the mouth of the medieval prince Charles Martel, whose soul greets Dante-protagonist with the warmth of an earthly friendship formed in Florence (*Par.* VIII. 55–57). Like Bongiunta in *Purgatorio*, he accompanies scathing comments on contemporary Italian political turbulence with an admiring allusion to Dante's career as a lyric poet. The encounter takes place in the sphere of Venus, the third heaven in the Ptolemaic planetary system, traditionally associated with love. Charles greets Dante by citing the first line of a *canzone* the latter composed before his exile, which opens with an appropriate planetary allusion: '*Voi che 'ntendendo il terzo ciel movete*' (*You who move the third heaven by intellection: Par.*VIII. 37). This is also the lyric on which the second book of the *Convivio* is based, which glosses the *canzone*'s amorous theme as signifying dedication to moral philosophy, and compares the different heavens to different intellectual disciplines (*Cvo* II. xii. 5–10, xv. 3–5). Venus corresponds to the art of rhetoric, both because of the appealing clarity ('*chiarezza [...] soavissima*') of its light, and because its morning and evening appearances correspond to the two types, oratorical and epistolary, of rhetorical performance (*Cvo* II. xiii. 13–14). Charles Martel, in the heaven of Venus, displays rhetorical discernment both in the tribute he pays to Dante's poetic skills and in his own responsible articulation of political and philosophical principles, displaying a command of the qualities appropriate, in the *Convivio*'s terms, to a political leader and to a man of noble temperament. Dante endows Charles with an admirable combination of practical and theoretical qualifications for leadership, making him an acute analyst of specific, historical problems in contemporary Italy, and also allowing him to comment on more general truths about human nature and human societies.

Charles's fine understanding of his political responsibilities as a ruler appears in his autobiographical statement (ll. 58–75). He concentrates less on his own actions than on the expectations and reactions of his subjects in various territories to his leadership, in conformity with the *Monarchia*'s declaration that rulers exist for the sake of the people and not vice-versa (*Mon.* I. xii. 10). In considering his father's less happy career, Charles stresses that '*mala seg-noria [...] sempre accora | li popoli suggetti*' ('bad governance always provokes its subject people': ll.73–74). Charles Martel, eldest son of Charles II of Anjou, was dynastic heir to numerous European possessions – the county of Provence and the kingdoms of Naples and of Hungary – while his marriage to the daughter of the Emperor Rudolf of Habsburg allied his family's Guelf-Angevin interests to those of the Ghibellines. Had he lived, Charles states, Italian political affairs in particular would have taken a turn for the better, with dynastic and party competition calmed both by Charles's personal probity and by his marriage's potential provision of heirs acceptable to all factions. The prince's awareness of responsibilities to his subjects and of his personal destiny as a leader make him resemble the noble Aeneas of *Convivio*, as Edward Peters notes; but death has left his regenerative mission, unlike Aeneas's, unfulfilled.[6] The virtuous and reflective political sensibility that Charles displays mark him as an ideal leader in the *Monarchia*'s as well as the *Convivio*'s terms: especially, his concern about cupidity (ll.82–84) and his location in the heavenly sphere of love, recall *Monarchia*'s insistence that the emperor's loving authority provides the best defence against division of the body politic by the destructive forces of greed (*Mon.* I. xi. 13–15).[7]

Venus is traditionally associated with '*folle amore*' (*Par.* VIII. 2), irrational and sensual love, rather than with political and moral *caritas*.[8] In the course of *Purgatorio*, the protagonist learned that disordered love is responsible for much of humanity's misguided pursuit of material, including sexual, objects (*Purg.* XVII–XVIII). The poets on the final terrace of Mount Purgatory reminded him, with their lament that '*non servammo umana legge*' ('we did not serve human law': XXVI. 83), that humans can and should learn to regulate their desires according to reason and morality. After concluding his political discourse, Charles Martel goes on in the second half of the present *canto* to outline the harmony of a duly regulated universe. Love has a central place in his discussion, which covers the physical love necessary for human reproduction, the moral or rational love that governs an individual's choices and the natural or divine love that orders the heavenly bodies and enables them to influence human temperaments. Charles's discourse embraces the whole universe: but he focuses most closely on humanity and on questions about social organisation, recognising the protagonist's need to understand the workings of the earthly life to which he must soon return.

Charles begins his discussion by emphasising the orderliness of the heavens, with their influence over earthly affairs, which take their perfection from the divine intelligence of the angels and of God; his explanation is concise, but outlines a minimum of essential details to help the protagonist follow his argument. His second statement, by contrast, is formulated with the utmost brevity and is immediately and unquestioningly accepted by the protagonist:

> 'Or dì: sarebbe il peggio
> per l'omo in terra, se non fosse cive?'
> 'Sì,' rispuos' io; 'e qui ragion non cheggio.'
>
> (*Par.* VIII. 115–117)

> 'Now tell me: would it be worse for man on earth, if he were
> not a citizen?' 'Yes,' I replied; 'and here I need no explanation.'

Charles and Dante-character concur unequivocally in the proposition that humanity requires the structure of the state in order to achieve successful existence on earth. This is recognisably the statement of the author of *Convivio* and *Monarchia*, convinced that nature, whose workings have just been described in some detail, has made humans instinctively social beings; the very conciseness of the exchange highlights its significance.

The necessity of social existence to human wellbeing is underlined conclusively in Charles's closing remarks on human diversity.

Aristotle, the unacknowledged source of the *'cive' dictum*, is cited specifically in support of Charles's explanation that within earthly society, *'si vive | diversamente per diversi offici'* ('humans live in different ways according to their different offices': ll. 118–119).[9] Classical and biblical examples illustrate the varied kinds of talents needed by the polity, in which the supports of law, defence, religion and material crafts all make vital contributions to community-wide wellbeing (ll. 124–126). These observations provide the direct link to Dante-character's original question about how a good parent can produce bad offspring (ll. 92–93): Charles explains that individuals each possess their own personal talents and temperament from nature and through celestial influence, not by inheritance, in a polished speech that celebrates diversity and the value of the individual.

He closes, however, with a more pessimistic corollary. Free will permits humans to abuse or neglect their talents: without expanding on the theological implications of such choices, Charles offers a stern condemnation of the social and political consequences of assigning any given office to an individual whose talents lie elsewhere. He provides two generic examples of the possible misallocation of roles:

> *Voi torcete a la religïone*
> *tal che fia nato a cignersi la spada,*
> *e fate re di tal ch'è da sermone.*
>
> (*Par.*VIII. 145–147)

> You twist towards religion one who is born to gird on a sword,
> and you make a king of one suited to sermons.

In the light of his earlier remarks on his own family, however, these generic examples take on a more specific resonance. After Charles Martel's own death his brother Louis, the legal heir, renounced the kingdom of Naples in favour of a religious vocation, responding correctly to his natural talents; but Robert, who then assumed power as third in the line of succession, has already been criticised for inadequate kingship (ll.76–84) and was attributed theological inclinations by his contemporaries.[10] Charles's remarks are thus obviously applicable to his own family but, as his use of *voi* to designate humanity at large indicates, the problem of misapplied talent is widespread. The speech concludes with a compelling general verdict on man's attempt to override nature's intentions and the tribulations consequent in human society thereof: '*la traccia vostra è fuor di strada*' ('your course strays off the path': l.148). The image recalls the stumbling misdirection of Dante-character at the start of the *Commedia*. Charles is concerned specifically with political misdirection, in a world that has forgotten the principles of fellowship and interdependence implied in his Aristotelian vision of social diversity and of gregarious human nature. His conclusion invites Dante's readers to return to the telling central question in his commentary, and to contemplate the reality that social organisation is an issue of pre-eminent importance to human beings whose natural mode of earthly existence is citizenship. For the poet, there is only one possible, affirmative answer to the question he attributes to the young prince, '*sarebbe il peggio | per l'omo in terra, se non fosse cive?*' ('would it be worse for man on earth, if he were not a citizen?').

AN IDEAL CITY: THE BONDS OF CIVIC FELLOWSHIP

Both the words and the personal history of Charles Martel invite the reader in *canto* VIII to concentrate on two specific political considerations: the question of how political leaders are formed and recognised; and the need for a variety of talents and activities to enable societies to function successfully. These themes reappear in the central *canti* of the *Paradiso*, another sequence in which a highly personal encounter provokes discussion of the needs and obligations inherent in human political life. The meeting in the heaven of Mars between Dante-character and his great-great-grandfather

Cacciaguida leads the two Florentines into an extended discussion of the past history and future prospects of their common birthplace. Of the three *canti* – XV, XVI and XVII – dedicated to the encounter, the first two are packed with local, day-to-day detail that gives them a strongly Florentine flavour, and even in the more elevated, prophetic passages of *canto* XVII, Florence and Florentine politics provide the background to the message of universal mission that Cacciaguida confides to Dante-character. But, as so often in the *Commedia*, Dante-poet uses the particulars of specific historical localities and events to illustrate general truths. Cacciaguida and Dante-character extrapolate from the example of their familiar polity broader insights into city-life and citizenship, which allow them to arrive at statements of general philosophical principle, rather as Charles Martel moved from reflection on Angevin policy in Italy into citations of Aristotle's political thought. The variety and complexity of the civic issues presented in this sequence is indicated in the way that different poetic voices are combined, offering varying images and accounts of city existence. Within the planet of Mars, Cacciaguida, the twelfth-century citizen-knight, and Dante-character, enmeshed on earth in the specifics of political office and present through divine grace in paradise, articulate two alternate visions of civic prosperity and decline. At the same time, the voice of Dante-author, commenting and supplying the words for these protagonists from the viewpoint of exile and of a consequently complex relation to his city, draws together the particular and the universal, investing urban experience with profound moral and political significance.

The physical realities of the city of Florence are accorded considerable importance in the sequence, in which Dante and Cacciaguida name and recognise Florentine streets and monuments with fervent local patriotism. Both of them identify their origins in a city affectionately labelled '*l'ovil di San Giovanni*' ('the sheepfold of St John': XVI. 25) as an essential part of their personal make-up; even in paradise, Cacciaguida is intensely interested in the history and experiences of his beloved Florence, and regularly punctuates his speeches with the city's name (XV. 97; XVI. 84, 111, 146, 149; XVII. 48). The biblical resonances of the sheepfold image echo New Testament references to Christ as Good Shepherd, to suggest that the city has spiritual and ethical, as well as geographical, dimensions. The Florentine sheepfold – as the crusader Cacciaguida emphasises – is a centre of Christian life and faith, protected by its patronal shepherd, St John the Baptist; this saint's church, one of the primary monuments of the physical city, is also a central symbolic presence in this sequence of Florentine exchanges.

Cacciaguida begins his self-presentation to Dante with a city description, detailing the appearance of Florence in his own lifetime.[11] The twelfth-century city is small, a compact urban space contained '*dentro de la cerchia antica*' ('inside the ancient circle': XV. 97) of its walls. The Baptistery stands out to mark the northern extent of the city limits, just as the presumed statue of Mars, standing by the natural boundary of the river, does to the south, so that the citizenry live '*tra Marte e 'l Batista*' ('between Mars and the Baptist': XVI. 47), physical monuments that measure and define the city space. Cacciaguida's definition of the city limits by these two monuments draws moreover on a fund of civic mythology stressing the character and antiquity of the town, set out in the legends of its privileged, Roman foundation that we have encountered earlier in this study. A sense of history and of political identity is encapsulated in these patriotic references, in which Dante uses the foundation mythology of his native town to remind the reader that membership of a city involves relationship with its past as well as with its present and future.

Dante's great-great-grandfather only reveals his personal name towards the end of his long speech about the city: he is so firmly a *cive*, in Aristotle's and Charles Martel's terms, that his individual identity is essentially connected to his community of origin. Cacciaguida's enthusiastic welcome to Dante-character hints at family relationship in its similarity with Anchises' encounter with Aeneas in the Elysian Fields (*Par.* XV. 25–27), and in his Latin greeting of 'sanguis meus' ('my blood': l.28).[12] Although the pilgrim's first request is that 'mi facci del tuo nome sazio' ('you satisfy me with your name': l.87), the spirit's elliptical reply defines his relation to Dante indirectly, in terms of their relationship to a third, unnamed individual (their respective son and great-grandfather: ll.91–94). The first name that he utters clearly is not that of a person but of the town, 'Fiorenza' (l.97), and this introduces a lengthy and detailed discussion of the city that Cacciaguida knew, in a passage that bears apparently no relation to Dante-character's question about his ancestor's name. Yet the sequence is far from a digression: rather, a central factor in Cacciaguida's identity is his sense of Florentine citizenship, and this passage gives as much information about the individual as does the plain fact of his name.

In the speech as a whole, nearly twice as much space is given to the city (ll.97–132) as to the individual (ll.133–148, and less directly, ll.91–96). The detailed description of Florence, contrasting his own virtuous community with modern degeneracy, unfolds over thirty-six lines in which Cacciaguida evokes the orderly and comforting routines that formed his own sense of citizenship. His relationship to Florence is unproblematic and, whereas Dante-character in purgatorial conversation with Forese Donati expressed some unease over his civic origins, Cacciaguida evokes a city where human fellowship and divine grace combine in creating an ideal sense of civic community:

> A così riposato, a così bello
> viver di cittadini, a così fida
> cittadinanza, a così dolce ostello,
> Maria mi diè, chiamata in alte grida;
> e ne l'antico vostro Batisteo
> insieme fui cristiano e Cacciaguida.
>
> (Par. XV. 130–135)

To so restful and fair a life of citizens, to such a trusty citizenry, to so sweet a shelter Mary gave me, called on with loud cries;

and within your ancient Baptistery I became at the same time
a Christian and Cacciaguida.

St John presides as patron over the city as a whole and also over
what legend held to be its most ancient sacred monument, the
Baptistery, where Florentines acquire identity as Christians, citizens
and individuals. Cacciaguida's long-delayed utterance of his name
takes place metaphorically within this church's walls, as if repeating
the ceremony of baptism that formally marked his membership of
the Christian and the Florentine communities.

Cacciaguida's speech is structured around a series of both
implied and explicit contrasts between two eras of the city's history, his own age and that of Dante. At the beginning of the crusader's speech, the virtuous quality of its ancient citizenship, which
is so insistently stressed in the repeated superlatives of lines
130–132, is manifested in the image of the city as a virtuous
woman:

> *Fiorenza dentro de la cerchia antica,*
> *ond'ella toglie ancora e terza e nona,*
> *si stava in pace, sobria e pudica.*
>
> (*Par.* XV. 97–99)

> Florence, within her ancient circle, from which she still takes
> the third and ninth hours, dwelled in peace, sober and modest.

The female figure of the city displays a physical simplicity or austerity summed up by her containment within a small geographical
space that shows a geometrical, circle-based purity of size and scale.
The space contained within the walls is clearly defined to the eye
by the man-made monuments – the walls, the Baptistery – that
Cacciaguida names. In the following *canto* too, the unnaturalness of
expansion beyond suitable limits is emphasised by reference to the
two great patriotic monuments, '*Marte e 'l Batista*' ('Mars and the
Baptist': XVI. 47), which should form almost sacred barriers to

Florentine expansion. The city-limits can be aurally, as well as visually, defined as lying within the carrying power of the bells of Badia, the abbey-church set next to the walls of the *cerchia antica*, measuring out the civic and religious day as they strike the hours.[13] The regular patterning of sound harmonises city activities and contributes to the orderly rhythms of life in this virtuous town, where life is described in terms of moderation and propriety, as sober, modest and, above all, peaceful. Even the natural landscape, Cacciaguida suggests, can be disturbed by excessive civic expansion, as he describes how, in his day:

> *Non era vinto ancora Montemalo*
> *dal vostro Uccellatoio, che, com' è vinto*
> *nel montar sù, così sarà nel calo.*
>
> (*Par.* XV. 109–111)

The [Roman hill of] Monte Mario was not yet overcome by that of your [hill of] Uccellatoio; just as the former has been outdone in rising up, so will it be in its fall.

The proportions of a whole city ought to be visible from a commanding hillside from which its size can be measured, like the walled towns seen in the background of Trecento paintings; Cacciaguida's image of the landscape itself in seismic shift warns vividly against Florentine attempts to outdo her mother-city of Rome.

THE DOMESTIC CIRCLE:
PROVING GROUND FOR CIVIC VIRTUE

Immediately after his opening description of the sobriety and peace of ancient Florence, Cacciaguida launches into a series of implied contrasts in which the characteristics of the ancient city are defined in relation to the degenerate habits of Dante's own time. The virtuous qualities of the past are initially affirmed by negatives, consisting simply of *not* indulging in ostentatious or immoral conduct. The political implications of the crusader's comments are emphasised by his comparisons of his contemporaries to figures of exemplary virtue in Roman history – Cincinnatus and Cornelia (l.129) – recalling the classical poets' evocations of the peace and justice that flourished under conditions of material austerity in the early centuries of Rome or in the mythical Golden Age.[14] Conspicuous consumption and material display are the first objects of Cacciaguida's criticisms: elaborate clothes, exaggerated dowries and over-sized palaces are treated as the visible markers not of privilege and success, but of degeneracy (ll.100–108). Dante's conservative disapproval of the fourteenth-century economic advances that favoured this kind of large-scale spending makes a virtue out of the opposite conduct, and Cacciaguida gives authoritative, paradisal expression to this disapproval in his praise for the austerity of dress and simplicity of domestic customs at an idealised period of political and moral probity in the life of the city (ll.112–126).[15]

Much of Cacciaguida's description of the virtue, or lack of vice, of his era is concerned with female, domestic activities: the '*bello | viver di cittadini*' ('fair life of the citizens': XV. 130–131) is one where women play an important part and can be identified as indicators of the moral wellbeing of the whole social order. Like Forese Donati or Bonagiunta da Lucca in *Purgatorio*, Cacciaguida displays an interest not only in the male sphere of governance, but in the evidence that female examples provide about wider issues of social morality.[16] The anthropomorphised figure of Florence and the individual figures of her female inhabitants often merge in his discussion of civic restraint and excess. Dress provides a preliminary measure of civic welfare, and the *Fiorenza pudica* of the twelfth century is praised for her, or her female citizens', modest garments:

Non avea catenella, non corona,

non gonne contigiate, non cintura

che fosse a veder più che la persona.

(*Par.* XV. 100–102)

She had no necklace, no diadem, no embroidered dresses, nor
belt more showy than its wearer.

The implied contrast tells us that in Dante's corrupt age an imbalance of values makes the human figure take second place to its
own extravagant attire. The glittering shell of clothes that conceals
contemporary women's real appearance becomes a symbol for the
city's new, false values, where impressive externals prevent appreciation of fundamental social and political realities. The criticism of
uselessly ostentatious dress is reinforced a little later by remarks on
male simplicity of attire in the *buon tempo antico*. Once again, an
implied comparison allows us to conclude that men, as well as
women, in Dante's time are showily over-dressed, for Cacciaguida
praises his male contemporaries who were '*cint[i] | di cuoio e d'osso*'
('belted with leather and bone': l.112–113) and '*contenti a la pelle
scoperta*' ('contented with undressed leather': l.116). Women in the
ancient city present themselves naturally in body as well as dress,
'*sanza 'l viso dipinto*' ('without a painted face': l.114): again, they
show a restraint not found in the later city, where even with cos-
metic help women cannot compete with clothes designed to be
seen '*più che la persona*' ('more than the wearer': l.102). By contrast
with the pointless ostentation of male and female dress in fourteenth-century Florence, Cacciaguida's own face and body in paradise are hidden in glittering light: but although his human form is
not visible, his essential humanity is all the more perceptible, for
the light expresses the joy of desires satisfied by loving commun-
ion with God, rather than by consumerist competition or self-
indulgence.[17]

Virtuous moral and financial restraint also characterises relationships between the sexes in the Florence of Cacciaguida:

Non faceva, nascendo, ancor paura
la figlia al padre, ché 'l tempo e la dote
non fuggien quinci e quindi la misura.

(*Par.* XV. 103–105)

Daughters did not yet at birth cause their fathers to fear, for
the time and the dowry did not yet escape due measure on this
side and on that.

The concept of '*misura*', morally equivalent to the Aristotelian
notion of moderation, is essential to the health of private and public life. When its balancing effect is disregarded, the family bonds
that form the foundation of virtuous civic life and that should be
spontaneous and affectionate become burdensome, even terrifying
(they induce '*paura*', 'fear'). The father–child relationship is cor-
rupted by financial considerations and the sacrament of marriage
becomes a de-sanctified economic bargain, entered into before due
time, and therefore inappropriately. Marriage becomes a cause of
family impoverishment and disrupted affection, in unions that link
man to man, father and bridegroom, not man to woman.[18] In the
city of *dismisura*, women's presence becomes paradoxically an
absence; they are physically invisible, overshadowed and hidden as
human figures by their own clothes, and they become powerless in
the vital human relationship of marriage, in which they are
reduced to the currency of a financial exchange.

In the virtuous city, by contrast, female figures are valued domestic partners and their activities make important contributions to
civic welfare. Dante describes the twelfth-century women as productive citizens, maintaining the domestic economy by their fru-
gality rather than dissipating the family fortune by narcissism and
display. They engage busily in producing humble, home-made
clothes for their household, '*al fuso e al pennecchio*' ('at the spindle
and the distaff': l.117) or '*traendo a la rocca la chioma*' ('drawing thread
from the distaff': l.124).[19] Just as Cacciaguida's opening list of negatives concentrated on issues concerning women, so his praise of

positive civic qualities takes female activity as a major indicator of the whole community's virtue, evoking the health and happiness of ancient Florence almost entirely in terms of women's domestic lives and personal relations. Women are seen at the centre of family life, contributing actively to the material and moral stability of the household, identified in *Convivio* and *Monarchia* as the base-unit of the political community.[20] Family and domestic relationships all find stability and meaning through their presence, and the content- ment and providential privilege of Florence's women, rather than any image of men or their activity in city-government, sum up civic wellbeing:[21]

> *Oh fortunate! ciascuna era certa*
> *de la sua sepultura, e ancor nulla*
> *era per Francia nel letto diserta.*
>
> (*Par.* XV. 118–120)

O fortunate women! Each was certain of her burial-place, and as yet none was left in her bed deserted for France.

These women are part of a truly secure cycle of life, in which even death can be seen as positive and reassuring, as an end in a known grave in their own family and religious neighbourhood, closing a fulfilled married life close to husbands who are involved in the fam- ily circle, not travelling abroad for trade. From birth (ll. 103–105), through marriage (ll. 112–126), to death (ll. 118–119), the life led by the women Cacciaguida describes matches that of the personified community as a whole, in its peace, sobriety and modesty.

In Cacciaguida's Florence, women also contribute importantly to the education of the citizenry, through their linguistic activity.[22] The importance given to female civic instruction recalls Dante's statements elsewhere about vernacular language. These include not only his expressions of idiosyncratic fondness for the Florentine vernacular (*DVE* I. vi. 2–3; *Cvo* I. x. 6–14, xii. 4–13), but also his emphasis that the particularity of local vernaculars creates affection among the citizenry and is the means of access to education and thereby to human rational perfection (*Cvo* I. xii. 4–7, xiii. 2–5). Florentine women in the past have used their local language for just these sorts of purposes. Cacciaguida describes how they teach their children to speak, in welcoming language that creates a reassuring atmosphere from infancy onwards. They later help their children and their household to learn about history and civic and cultural concerns, through telling stories about the towns and civilisations that helped to form Florence, according to the foundation legends explored in Chapter 1:

> L'una vegghiava a studio de la culla,
> e, consolando, usava l'idïoma
> che prima i padri e le madri trastulla;
> l'altra, traendo a la rocca la chioma,
> favoleggiava con la sua famiglia
> d'i Troiani, di Fiesole e di Roma.

(*Par.* XV. 121–126)

One woman would be occupied with watching the cradle and, soothing, spoke in the tongue that first gives delight to fathers and mothers; another, drawing thread from the distaff, would tell stories with her household about the Trojans and Fiesole and Rome.[23]

The positive moral and linguistic productivity of female storytelling is matched by the positive material productivity of the women's simultaneous engagement in spinning. Both are peaceful, unpretentious pursuits, using the humble materials of woollen thread and vernacular language, but are also creative, clothing the citizens with warm garments and with strong civic values that give comfort and protection. Through storytelling and the use of the local language of Florence, private domestic experience is linked to, and provides training for, public life and an appreciation of civic and Florentine values. The 'municipal' vernacular is elevated to

212

noble purposes as it links the local and particular with other civilisations, and traces fundamental connections between Florence and
the universal authority of Rome. The history, learning and values
of the past are thus made relevant to local experience via the setting of the household, a solid, affectionate unit that lies at the heart
of civic development. The philosophical analysis of the *Convivio*
and the *Monarchia* sets out the close links between family, neighbourhood and city, as essential units within the political hierarchy
that enables humans to seek sufficiency and the good life; but it is
the poetry of the *Paradiso* that provides the most compelling
human picture of the value of these units and of the interconnections between familial and civic wellbeing.

PUBLIC AFFAIRS: THE EXERCISE OF CIVIC VIRTUE

Cacciaguida's first speech traces an almost apolitical picture of the
moral prosperity of the Florence that he knew in life. Dante-character responds enthusiastically to his ancestor's words, but the more
conventionally political interests of a figure who in 1300 was
actively involved in urban administration are displayed in his
request for statistical, governmental and genealogical information:

> *Ditemi de l'ovil di San Giovanni*
> *quanto era allora, e chi eran le genti*
> *tra esso degne di più alti scanni.*
>
> (*Par.* XVI. 25–27)

> Tell me about the sheepfold of St John, how large it was then,
> and who were the people there worthy of the highest positions.

The emphasis in this new *canto* shifts from the private detail of the
domestic scene to the consideration of families as aggregates of
their individual members, highlighting the collective nature of citizenship and civic activity.

A large proportion of the *canto* is dedicated to a list of names and facts that individually identify more than forty Florentine aristocratic families.[24] In the previous *canto*, a mere five or six individual names – Bellincion Berti (XV. 112), Lapo Salterello (l.128), Moronto and Eliseo (l.136), and so on – have already given a strong local flavour to the sequence; some critics have found the dense accumulation of patronymics in *canto* XVI bathetic, disrupting the simplicity and lyricism of Cacciaguida's discourse with dry or trivial data.[25] It is true that for about half the *canto*, virtually whole terzine are composed simply of surnames:

> *Io vidi li Ughi e vidi i Catellini,*
> *Filippi, Greci, Ormanni e Alberichi,*
> *già nel calare, illustri cittadini.*
>
> (*Par.* XVI. 88–90)

I saw the Ughi and I saw the Catellini, Filippi, Greci, Ormanni and Alberichi, illustrious citizens, already in decline.

But details of this kind can provide a significant contribution to our understanding of Dante's attitude towards cities and citizenship, as well as towards Florentine history, which are vital in turn to our reading of his statements about politics and exile in the next *canto*. Both the pilgrim's question and the particularity of his ancestor's reply highlight a variety of issues that are central to Dante's conception and experience of city life. Notions about moderation, virtue and nobility meld with an awareness of fortune and historical pattern, in which the details of Florentine politics both reflect and form part of a providential plan for humanity that becomes perceptible via small-scale events within a known city community. The concern with order in human affairs that we saw in Charles Martel's discourse is again apparent, in a *canto* that returns to the theme of leadership and urges that individuals should only assume responsibilities for which they are fitted by nature.

The list of family names stresses the small size and containment of the ancient city as almost moral qualities in themselves. The families are members of a city that holds only *'il quinto di quei ch'or son vivi'* ('a fifth of the number of those now alive': XVI. 48), but they form a unified and close-knit community. A relatively small ruling caste can be identified by name as the *'illustri cittadini'* ('illustrious citizens': l.90) who fill the prominent positions of government. The histories of these families were often closely linked by the realities of civic life – several of Cacciaguida's references describe how the dynasties intermarried, formed partnerships and bought and sold each other's land or houses. In the idealised city of Cacciaguida's era, such ties of blood and association draw together the leading citizenry into a unified and responsible collective, fitted by birth and training for the duties of government. Dante-poet laments that, by his own time, not only have many of these families been entirely eclipsed (ll.86–87), but the remainder are embroiled in the bitterness and violence raised by the factional conflicts between the Guelfs and Ghibellines or the Blacks and Whites, several of the Ghibelline families having been permanently expelled from Florence on faction grounds.[26]

The list is constructed not only so as to celebrate the virtues of the leading families of the past, but also to remind its audience of how, since Cacciaguida's age, family lines have been attenuated or extinguished in bloodshed, internal divisions have split family groups into rival branches, and family alliances been disrupted – paradigmatically, when Bondelmonte's broken marriage pact with the Amidei (ll. 140–147) triggered the thirteenth-century cycle of vendetta and faction that destroyed the city's former unity and stability. Many of the families of traditional aristocratic or consular rank named by Cacciaguida were those whom the Florentine *Secondo Popolo* of the 1290s classified as 'magnates' and excluded from government participation, punishing the violence with which they manifested their aristocratic sense of superiority and of honour in vendetta and faction-politics. The descendants of these illustrious citizens, *'grandi come antichi'* ('as great as they were

ancient': l.91), have thus become the victims of legislation that formally marks the profundity of the modern rupture across the social
ranks with the city's history and traditions.[27]

The vocabulary of the passage emphasises the importance of
authentically Florentine origins for good citizenship. While the poet
acknowledges the risibility of genealogical snobbism (ll. 1–15), there
is a strong sense of the importance to society of moral nobility of the
kind discussed in Book IV of *Convivio*. Cacciaguida tells Dante-
character that in his age, patriotism and loyalty to civic origins constituted the qualification for citizenship as much as wealth or name:

> Ma la cittadinanza, ch'è or mista
> di Campi, di Certaldo e di Fegghine,
> pura vediesi ne l'ultimo artista.
>
> (*Par.* XVI. 49–51)

> But the citizenry, which now is mixed with that of Campi,
> Certaldo and Figline, was then pure even in the humblest
> artisan.

Even the lowly artisan was Florentine and therefore worthy of at
least passing mention among the list of good citizens. In the discussion of the notable families, Dante repeatedly emphasises their
antiquity in a way that exalts noble genealogy but also, more importantly, stresses the length of association with Florence and with her
historical fortunes that is seen as essential to good citizenship.
Family origins and alliances are an important part of civic identity,
and the sequence is densely patterned with references that stress
family continuity: '*è disceso*' ('is descended from': l.97), '*lo ceppo di che
nacquero*' ('the root from which were born': l.106), '*i padri di coloro*'
('the fathers of those': l.112), '*la casa di che nacque*' ('the house from
which was born': l.136). Networks of kinship and alliance spread
across the ancient city among its small nucleus of citizens, drawing
them together as members of a community which Cacciaguida can
proudly call '*glorioso | e giusto*' ('glorious and just': ll.151–152) – a

phrase that clearly anticipates and contrasts with the poet's final verdict on modern Florence at his entry into the Empyrean: '*ïo [...] era venuto [...] di Fiorenza in popol giusto e sano*' ('I had come from Florence to a just and healthy people': XXXI. 37–39).

The closing part of Cacciaguida's speech changes focus from the specifics of family names. The city is again spoken of as a single people ('*popol*': l.152), whose shared Florentine citizenship unites the whole community. As before, the contrast between Cacciaguidan unity, glory and justice, and the confusion and discord of Dante's own era is brought out through the personification of the city:

> *Con queste genti, e con altre con esse,*
> *vid' io Fiorenza in sì fatto riposo,*
> *che non avea cagione onde piangesse.*
>
> (*Par.* XVI. 148–150)

With these families, and with others besides, I saw Florence in such repose that she had no reason to weep.[28]

Just as the anthropomorphised Florence of the preceding *canto* resembled her female inhabitants in dress, the Florence of this political *canto* displays a physical resemblance to her male citizens in that, like the noble families, she bears an identifying coat of arms. The disruption of Florentine history is vividly dramatised in the image of the change to this crest: the symbol of shared unity and loyalty is dishonourably reversed, and changes colour to match and to indicate the citizens' new characteristics of division and disloyalty, as the traditional white lily emblem is dyed red by the bloodshed of civil war:

> *Con queste genti vid' io glorïoso*
> *e giusto il popol suo, tanto che 'l giglio*
> *non era ad asta mai posto a ritroso,*
> *né per divisïon fatto vermiglio.*
>
> (*Par.* XVI. 151–154)

With these families I saw her people so glorious and just that the lily was never reversed on the staff nor turned red by division.[29]

Dante tells us that the ancient town's peace, justice and unity have been replaced, in his own time, by avarice, violence and rivalry. The start of Cacciaguida's speech reveals this to be hardly surprising, for the city has filled with immigrants whose origins outside the city walls mean that they have no sense of the moral connotations of Florentine citizenship. With no experience of the probity, stability and austerity of the ancient Florence described in *canto* XV, they cannot perpetuate its traditions. Cacciaguida extrapolates a broader political principle from this fact which, like Charles Martel's philosophical statements, derives from Aristotle – although in this case, is somewhat distorted from the original:

> *Sempre la confusion de le persone*
> *principio fu del mal de la cittade,*
> *come del vostro il cibo che s'appone.*
>
> (*Par.* XVI. 67–69)

The confusion of persons was always the origin of hurt for the city, as for you to pile up food [hurts the body].[30]

Like over-indulgence in food, over-extension of the city leads to the loss of comfort and dignity; the same striking imagery of immigration as gluttony reappears when Cacciaguida comments that the people of a city *sestiere* were happier when 'starved' of new neighbours ('*di novi vicin [...] digiuni*':l.135). Another vivid sensory image portrays immigration as polluting the city with the 'stink' of outsiders:

> *Oh quanto fora meglio esser vicine*
> *quelle genti ch'io dico, e al Galluzzo*
> *e a Trespiano aver vostro confine,*
> *che averle dentro e sostener lo puzzo*

del villan d'Aguglion, di quel da Signa,
che già per barattare ha l'occhio aguzzo!

(*Par.* XVI. 52–57)

O how much better it would be to have the people that I am
naming as neighbours, and to have your borders at Galluzzo
and Trespiano, than to have them inside the city and have to
support the stink of the peasant of Aguglione and of him of
Signa, who already has his eyes peeled for dirty work!

Dante's strong sensory imagery leaves us in no doubt that the
changed habits of his own age are profoundly contaminated, nor
that they have been brought to the city from outside.

The poet's distaste in these lines seems directed against the low
birth of the newcomers, labelling the immigrants peasants, but this
is true only in part; Cacciaguida also identifies the immigration of
noble or prominent families as contributing to the city's ills, when
he condemns the transfer to Florence of three of the city's most
prominent fourteenth-century dynasties:

Sariesi Montemurlo ancor de' Conti;
sarieno i Cerchi nel piovier d'Acone,
e forse in Valdigrieve i Buondelmonti.

(*Par.* XVI. 64–66)

Montemurlo would still belong to the Counts [Guidi]; the
Cerchi would be in the parish of Acone and the Bondelmonti
perhaps in Val di Greve.

By leaving their castles, towns and villages for Florence, the immigrants deny their own origins and the civic duties binding them to
their place of birth, so it is hardly surprising that they fail to contribute to the welfare of their adopted town. Continuity of residence and involvement in the community are an essential part of
civic formation at any social level, from the Conti Guidi of

Montemurlo as leaders to the peasants of Aguglione or Signa, or the humble artisan of ancient Florence. Immigration, on the other hand, is by definition discontinuous, breaking the stabilising influences of tradition and responsibility.

The sign of the moral degradation of the city's new *'cittadinanza [...] mista'* ('mixed citizenry': l.49) can be found in the degraded occupations they have introduced into the city. Their attitude to civic life is exploitative rather than contributory and is shown to be degradingly materialistic, bringing corruption to the old, simple order. The newcomer's energies are not turned to civic duty and the *'più alti scanni'* ('highest positions': l.27) of government administration, in which the good Florentine Dante-character was interested; instead he seeks to corrupt public life by *'barattare'* ('committing barratry': l.57). He assumes the name of citizenship but not its responsibilities, concentrating instead on personal profit: *'tal fatto è fiorentino e cambia e merca'* ('such a one has become Florentine and changes money and trades': l.61). As Cacciaguida's speech in the previous *canto* has already shown, this competitive emphasis on personal gain debases both public and private life: dress, habits, and family and personal relationships are all negatively affected by commercialism. *Canto* XV even showed that the new habits have led to the emigration of true Florentines from the city, leaving their wives *'per Francia nel letto disert[e]'* ('left in their beds deserted for France': XV. 120) – a total reversal of natural order is achieved when the original inhabitants adopt the values of the outsiders and voluntarily abandon their family and community.

FLORENCE AND FORTUNE: THE CITY, THE CHURCH AND THE EMPIRE

Cacciaguida firmly attributes the corruption of civic identity and responsibility to imbalance between institutions at a higher level than the city. The rising tide of immigration and commercialisation could have been stemmed, he claims:

se la gente ch'al mondo più traligna
non fosse stata a Cesare noverca,
ma come madre a suo figlio benigna.

(*Par.* XVI. 58–60)

if the people most degenerate in the world had not acted towards
Caesar as a stepmother, but as benignly as a mother to her son.

The human community that Dante feels has degenerated furthest
from its ideal form is the Church which, as we know from the
Monarchia as well as from evidence elsewhere in the *Commedia*, has
fatally undermined its spiritual mission by intervention in secular
affairs.[31] The imbalance between the powers of Church and empire
lies at the root of the imbalances in the life of the city. The voice of
Cacciaguida carries conviction, for he himself is a good citizen of
the ancient, virtuous Florence and a crusader who followed his
emperor to defend the Church in a holy war, in an age of harmony
when political service of both city and empire, and religious service of the Christian faith, were all compatible with one another.

The relation of the Church to the empire is expressed in the language of the family, implying obligations of mutual attention,
respect and reciprocity. Cacciaguida's biography illustrates their
proper working in an earlier age, but he and his descendant are
painfully aware of the disruption that has occurred between the
powers by the 1300s. This broken relationship metaphorically
changes the natural parent into the unnatural step-parent and dis-
rupts the whole pattern of human affairs, breaking the links
between individuals and institutions at every level. In Florence, territorial upheaval and immigration take people from their fundamental duties and stations, or capacities, in life and bring down a
whole structure of natural positions and relationships, to be
replaced with mistrust, division and violence. As we know from
Monarchia, Dante saw the good relations of Church and empire as
vital to the order and wellbeing of humanity, and of the city units
in which people naturally congregate. The enmity between the

two divinely sanctioned institutions in Dante's time has reduced their holy authority to the same status as merely human institutions which, Cacciaguida tells us, *'tutte hanno lor morte, | sì come voi'* ('all have their death, just as you do': XVI. 79–80).

Cacciaguida comments that, to mortal eyes, the fluctuations in the fortunes of earthly families or urban polities appear random and meaningless. Apparently stable institutions and landmarks – even whole cities – prove subject to temporal forces of growth and decay. The inevitability of the historical process of change is stressed when Cacciaguida once again anthropomorphises human cities, whose individual periods of growth and disappearance are similar to the birth-to-death cycle of human life:

> *Se tu riguardi Luni e Orbisaglia*
> *come sono ite, e come se ne vanno*
> *di retro ad esse Chiusi e Sinigaglia,*
> *udir come le schiatte si disfanno*
> *non ti parrà nova cosa né forte,*
> *poscia che le cittadi termine hanno.*
> *Le vostre cose tutte hanno lor morte,*
> *sì come voi; ma celasi in alcuna*
> *che dura molto, e le vite son corte.*
>
> (*Par.* XVI. 73–81)

If you look at how Luni and Orbisaglia have fled, and how Chiusi and Senigallia are following after them, to hear how families come to nought shall not seem to you strange or hard, since cities themselves come to an end. All your affairs have their death, just as you do; but this is hidden in some things that last a long time, while lives are short.

The general statement, using the examples of cities from antiquity, Etruscan Luna and Roman Urbs Salvia, whose ruins were well-known in Dante's day, allow Cacciaguida to introduce a political maxim that he then, more challengingly, applies to Florence:

> *E come 'l volger del ciel de la luna*
> *cuopre e discuopre i liti sanza posa,*
> *così fa di Fiorenza la Fortuna.*
>
> (*Par.* XVI. 82–84)

And just as the circling of the heaven of the moon covers and uncovers the seashore unceasingly, so does Fortune act on Florence.

The observable cycle of the lunar month and its effect on the sea-tide provides a comprehensible, small-scale image to illustrate the cyclical repetitions of providential history in a human community. The processes of Fortune are like those of nature, apparently arbitrary in their single, local manifestations but forming an orderly pattern when viewed over time. Dante-character learned from Virgil early in the journey that Fortune is an instrument of divine will, ruling over the patterns of human history (*Inf.* VII. 67–96); using this information, his perception of events from the limited perspective of the human lifespan is now replaced with an understanding of the wider scale of human history and of its internal logic, illustrated in the example of his own native city. Legends about Florentine history, as we know, already identified at least two periods of destruction and renewal in the city's past, imposed by Fortune's 'tidal' action of decay and regeneration – the city's foundation by Caesar, destruction by Totila and subsequent Roman re-foundation. Dante-poet's image makes the apparent lack of order in the city at a third troubled turn of the tide of history, in 1300, fall into place as part of this pattern. The Florence of Cacciaguida's lifetime took stability and order as natural, but now disorder, apparently perverse, is also seen to be natural to the city, part of a process that fits into the divine plan for the city and in which renewal is surely implicit in the decline.[32]

The providential logic underlying human affairs is revealed only gradually to Dante-character, and not made fully explicit until the end of the next *canto*. For the moment, Cacciaguida deals specifically with the patterns of Florentine history, and the concept of

Fortune is at issue at both the start and the close of his list of the ancient city's illustrious citizens. Cacciaguida's speech in *canto* XVI is carefully constructed, with these general observations on human polities and on the processes of history and Fortune in empire, Church and city providing a general preface to the strongly Florentine list of family details in the centre of the *canto*. The speech concludes with a set of reflections on a single historical event that, though still local and Florentine, demonstrates the connections between local affairs and the wider historical and political forces associated with the city's myth of origins:

> *O Buondelmonte, quanto mal fuggisti*
> *le nozze süe per li altrui conforti!*
> *Molti sarebber lieti, che son tristi,*
> *se Dio t'avesse conceduto ad Ema*
> *la prima volta ch'a città venisti.*
> *Ma conveniesi, a quella pietra scema*
> *che guarda 'l ponte, che Fiorenza fesse*
> *vittima ne la sua pace postrema.*
>
> (Par. XVI. 140–147)

Oh Bondelmonte, how wickedly you fled from marriage [with the Amidei], encouraged by another! Many would be happy, who are sad, if God had committed you to the River Ema the first time you came into the city. But it was necessary that Florence, in her last peace, should give a victim to that broken stone that stands at the bridge.

Couched in the language of pagan religion and sacrifice, this reference fits the violent event of Bondelmonte dei Bondelmonti's assassination in 1215 into the orderly rhythms of Florentine fortune, patterned by periods of struggle and redirection. Cacciaguida's reference to the '*pietra scema*', the broken stone image identified by the Florentines as the city's ancient cult idol of Mars, initially suggests a malevolent connection between the god of war and the city of Florence.[33] The planet Mars, where Dante and Cacciaguida's meeting takes place in the *Paradiso*, is traditionally associated with war, but is described in *Convivio* as the star of music and harmony (*Cvo* II. xiii. 20–24). The '*pietra scema*' is thus a sign both of civic discord and of providential harmony in the affairs of Florence.[34] The statue is associated in legend with the founding and re-founding of the town under Roman, imperial auspices, and so with epochs of world history when empire, too, was being founded or revived to give the direction to human secular affairs that Dante believes to be so crucial for the wellbeing of smaller political units, such as the city. The history of Florence is seen to be closely linked to the varying stability of empire and to the state of relations between pope and emperor. In Cacciaguida's time, with both in accord, Florence's Mars-inspired energies create harmony, and the good citizen's warrior qualities are placed in the service of a holy enterprise – crusade – that fits into the divine plan for world religion and universal empire under these twin leaders. In Dante's time, the broken relationship between higher authorities creates disunity at world and civic level, and the town's Mars-derived energies turn inwards to produce discord and violence, degenerating into civil war between the factions of Guelfs and Ghibellines.

The Bondelmonte murder brings Cacciaguida's survey of the political fortunes of ancient Florence to an end. In the next *canto*, Dante-character raises the question of the political future of the city and indeed of himself. Here, too, Cacciaguida outlines a pattern of events in which surface turmoil is fitted into a broader pattern ordered by Fortune. From the viewpoint of eternity, '*il punto | a cui tutti li tempi son presenti*' ('the point to which all times are present': XVII. 17–18), Cacciaguida can see Dante's heaviest personal tragedy, his exile, as part of the musical rhythm and order of providential history. He compares his prevision to a '*dolce armonia da organo*' ('sweet harmony on the organ': l.44), recalling the *Convivio*'s connection between Mars and the discipline of music, which stressed harmonious relationships and mathematical pattern, and which reflected on the association of Mars with prophecies of change and upheaval:

Né per ambage, in che la gente folle
già s'inviscava pria che fosse anciso
l'Agnel di Dio che le peccata tolle,
ma per chiare parole e con preciso
latin rispuose quello amor paterno,
chiuso e parvente del suo proprio riso.

(*Par.* XVII. 31–36)

Not with enigmatic words, in which foolish people used to entrap themselves before the Lamb of God who takes away sin was slain, but in clear words and with precise language that paternal love replied, enclosed and revealed in his own smile.

Human events, if properly understood, can be discussed with clearness and precision, however difficult they may appear, and Cacciaguida actively rejoices in disclosing the pattern of divine will.

The long section (ll.46–99) dealing with the factual and emotional realities of exile is notable for its simplicity, clarity and directness, creating a moving poetic effect that make this one of the most famous passages of the *Commedia*. Exile is, at its simplest level, the loss of '*ogne cosa diletta | più caramente*' ('everything beloved most dearly': ll.55–56). Cacciaguida sums up these losses in everyday realities, where the most ordinary activities are conducted with a sense of disorientation:

Tu proverai sì come sa di sale
lo pane altrui, e come è duro calle
lo scendere e 'l salir per l'altrui scale.

(*Par.* XVII. 58–60)

You will experience how salty is the taste of other people's bread, and how hard a path it is to ascend and descend by another's stairs.

But beyond the evocation of personal suffering, Cacciaguida emphasises that Dante's banishment forms part of a meaningful historical order. His first direct reference to the protagonist's impending exile already contains both these elements, although the pattern here is a gloomy one:

> Qual si partio Ipolito d'Atene
> per la spietata e perfida noverca,
> tal di Fiorenza partir ti convene.

(*Par.* XVII. 46–48)

Just as Hippolytus left Athens because of his pitiless and treacherous stepmother, so you will be compelled to leave Florence.

Dante's exile is placed in relationship to Hippolytus, in a model that balances the patterns of injustice and suffering across human and civic history – the patterns of Fortune recur in human experience between different people, cities and states. In the story of Hippolytus too, perverted relationships between the supposed representatives of order – king, queen and heir; husband and wife; parent and child – lie at the root of undeserved exile, as in Dante's case do the corrupt relations of empire and Church (the *madre* turned Phaedra-like *noverca*, XVI. 59–60), and the perversities of faction in his city's government. Cacciaguida stresses that even the hardest patterns of history and repetition are meaningful, promising a future turn of the tide of history in which the exile will be vindicated ('*vendetta*': l.53), and underlying providential truths ('*ver*': l.54) made manifest.

This will involve play between the two different but interdependent strands of Florentine historical fortune, those of downfall and regeneration. The general course of civic events and the individual case of Dante bear on each other closely, and are illustrated by the mass nature of exile, within which Cacciaguida tells the protagonist that he will establish a '*parte per te stesso*' ('party for yourself': l.69), clearly distinguished from the '*compagnia malvagia e scempia*' ('wicked and senseless company': l.62) of the failed White politicians expelled from Florence in the Black coup of 1301. Both kinds of exile illustrate the nature of the Florentine historical cycle of periodic upheaval and destruction, and its links to the wider pattern of world events. Factionalism resulting from papal–imperial opposition absorbs the energies and ideas of the other exiles, who concentrate blindly on their own sufferings and attempt to perpetuate violence and injustice, in their struggle to regain Florence and exile their opponents in turn. Their attempt to impose their own patterns on history, rather than perceiving and following God's, betrays both faith and reason, and Cacciaguida labels their conduct '*bestialitate*' ('bestiality': l.67). The full extent of the city's political perversity is indicated when the cause of truth and moderation must become a third 'party' in the struggle for civic direction, Dante ironically applying the hated terminology of factionalism to his own conduct.[35] The *Commedia* is hailed by Cacciaguida as the manifesto, as it were, of this party, revealing to its readers the providential model for human affairs and the key position of city communities in human history at large, represented through the example of Florence.

Cacciaguida's account of Dante's political future is uncompromising. He looks ahead to the disappointment of future imperial hopes, embodied by Henry VII, and confirms the difficulties that lie ahead. The failure of Henry VII's Italian mission (l.82) does not however invalidate its providential rightness, or the necessity of energetic support for attempts to restore the true relationship between Church and empire, as truly universal and complementary institutions. After Dante-character's entry into the Empyrean, almost the last political comment in the poem will appear when Beatrice points out the place reserved for Henry in paradise (XXX. 133). Although Henry VII's energetic attitude to the rights and responsibilities implied by the imperial title offered the last really practical hope for a renewed Roman empire in Dante's lifetime, his death is shown by Cacciaguida by no means to invalidate the need for Dante to inspire political zeal and to correct mistaken political assumptions among his contemporaries. Dante's own life pattern and its effects will be extended in a dynamic *infuturare* ('enfuturing': l.98), until history reveals the value of his activities. In the future of eternity, too, Dante-character is promised the ultimate vindication of a place in paradise (XXX. 135); whereas *Inferno* was packed with the representatives of faction and corrupt citizenship, all too many of them from Florence.

Dante-character accepts the sentence of exile stoically, but remains unclear as to his own role and asks Cacciaguida anxiously about his responsibilities not only in political but also in poetic terms. In the course of the journey, he reminds his ancestor:

> *ho io appreso quel che s'io ridico,*
> *a molti fia sapor di forte agrume;*
> *e s'io al vero son timido amico,*
> *temo di perder viver tra coloro*
> *che questo tempo chiameranno antico.*
>
> (*Par.* XVII. 116–120)

I have learned things which, if I report them, will taste bitter to many; and if I am a timid friend to truth I fear to lose life among those who will call this time ancient.

The response to this anxiety provides the poet's vindication of his own work, placed in the mouth of Cacciaguida, spokesman both for Florence and for Providence. The plan of Providence for humanity must be communicated in its entirety or not at all: '*tutta tua visïon fa manifesta*' ('make manifest all that you have seen': l.128), the protagonist is urged.[36] The crusading martyr knows that truth may have to be defended through personal suffering and sacrifice in the cause of the divine plan for humanity and that these should not be avoided to maintain personal comfort. His exhortation ends with a strong, even crude, image for the necessity of communicating the truth accessibly and in entirety: '*lascia pur grattar dov'è la rogna*' ('let them scratch where the scabs itch': l.129). Just as the itch of disease cannot be ignored, nor, in a shift of image, can Dante's poem, which brings a combination of irritation and relief to human affairs, like the curative effects of an unpleasant-tasting medicine:

> Ché se la voce tua sarà molesta
> nel primo gusto, vital nodrimento
> lascerà poi, quando sarà digesta.
>
> (Par. XVII. 130–132)

For if your voice is unwelcome at first taste, it will leave behind vital nourishment, when it has been digested.

In the political discourse of *Purgatorio*, the emperor was the metaphorical doctor for secular ills (*Purg.* VI. 110), but this role is now taken over by a poet. Dante's poem is vital to the moral prosperity of papacy, empire and city, bringing a prophetic message of truth to its readers.

Cacciaguida closes with a striking final image for the poem:

> Questo tuo grido farà come vento,
> che le più alte cime più percuote.
>
> (Par. XVII. 133–134)

This cry of yours will act like the wind, which strikes hardest on the highest peaks.

The poet achieves prophetic status with his urgent '*grido*' ('cry') of witness and reform, reminiscent of John the Baptist's 'voice crying in the wilderness':[37] an appropriate role for a Florentine to fill. His words in the wilderness of exile bear witness to the divine plan for humanity and to the working of historical pattern in human affairs. The message of reform looks first to the leaders of the people (ll. 136–142), examining their failure to act responsibly; its providential revelations are intended to restore meaning and fruitfulness

both to the human community of the city, and to the ruling institutions of Church and empire. The forcefulness of the *Commedia*'s
comic, vernacular language ensure the dissemination of Dante's
ideas on both secular and spiritual matters both to princes and to
the popular audience found on an Italian city *piazza*, and invites
both groups to change their conduct in reaction to the poem's
words.[38]

RESTORING THE SECULAR ORDER:
EXILE AND HOMECOMING IN THE POETIC IMAGINATION

The intensely personal exchanges that Dante-poet imagines
between his protagonist and the father-figure of Cacciaguida draw
a tight network of links between the affairs of Florence and those
of the universal institutions. He chooses to illustrate the importance of community existence to human wellbeing through the
familiar, specific example of Florence, but the insertion of frequent
reflections of a more philosophical character point towards the
general conclusions that can be drawn from his chosen example.
Significantly, the Florentine meditations of the heaven of Mars are
followed, in the heaven of Jupiter, by reflections on the principle of
justice, where the imperial eagle symbol formed by the planet's
souls speaks and moves with a single, totally unified voice and will.
The lofty lessons that the eagle offers Dante about justice and
judgement can be assimilated more easily in the light of
Cacciaguida's discourse about the urban polity, where Florentine
specifics made concrete Dante-poet's conclusions about moderation, peace, unity and justice.

Florentine concerns re-emerge with surprising vehemence several *canti* later, in the middle of Dante-character's examination on
the theological virtues. The passage imagines a future return to
Florence which implies the turning of Fortune's tide back towards
unity, peace and justice:

Se mai continga che 'l poema sacro
al quale ha posto mano e cielo e terra,
sì che m'ha fatto per molti anni macro,
vinca la crudeltà che fuor mi serra
del bello ovile ov' io dormi' agnello,
nimico ai lupi che li danno guerra;
con altra voce omai, con altro vello
ritornerò poeta, e in sul fonte
del mio battesmo prenderò 'l cappello.

(*Par.* XXV. 1–9)

If it ever comes to pass that the sacred poem, to which heaven and earth have set their hands so that it has kept me thin for many years, should overcome the cruelty that shuts me out from the fair sheepfold where I slept as a lamb, enemy to the wolves that wage war on it, with a voice altered by now and with altered fleece I shall return a poet, and at the font of my baptism take the crown.

Again, these lines make impressive claims about the role of Dante and his poem, both in relation to Florence and to the wider world. The prophetic nature of the poem is confirmed when it is identified unequivocally as a '*poema sacro*' ('sacred poem') forged by both heaven and earth – the earthly contribution reminding us that the *Commedia* is a human, practical and moral, as well as a religious and theological, work.

The poet's essential sense of loyal, Florentine citizenship is manifested in his wish to return to the sheepfold of Florence and, in the Baptistery Church that lies at the symbolic heart of the city, receive the crown of a poet laureate; but he is prepared to wait on Providence for the fulfilment of a desire expressed with a hypothetical, subjunctive '*continga*' ('should it come to pass'). The imagined return to Florence and to the Baptistery that constitutes its symbolic civic and religious centre, recall indirectly the similarities between the Florentine poet and the Florentine patron-saint that were drawn at the end of the Cacciaguida episode. St John is the last of the prophets of the Messiah, who takes up a position outside the city walls, in the wilderness, and addresses a message of reform to towns whose excessive arrogance is bringing them into moral and spiritual danger.[39] Dante describes him in *Paradiso* XXXII as one who *''l diserto e 'l martiro | sofferse*' ('suffered the desert and martyrdom': ll.32–33). For Dante-poet, and for his alter ego, the poem's protagonist, the journeys of exile and of poetry-writing from the '*selva selvaggia e aspra e forte*' ('wild and harsh and fierce wood': *Inf.* I. 5) that opens the narrative, to the '*vera città*' ('true city', *Purg.* XIII. 95, XVI. 96) of heaven, mimic that of the martyr whose execution won him a seat in paradise. But there remains a constant concern with Florence, the city of the Baptist, and with the need to convey an urgent spiritual message to the inhabitants of this and other cities. The ideal model of citizenly experience depicted in the *Paradiso* tells us more about Dante's political values than do his theoretically based idealisations of the empire in *Convivio* or *Monarchia*, by bringing the realities of human experience alive through the vivid, vernacular idiom of the *poema sacro*. Cacciaguida articulates Dante-poet's most lively and serious self-justification, showing how his words in the wilderness of exile bear witness to the divine plan for humanity, and to the working of historical pattern in human affairs. The poem brings the voice of the exile out of the desert and into the heart of the city, to urge its moral and political re-foundation.

7

CONCLUSION

Over the course of the preceding chapters, the city has been found to occupy a cardinal place in Dante's political thinking, even when he develops his theories of the necessity *also* of empire. The close reading of his theoretical works, but even more, the investigation of his practice in the writing of the *Commedia*, has shown that Dante displays a central interest in the small community of the city and in the interactions of the individuals who live there. As he depicts it, the urban community is small enough for moral and social responsibilities to lie on each of its members, and for a shared vernacular to flourish through use in the legislation, historiography and literature that form bonds between citizen and citizen, and between citizen and place. The native population of a city is intimately bound to its place of origin, and should take an active part in the private and the political functions that maintain urban harmony and stability.

Much of his interest in cities is plain from Dante's statements in *Convivio* and even in *Monarchia*, despite their obviously imperial content. But theory comes to life for Dante in the detail of historical example and of individual words or actions and reactions to specific circumstances. In this perspective, his greatest political work is not the *Monarchia*, but the *Commedia* – the *Commedia*, precisely because it argues through poetry and historical detail rather than through philosophical exposition, and seeks out a wide audience for its vernacular, accessible narrative. In the poem, Dante communicates his ideas about general human problems through the dramatisation of individual lives, playing off his characters' words against the evidence of their historical or literary biographies. The narrative of the *Commedia* constantly challenges the truth of its protagonists' stories, echoing the kinds of ethical activity that we have found Dante to associate with the life of the city, as the forum where the public and the private, the individual and the political, coincide and are put to the test.

From the very beginning of Dante's narrative in the *Commedia*, the reader knows of his reforming intentions: the poem is written to '*trattar del ben*' ('treat of the good': *Inf.* I. 8) that can be found amongst even the most perplexing of human circumstances. This good is one that ultimately transcends human and earthly concerns: but it is also intimately connected to them. As the long sequence of encounters with individuals that makes up the narrative of the *Commedia* reminds us, access to the supreme goods of the celestial world is dependent upon behaviour and choices pursued in the earthly world. The apparent valediction to human concerns that is pronounced as the protagonist enters the Empyrean at the end of his journey reminds us of this very forcefully, by combining abstract pronouncements on the nature of eternity with specific allusions to human cities:

> *Se i barbari, venendo da tal plaga*
> *che ciascun giorno d'Elice si cuopra,*
> *rotante col suo figlio ond' ella è vaga,*
> *veggendo Roma e l'ardüa sua opra,*
> *stupefaciensi, quando Laterano*
> *a le cose mortali andò di sopra;*
> *ïo, che al divino da l'umano,*
> *a l'etterno dal tempo era venuto,*
> *e di Fiorenza in popol giusto e sano,*
> *di che stupor dovea esser compiuto!*
>
> (*Par.* XXXI. 31–40)

If the barbarians – coming from such realms as are daily covered by Helice, wheeling with her son whom she loves – seeing Rome and its noble works at the time when the Lateran rose above all mortal things, were stupefied; then I, who had come to the divine from the human, to the eternal from time, and from Florence to a just and healthy people – what wonder must have filled me!

Rome and Florence, two cities whose destinies have proved in the course of the *Commedia* to be persistently linked together, appear as a pair once again, in a forceful summation of the imperfections of contemporary society. Florence is evoked as the antithesis of heavenly justice and wellbeing; Rome, as the emblem of the greatest secular and spiritual achievements of human history.

But the transcendence of Florentine injustice and moral ill-health in the heavenly '*Roma onde Cristo è romano*' ('Rome of which Christ is a Roman': *Purg.* XXXII. 102) is nonetheless made with the earthly communities of Florence, Rome and other cities in mind. As Cacciaguida told the protagonist in the central *canti* of *Paradiso*, the point of the journey is not simply to win Dante-character's personal redemption. It is because he is a poet and can communicate what he has seen to the wider earthly audience, that he is accorded the privilege of his journey through the afterworld. The poem's narrative is predicated on circular chronologies of departure and return that maintain a continual tension – for protagonist, poet and reader – between yesterday, today and tomorrow. Dante remains continuously committed to his interest in questions about social and political life, and urges his audience to share his concerns.

At the end of *Paradiso*, his comment on the injustice of his own *patria* is succeeded almost immediately by a statement that focuses these concerns anew. In a reversal of the traditional Christian imagery of the earthly and the heavenly 'Jerusalems', which defines temporal existence as an exile from the homeland of God, Dante-character in heaven is represented as a pilgrim intent on making a journey home to his point of origin – that is, presumably, to

Florence and the earthly world – as he reacts delightedly to the vision of celestial harmony and happiness,

> *quasi peregrin che si ricrea*
> *nel tempio del suo voto riguardando,*
> *e spera già ridir com'ello stea.*
>
> (*Par.* XXXI. 43–45)

like a pilgrim who takes delight in looking around the temple
of his vow, and already hopes to recount what it was like.

The poet has a duty to address his fellow-citizens about what he has experienced and even in the spiritual homeland of heaven is aware of a pressing concern with the wellbeing of his earthly homeland.

Dante's home city was characterised only a few lines previously as a place of absolute depravity, but nonetheless, its exiled representative can express a determination to achieve a reversal of the patterns of exclusion, conflict and betrayal that punctuate its history, bringing it back to a more positive phase in the historical cycle. Playing on a complex range of allusions to *patriae* and patriotisms (Florentine and heavenly and related both to exile and to pilgrimage), the poet reminds the reader that his poetic activity in the *Commedia* has an intensely serious purpose. Excluded from the field of practical politics by one set of exile experiences, Dante (man and poet) represents himself in his own fiction as an exile or pilgrim of a different, moral and spiritual sort, and uses the narrative as a vehicle for expressing social and ethical concerns, and for urging the political world to reformatory action.

All Dante's depictions of city life, whether in the *Monarchia*, *Convivio* or *Commedia*, emphasise a similar finely tuned conjunction between personal and public considerations. Dante's cities are not places where technical efficiency alone can assure the smooth running of public affairs – instead, the personal virtues of the individual citizens who assume governmental responsibilities provide the main guarantees of political order. The *Commedia* in particular

emphasises an almost organic link between city patriotism and citizenly virtues in the political life, involving loyalties to place, language and customs. Our survey of episodes from the *Inferno*,
Purgatorio and *Paradiso* has stressed that even the activities of private
life – ranging from poetry-writing to interests in food or clothes –
and of those marginal to political institutions, like women, children
or artisans, have political import for Dante, because of the close ties
that connect all the members of city society in material, and in
moral, exchanges with one another.

Linguistic questions are never far removed from the attention of
Dante, the poet and philosopher who came to depend on writing as
his sole means of access to the political sphere after his exile. Speech
is an essential element in the forming of human relationships and as
the *De vulgari* stresses, it pertains to the rational capacities that distinguish humans as social and moral beings. The *De vulgari*'s theory of
an elevating and unifying *vulgare illustre* looks to the two groups of
poets and governors to provide its exponents – and finds them only
among the former. Dante's linguistic views, as the treatise might lead
us to expect, evolved over the course of his literary development; the
Commedia's very title indicates revision of the treatise's neat linguistic
categorisations. This book's chapters on the *Commedia* have shown
Dante tacitly revising his earlier pronouncements on 'municipal' and
on comedic language and endowing a range of different, and often
unexpected, speakers (Forese and Bonagiunta) with moral authority,
while questioning the authority assumed by others (Pope Nicholas
and the *Frati Gaudenti*). Linguistic skill and awareness are importantly linked to political insight, by promoting a sense of fellowship
among members of the linguistic community whether, like
Guinizelli and Arnaut Daniel, they share the elevated, 'illustrious'
idiom of the lyric poetry of *gentilezza* that appeals initially to a small
élite of *amici di virtù*, or depend instead on the local vernacular of a
city where moral nobility is widespread, like the women of ancient
Florence in *Paradiso* XV.

Dante's interests in the city clearly derive from his own senti-
mental and political relationship to Florence. Even in his earliest

writing, in the *Vita Nova*, the city mattered because it was the place where Beatrice lived and so was a place of *gentilezza*. It was in Florence that he first encountered discussion of political ethics and organisation, fostered by figures like Brunetto Latini, and where he chose to pursue an active governmental career. In exile, Dante retains a sense of the city as testing-ground of curiality and ethical values. Even when he feels the need to place the city within the universal framework of empire Dante seeks, in the *Commedia* above all, to find in the city the possibility of human political order by which to reassess the disorderly events of his own life, a need writ large in the *canti* of Cacciaguida. And so the *Commedia* enables him to become once more a political agent, urging his fellows, and especially his fellow Florentines, to recognise that political success depends on acceptance of one's identity and origins, and on the whole-hearted enactment of civic obligations.

Within the poem, the city becomes an essential paradigm in political matters, and provides Dante with a constant point of reference in his examination of how and why individuals and societies achieve success or failure, in political and secular terms, as well as spiritual and eschatological ones. In the *Commedia* which places himself, as protagonist, at the centre of the action, Dante reminds his readers that political matters are not abstract affairs but are vitally important to the personal and social interests of real historical individuals such as himself or themselves. The city appears in the *Commedia* as a polity where such interests can find full expression, and where the histories of Florence and Rome, Lucca and Bologna, and a host of other cities, take on symbolic significance in inviting Dante's audience to examine the pleasures and pitfalls of human social existence. The compelling dramas of the poem's narrative repeatedly echo the author's statements elsewhere on cities, citizenship and the human desire for companionship and happiness. Dante remains constantly concerned with exploring these desires, and in whatever medium he addresses the issues, the city always retains a central place in his political and poetic imagination.

BIBLIOGRAPHY

PRIMARY SOURCES

WORKS BY DANTE

La Commedia secondo l'antica vulgata, ed. Giorgio Petrocchi, 4 vols, Milan: Mondadori, 1966–1967.

La Divina Commedia, ed. Attilio Momigliano, Florence: Sansoni, 1950.

La Divina Commedia, ed. Natalino Sapegno, 3 vols, Florence: La Nuova Italia, 1962.

La Divina Commedia, ed. Umberto Bosco and Giovanni Reggio, 3 vols, Florence: Le Monnier, 1980.

La Divina Commedia, ed. Luigi Scorrano and Aldo Vallone, 3 vols, Naples: Ferraro, 1986.

La Divina Commedia, ed. Giuseppe Giacalone, 2nd edn, 3 vols, Rome: Signorelli, 1988.

The Divine Comedy, ed. and trans. Charles S. Singleton, 3 vols, Princeton: Princeton University Press, 1977.

Convivio, ed. Cesare Vasoli and Domenico De Robertis, (*Opere minori* I. 2), Milan: Ricciardi, 1998.

Il convivio ridotto a miglior lezione, ed. G. Busnelli and G. Vandelli, 2 vols, Florence: Le Monnier, 1934–1938.

Dante: The Banquet, trans. Christopher Ryan, Stanford: Anma Libri, 1989.

De vulgari eloquentia, ed. and trans. Steven Botterill, Cambridge: Cambridge University Press, 1996.

De vulgari eloquentia, ed. Pier Vincenzo Mengaldo, (*Opere minori* II), Milan: Ricciardi, 1979.

Epistole, ed. Giorgio Brugnoli and Arsenio Frugoni, (*Opere minori* II), Milan: Ricciardi, 1979.

Dantis Alagherii Epistolae, ed. Paget Toynbee, 2nd edn, Oxford: Clarendon, 1966.

Monarchia, ed. and trans. Prue Shaw, Cambridge: Cambridge University Press, 1995.

Dante's Monarchia, ed. and trans. Richard Kay, Toronto: Pontifical Institute of Mediaeval Studies, 1998.

Monarchia, ed. and trans. Gustavo Vinay, Florence: Sansoni, 1950.

Monarchia, ed. Pier Giorgio Ricci, Milan: Mondadori, 1965.

Monarchia, ed. Bruno Nardi, (*Opere minori* II), Milan: Ricciardi, 1979.

Rime, ed. Gianfranco Contini, (*Opere minori* I. 1) Turin: Einaudi, 1946.

Rime, ed. Gianfranco Contini, Milan: Ricciardi, 1984.

Dante's Lyric Poetry, ed. and trans. K. Foster and P. Boyde, 2 vols, Oxford: Clarendon, 1967.

Vita nuova, ed. Domenico De Robertis, (*Opere minori* I. 1), Milan: Ricciardi, 1984.

Vita Nova, ed. Guglielmo Gorni, Turin: Einaudi, 1996.

OTHER WORKS CITED

Alighieri, Pietro, *Petri Allagherii super Dantis ipsius genitoris Comoediam Commentarium nunc primum in lucem editum sumptibus G. J. Bar. Vernon*, ed. Vincenzo Nannucci, 8 vols, Florence: Piatti, 1846.

Anonimo Fiorentino, *Commento alla Divina Commedia d'Anonimo Fiorentino del secolo XIV*, ed. Pietro Fanfani, 3 vols, Bologna: Romagnoli, 1866–1874.

Aristotle, *Ethica Nicomachea*, trans. H. Rackham, Cambridge, Mass.: Harvard University Press (Loeb), 1934.

—*The Nicomachean Ethics*, trans. J.K. Thompson, 2nd edn, Harmondsworth: Penguin, 1976.

—*Metaphysics*, trans. John Warrington, London: Dutton, 1961.

—*The Metaphysics: Books 1–9*, trans. Hugh Tredennick, Cambridge, Mass.: Harvard University Press (Loeb), 1933.

—*Politics*, trans. T.A. Sinclair and Trevor J. Saunders, Harmondsworth: Penguin, 1979.

—*Politics*, trans. H. Rackham, Cambridge, Mass: Harvard University Press (Loeb), 1959.

—*Politica*, ed. P. Michaud-Quentin, *Aristoteles Latinus: Opera*, vol. 29, 1, ed. L. Minio-Paluello and G. Verbeke, Leiden: Brill, 1953– (1961).

—*Politicorum libri octo cum vetusta traslatione Gulielmi de Moerbeka*, ed. F. Susemihl, Leipzig: Teubner, 1872.

Augustine, St, *De Civitate Dei contra paganos*, ed. Bernard Dombart and Alphonse Kalb, 2 vols, Turnholt: Brepols, 1955. (*Corpus Christianorum, Series Latina* 47–48).

—*Concerning the City of God against the Pagans*, trans. Henry Bettenson, Harmondsworth: Penguin, 1972.

Benvenuto da Imola, *Comentum super Dantis Aldighierij Comoediam*, ed. J.P. Lacaita, 5 vols, Florence: Barbera, 1887.

Biblia Sacra iuxta Vulgatam versionem, ed. Robert Weber, 2 vols, Stuttgart: Württembergische Bibelanstalt, 1969.

—*The Holy Bible: Authorised (King James) Version*, London: Eyre and Spottiswoode, 1977.

Boccaccio, Giovanni, *Decameron*, ed. Cesare Segre, Milan: Mursia, 1966.

Bruni, Leonardo, *Vita di Dante, Le vite di Dante e del Petrarca*, ed. Antonio Lanza, Rome: Archivio Guido Izzi, (1987), 31–52.

Chronica de origine civitatis. Quellen und Forschungen zur Ältesten Geschichte der Stadt Florenz, ed. Otto Hartwig, 2 vols, Marburg: Halle, (1875), I. 35–69.

Cicero, *Rhetorici libri Duo qui vocantur De inventione*, ed. E. Stroebel, Stuttgart: Teubner, 1965.

—*De inventione, De optimo genere oratorum, Topica*, trans. H.M. Hubbell, Cambridge, Mass: Harvard University Press (Loeb), 1949.

—*De officiis*, trans. Walter Miller, Cambridge, Mass: Harvard University Press (Loeb), 1961.

Compagni, Dino, *Cronica*, ed. Gino Luzzatto, Turin: Einaudi, 1968.

Contini, Gianfranco, ed., *Poeti del Duecento*, 2nd edn. 2 vols, Milan: Mondadori-Ricciardi, 1995.

Daniel, Arnaut, *Le Canzoni*, ed. Maurizio Perugi, 2 vols, Milan: Ricciardi, 1978.

Della Lana, Jacopo, *Comedia di Dante degli Allagheri col Comento di Jacopo della Lana, Bolognese*, ed. Luciano Scarabelli, 3 vols, Bologna: Tipografia Regia, 1866–1867.

Folquet of Marseilles, *Le Troubadour Folquet de Marseilles*, ed. Stanislaw Stronski, Kraków: Spolka Wydawnicza Polska, 1910.

Francesco da Buti, *Commento di Francesco da Buti sopra la Divina Comedia di Dante Allighieri*, ed. Crescentino Giannini, Pisa: Nistri Lischi, 1989.

Giovanni da Viterbo, *Liber de Regimine Civitatem*, ed. Gaetano Salvemini, *Bibliotheca Juridica Medii Aevi*, ed. Augustus Gaudentius, 3 vols, Bologna: Monti, (1901), III, 215–280.

Guittone d'Arezzo, *Le Rime*, ed. Francesco Egidi, Bari: Laterza, 1940.

Guido da Pisa, *Guido da Pisa's Expositiones et Glose super Comediam Dantis: or Commentary on Dante's Inferno*, ed. Vincenzo Cioffari, Albany, NY: State University of New York Press, 1974.

Justinian, *The Digest of Justinian*, ed. and trans. Theodor Mommsen, Paul Kreuger, and Alan Watson, 4 vols, Philadelphia: University of Pennsylvania Press, 1985.

—*The Institutes of Justinian*, ed. and trans. J.A.C. Thomas, Amsterdam:

North-Holland, 1975.

Latini, Brunetto, *Li Livres dou Tresor*, ed. Francis J. Carmody, Berkeley: University of California Press, 1948.

—*Tesoretto*, ed. Julia Bolton Holloway, New York: Garland, 1981.

L'Ottimo Commento della Divina Commedia: Testo inedito d'un contemporaneo di Dante, ed. Alessandro Torri, 3 vols, Pisa: Capurro, 1827–1829.

Ovid, *Metamorphoses*, trans. Frank Justus Miller, 2 vols, Cambridge, Mass.: Harvard University Press (Loeb), 1976.

Sordello, *Le Poesie*, ed. Marco Boni. Bologna: Libreria Antiquaria Palmaverde, 1954.

Statius, *Thebaid*, trans. J.H. Mozley, Cambridge, Mass.: Harvard University Press (Loeb), 1928.

Villani, Giovanni, *Nuova cronica*, ed. Giuseppe Porta, 3 vols, Parma: Guanda, 1990–1991.

Virgil, *Aeneidos, I–VI*, ed. R.G. Austin, Oxford: Clarendon, 1971–1977.

—*Eclogues, Georgics, Aeneid, Minor Poems*, trans. H. Rushton Fairclough, 2 vols, Cambridge, Mass.: Harvard University Press (Loeb), 1986.

SECONDARY SOURCES

Alfie, F., 'For Want of a Nail: the Guerri-Lanza-Cursietti Argument regarding the *Tenzone*.' *Dante Studies* 116, (1998), 141–159.

Anselmi, Giano Mario, '*Il sangue e le piaghe: immagini della città partita.*' *Letture classensi* 15, (1986), 27–39.

Armour, Peter, *The Door of Purgatory. A Study of Multiple Symbolism in Dante's Purgatorio*, Oxford: Clarendon, 1983.

—*Dante's Griffin and the History of the World. A Study of the Earthly Paradise (Purgatorio, cantos xxix–xxxiii)*, Oxford: Clarendon, 1989.

—'Dante's *Contrapasso*: Contexts and Texts.' *Italian Studies* 55, (2000), 1–20.

Artifoni, Enrico, 'I podestà professionali e la fondazione retorica della politica comunale.' *Quaderni storici* n.s. 63, (1986), 687–719.

Auerbach, Erich, *Dante, Poet of the Secular World*, trans. Ralph Manheim, Chicago: University of Chicago Press, 1961.

—*Studi su Dante*, trans. Maria Luisa De Pieri Bonino and Dante Della Terza, Milan: Feltrinelli, 1966.

Barański, Zygmunt G., '*Comedía*: Notes on Dante, the Epistle to Cangrande and Medieval Comedy.' *Lectura Dantis* 8, (1991), 26–55.

—'*Sole nuovo, luce nuova.*' *Saggi sul rinnovamento culturale in Dante*, Turin: Scriptorium, 1996.

—*Dante e i segni. Saggi per una storia intellettuale di Dante Alighieri*, Naples: Liguori, 2000.

—'Three Notes on Dante and Horace.' *Reading Medieval Studies* 27, (Special Issue: *Current Trends in Dante Studies*, ed. C.E. Honess), (2001), 5–37.

Barbi, Michele, *Problemi di critica dantesca*, 2 vols, Florence: Sansoni, 1941.

Barnes, John C., 'Uno, nessuno e tanti: il Fiore attribuibile a chi?' *The Fiore in Context: Dante, France, Tuscany*, ed. Zygmunt G. Barański and Patrick Boyde, Notre Dame: University of Notre Dame Press, (1997), 331–362.

Barolini, Teodolinda, *Dante's Poets: Textuality and Truth in the Commedia*, Princeton, N.J.: Princeton University Press, 1984.

Bemrose, Stephen, *A New Life of Dante*, Exeter: Exeter University Press, 2000.

Bisson, Lillian M., 'Brunetto Latini as a Failed Mentor.' *Medievalia et Humanistica* n.s. 18, (1992), 1–15.

Bloch, R. Howard, *Medieval Misogyny and the Invention of Western Romantic Love*, Chicago: Chicago University Press, 1991.

Boase, Roger, *The Origin and Meaning of Courtly Love: A Critical Study of European Scholarship*, Manchester: Manchester University Press, 1977.

Boyde, Patrick, *Dante's Style in his Lyric Poetry*, Cambridge: Cambridge University Press, 1971.

—*Dante, Philomythes and Philosopher. Man in the Cosmos*, Cambridge: Cambridge University Press, 1981.

—*Perception and Passion in Dante's Comedy*, Cambridge: Cambridge University Press, 1993.

—'*Summus Minimusve Poeta*? Arguments For and Against Attributing the *Fiore* to Dante.' *The Fiore in Context: Dante, France, Tuscany*, ed. Zygmunt G. Barański and Patrick Boyde, Notre Dame: University of Notre Dame Press, (1997), 13–45.

—*Human Vices and Human Worth in Dante's Comedy*, Cambridge: Cambridge University Press, 2000.

Capitani, Ovidio, '*Monarchia*: il pensiero politico.' *Cultura e scuola* 13, (1965), 722–738.

Carpi, Umberto, 'La nobiltà di Dante (a proposito di *Paradiso* XVI).' *Rivista di letteratura italiana* 8, (1990), 229–260.

Catto, Jeremy, 'Florence, Tuscany and the World of Dante'. *The World of Dante: Essays on Dante and his Times*, ed. Cecil Grayson, Oxford: Clarendon, (1980), 1–17.

Charity, A.C., *Events and their Afterlife: The Dialectics of Christian Typology in the Bible and Dante*, Cambridge: Cambridge University Press, 1966.

Contini, Gianfranco, *Varianti e altra linguistica. Una raccolta di saggi (1938–1968)*, Turin: Einaudi, 1970.

Corti, Maria, *Dante a un nuovo crocevia*, Florence: Sansoni, 1981.

—*La felicità mentale. Nuove prospettive per Cavalcanti e Dante*, Turin: Einaudi, 1983.

—*Percorsi dell'invenzione. Il linguaggio poetico e Dante*, Turin: Einaudi, 1993.

Cox, Virginia, 'Ciceronian Rhetoric in Italy, 1260–1350.' *Rhetorica* 17, (1999), 239–288.

Cursietti, Mauro, *La falsa Tenzone di Dante con Forese Donati*, Anzio: De Rubeis, 1995.

Davidsohn, Robert, *Forschungen zur Geschichte Florenz*, 4 vols, Berlin: Mitter, 1908.

Davis, Charles T., *Dante and the Idea of Rome*, Oxford: Clarendon, 1957.

—'Il *buon tempo antico*.' *Florentine Studies: Politics and Society in Renaissance Florence*, ed. Nicolai Rubinstein, London: Faber and Faber (1968), 45–69.

—*Dante's Italy and Other Essays*, Philadelphia: University of Pennsylvania Press, 1984.

—'Topographical and Historical Propaganda in Early Florentine Chronicles and in Villani', *Medioevo e rinascimento* 2, (1988), 33–51.

Dell'Aquila, Michele, 'Gli spiriti amanti del cielo di Venere (*Paradiso canti VIII e IX*).' *Lectura Dantis (Potenza, 1986–87)*, ed. Michele Dell'Aquila et al., Potenza: Congedo, (1990), 45–55.

D'Entrèves, A. Passerin, *Dante as a Political Thinker*, Oxford: Clarendon, 1952.

De Robertis, Domenico, *Il libro della Vita nuova*, 2nd edn, Florence: Sansoni, 1970.

Di Pino, Guido, 'Firenze nell'immaginativa oltremondana di Dante.' *Miscellanea di studi danteschi in memoria di Silvio Pasquazi*, ed. Alfonso Paolella, Vincenzo Placella, and Giovanni Turco, 2 vols, Naples: Federico e Ardia, I, (1993), 325–339.

Donati, Claudio, *L'idea di nobiltà in Italia: secoli XIV–XVIII*, Bari: Laterza, 1988.

Durling, Robert M., and Ronald L. Martinez, *Time and the Crystal. Studies in Dante's Rime petrose*, Berkeley: University of California Press, 1990.

—'The Audience(s) of the *De vulgari eloquentia* and the *Petrose*', *Dante Studies* 110, (1992), 25–35.

Ellis, Steve, 'Controversial Comedy', *Lectura Dantis: Inferno. A Canto-by-Canto Commentary*, ed. Allen Mandelbaum, Anthony Oldcorn, and Charles Ross, Berkeley and Los Angeles: Univeristy of California Press, (1998), 287–296.

—*Enciclopedia Dantesca*, ed. Umberto Bosco, 6 vols, Rome: Istituto della Enciclopedia Italiana, 1970–1978.

Ercole, Franceso, 'Mario Chiaudano: *Dante e il Diritto Romano*', *Bullettino della Società Dantesca Italiana*, 20, (1913), 161–178.

Fanelli, Giovanni, *Firenze*, 5th edn, Rome: Laterza, 1993.

Fasoli, Gina, 'Bologna, Dante e i commentatori antichi', *Dante e Bologna nei tempi di Dante*, ed. Facoltà di Lettere e Filosofia, Università di Bologna, Bologna: Commissione per i testi di lingua, (1967), 251–263.

Ferrante, Joan M., *The Political Vision of the Divine Comedy*, Princeton, N.J.: Princeton University Press, 1984.

Figurelli, F., 'I canti di Cacciaguida', *Cultura e scuola*, 13, (1965), 634–661.

Foster, Kenelm, *The Two Dantes and Other Studies*, London: Darton, Longman and Todd, 1977.

Freccero, John, *Dante: The Poetics of Conversion*, ed. Rachel Jacoff, Cambridge, Mass.: Harvard University Press, 1986.

Gilson, Etienne, *Dante the Philosopher*, trans. David Moore, London: Sheed and Ward, 1948.

Gorni, Guglielmo, 'Il metafora di testo', *Strumenti critici* , 38, (1979), 18–32.

Goudet, Jacques, *La Politique de Dante*, Lyon: L'Hermès, (First published Paris, Montaigne, 1969), 1981.

Gozzadini, Giovanni, *Cronaca di Ronzano e memorie di Loderingo d'Andalò Frate Gaudente*, Bologna: Società tipografica Bolognese, 1851.

Havely, Nicholas R., 'The Self-Consuming City: Florence as Body-Politic in Dante's *Commedia*', *Deutsches Dante-Jahrbuch*, 61, (1986), 99–113.

Heers, Jacques, *Family Clans in the Middle Ages: A Study of Political and Social Structures in Urban Areas*, trans. Barry Herbert, Amsterdam: North-Holland, 1977.

Holmes, George, 'The Emergence of an Urban Ideology at Florence, *c*.1250–1450', *Transactions of the Royal Historical Society* 23 (5th series), (1973), 111–134.

Hollander, Robert, *Allegory in Dante's Commedia*, Princeton: Princeton University Press, 1969.
—*Il Virgilio dantesco: tragedia nella Commedia*, Florence: Olschki, 1983.
—'Il dibattito odierno attorno all'*Epistola a Cangrande*', *Pour Dante. Dante et l'Apocalypse. Lectures Humanistes de Dante*, ed. Bruno Pinchard, Paris: Champion, (2001), 255–268.

Holloway, Julia Bolton, *Twice-Told Tales: Brunetto Latini and Dante Alighieri*, New York: Peter Lang, 1993.

Honess [Rose], Claire E., 'Dante's Hell and the Medieval Idea of Jerusalem', *The Italianist*, 11, (1991), 7–28.
—'City, Garden, Wilderness. Insiders and Outsiders in Dante's *Commedia*', *New Readings*, 1, (1995), 5–40.

—'Expressing the Inexpressible: the Theme of Communication in the Heaven of Mars', *Lectura Dantis*, 14–15, (1994), 42–60.

—'*Di Fiorenza in popol giusto e sano': The Concept and Image of the City in Dante*, unpublished PhD thesis, University of Reading, 1997.

—'Feminine Virtues and Florentine Vices: Citizenship and Morality in *Paradiso* XV–XVII', *Dante and Governance*, ed. J.R. Woodhouse, Oxford: Clarendon, (1997), 102–120.

Hyde, J.K., *Society and Politics in Medieval Italy: The Evolution of the Civil Life, 1000–1350*, Basingstoke: Macmillan, 1973.

Iannucci, A., 'Virgil's Erichthean Descent and the Crisis of Intertextuality', *Forum Italicum*, 33, (1999), 13–26.

Jacoff, Rachel, 'Dante, Geremia e la problematica profetica', *Dante e la Bibbia*, ed. Giovanni Barblan, Florence: Olschki, (1988), 113–123.

Jones, Philip, *The Italian City-State: From Commune to Signoria*, Oxford: Clarendon, 1997.

Kantorowicz, Ernst H., *The King's Two Bodies: A Study in Mediaeval Political Theology*, Princeton, N.J.: Princeton University Press, 1957.

Kay, Richard, *Dante's Swift and Strong: Essays on Inferno XV*, Lawrence: Regents Press of Kansas, 1978.

Keen, Catherine, 'Signs of *fiorentinità*: the Baptistery and its Meanings in Dante's Florence', *Sguardi sull'Italia: Miscellanea dedicata a Francesco Villari*, ed. Gino Bedani, Zygmunt Barański, Anna Laura Lepschy, and Brian Richardson, Leeds: Society for Italian Studies, (1997), 29–42.

Keen, Maurice, 'The Debate over Nobility: Dante, Nicholas Upton and Bartolus', *The Culture of Christendom: Essays in Medieval History in Commemoration of Denis L.T. Bethel*, ed. Marc Anthony Meyer, London: Hambledon, (1993), 257–268.

Kent, D.V. and F.W., *Neighbours and Neighbourhood in Renaissance Florence. The District of the Red Lion in the Fifteenth Century*, Locust Valley, N.Y.: J.J. Augustin, 1982.

Kirkpatrick, Robin, 'The Principle of Courtesy in the *Convivio* and the *Comedy*', *Italian Studies*, 35, (1980), 25–30.

—'Courtesy and Imagination: A Study of *Purgatorio* XIV', *The Modern Language Review*, 76, (1981), 67–80.

—*Dante's Inferno: Difficulty and Dead Poetry*, Cambridge: Cambridge University Press, 1987.

—'Dante's Beatrice and the Politics of Singularity', *Texas Studies in Literature and Language* 32, (Special Issue: *Beatrice Dolce Memoria*,

1290–1990: Essays on the Vita Nuova and the Beatrice-Dante Relationship, ed. David Wallace), (1990), 101–119.

Kleinhenz, Christopher, 'Deceivers Deceived: Devilish Doubletalk in *Inferno* 21–23', *Quaderni d'italianistica* 10 (Special Issue: *Dante Today*, ed. Amilcare A. Iannucci), (1989), 133–156.

Ladner, Gerhart B., '*Homo Viator*: Mediaeval Ideas on Alienation and Order', *Speculum*, 42, (1967), 233–259.

Lansing, Carol, *The Florentine Magnates. Lineage and Faction in a Medieval Commune*, Princeton, N.J.: Princeton University Press, 1991.

Lansing, Richard, 'Dante's intended audience in the *Convivio*', *Dante Studies*, 110, (1992), 17–24.

Le Goff, Jacques, 'L'immaginario urbano nell'Italia medievale (secoli V–XV)', *Storia d'Italia. Annali 5: Il paesaggio*, ed. Cesare De Seta, Turin: Einaudi, 1982.

—*The Birth of Purgatory*, trans. Arthur Goldhammer, London: Scolar Press, 1984.

—*The Medieval Imagination*, trans. Arthur Goldhammer, Chicago: University of Chicago Press, 1988.

Lenkeith, Nancy, *Dante and the Legend of Rome*, London: Warburg Institute, 1952.

Leo, Ulrich, 'The Unfinished *Convivio* and Dante's Re-Reading of the *Aeneid*', *Mediaeval Studies*, 13, (1951), 41–64.

Limentani, Uberto, *Dante's Comedy: Introductory Readings of Selected Cantosh*. Cambridge: Cambridge University Press, 1985.

Lopes-Pegna, Mario, *Firenze dalle origini al medioevo*, Florence: Del Re, 1962.

Luscombe, David, 'City and Politics before the Coming of the *Politics*: Some Illustrations', *Church and City, 1000–1500: Essays in Honour of Christopher Brooke*, ed. David Abulafia, Michael Franklin and Miri Rubin, Cambridge: Cambridge University Press, (1992), 41–55.

McLaughlin, Martin, 'Pier della Vigna, Dante, and the Imagery of Empire', *Dante and Governance*, ed. John Woodhouse, Oxford: Clarendon, (1997), 121–136.

Mancusi-Ungaro, Donna, *Dante and the Empire*, New York: Lang, 1987.

Martines, Lauro, *Power and Imagination: City-States in Renaissance Italy*, New York: Knopf, 1979.

Maissen, Thomas, 'Attila, Totila e Carlo Magno fra Dante, Villani, Boccaccio e Malispini: per la genesi di due leggende erudite', *Archivio storico italiano*, 152, (1994), 561–639.

Mazzotta, Giuseppe, *Dante, Poet of the Desert. History and Allegory in the Divine Comedy*, Princeton, N.J.: Princeton University Press, 1979.

—*Dante's Vision and the Circle of Knowledge*, Princeton, N.J.: Princeton University Press, 1993.

Mengaldo, Pier Vincenzo, *Linguistica e retorica di Dante*, Pisa: Nistri-Lischi, 1978.

Milner, Stephen, 'Citing the *Ringhiera*: The Politics of Place and Public Address in Trecento Florence', *Italian Studies*, 55, (2000), 53–82.

Minio-Paluello, Lorenzo, 'Dante's Reading of Aristotle', *The World of Dante: Essays on Dante and his Times*, ed. Cecil Grayson, Oxford: Clarendon, (1980), 61–80.

Momigliano, Attilio, *Dante, Manzoni, Verga*, Messina: D'Anna, 1976.

Musa, Mark, '"E questo sia suggel ch'ogn' uomo sganni" (*Inferno* XIX, 21)', *Italica*, 41, (1964), 134–138.

Najemy, John M., *Corporation and Consensus in Florentine Electoral Politics, 1280–1400*, Chapel Hill: University of North Carolina Press, 1982.

—'Dante and Florence', *The Cambridge Companion to Dante*, ed. Rachel Jacoff, Cambridge: Cambridge University Press, 1993.

—'Brunetto Latini's "Politica"', *Dante Studies*, 112, (1994), 33–51.

Nardi, Bruno, *Nel mondo di Dante*, Rome: Edizioni di storia e letteratura, 1944.

—*Dal "Convivio" alla "Commedia". Sei saggi danteschi*, Rome: Istituto storico italiano per il Medio Evo, 1960.

—'Il preludio alla *Divina Commedia*', *L'Alighieri*, 4, (1963), 3–17.

—*Saggi di filosofia dantesca*, 2nd edn, Florence: La Nuova Italia, 1967.

Noakes, Susan, 'Dino Compagni and the Vow in S. Giovanni: *Inferno* XIX, 16–21', *Dante Studies*, 86, (1968), 41–63.

Padoan, Giorgio, *Il pio Enea, l'empio Ulisse*, Ravenna: Longo, 1977.

Parker, Deborah, 'Ideology and Cultural Practice: the Case of Dante's Treatment of Beatrice d'Este', *Dante Studies*, 111, (1993), 131–147.

Pertile, Lino, '*Canto – cantica – comedia e l'Epistola a Cangrande*', *Lectura Dantis* 8, (1991), 105–123.

—'Dante's *Comedy* beyond the *Stilnovo*', *Lectura Dantis* 13, (1993), 47–77.

—'Il nodo di Bonagiunta, le penne di Dante e il dolce stil novo', *Lettere italiane*, 46, (1994), 44–75.

—*La puttana e il gigante: dal Cantico dei Cantici al Paradiso Terrestre di Dante*, Ravenna: Longo, 1998.

—'Dante popolare', *Dante, poète et narrateur*, ed. M. Marietti and C. Perrus, Paris: Presses de la Sorbonne Nouvelle, (2001), 67–90.

Peters, Edward, '*Pars, parte*: Dante and an Urban Contribution to Political Thought', *The Medieval City*, ed. H.A. Miskimin, D. Herlihy and A.L. Udoritch, New Haven: Yale University Press, (1977), 113–140.

—'Human Diversity and Civil Society in *Paradiso* VIII', *Dante Studies*, 109, (1991), 51–70.

Pézard, André, *Dante sous la pluie de feu (Enfer, chant XV)*, Paris: Vrin, 1950.

Picone, Michelangelo, *Vita nuova e tradizione romanza*, Padua: Liviana, 1979.

Pietrobono, Luigi, 'Il canto degli ipocriti (XXIII dell'*Inferno*)', *Lectura Dantis romana*, AA.VV., Turin: Società editrice internazionale, 1961.

Quinones, Ricardo J., *Foundation Sacrifice in Dante's Commedia*, University Park, PA: Pennsylvania State University Press, 1994.

Raimondi, Ezio, *Metafora e storia: studi su Dante e Petrarca*, Turin: Einaudi, 1970.

Ramat, Raffaello, *Il mito di Firenze e altri saggi danteschi*, Messina: D'Anna, 1976.

Ricci, Pier Giorgio, '*Monarchia*', *Enciclopedia dantesca* vol. 3. Rome: Istituto dell'enciclopedia italiana, (1970), 993–1003.

Rubinstein, Nicolai, 'The Beginnings of Political Thought in Florence: a Study in Mediaeval Historiography', *Journal of the Warburg and Courtauld Institutes*, 5, (1942), 198–227.

Russo, Vittorio, *Esperienze e/di letture dantesche (tra il 1966 e il 1970)*, Naples: Liguori, 1971.

Ryan, Christopher J., 'Virgil's Wisdom in the *Divine Comedy*', *Medievalia et Humanistica* n.s., 11, (1982), 1–38.

Scaglione, Aldo D., *Knights at Court: Courtliness, Chivalry and Courtesy from Ottonian Germany to the Italian Renaissance*, Berkeley: University of California Press, 1991.

Schnapp, Jeffrey T., *The Transfiguration of History at the Center of Dante's Paradise*, Princeton, N.J.: Princeton University Press, 1986.

Scorrano, Luigi, 'Da Firenze a Firenze: vicenda politica nella *Commedia*', *Letture classensi*, 16, (1987), 51–68.

Scott, John, *Dante's Political Purgatory*, Philadelphia: University of Pennsylvania Press, 1996.

Singleton, Charles S., *Dante Studies 1: Commedia: Elements of Structure*, Cambridge, Mass.: Harvard University Press, 1954.
—*Dante Studies 2: Journey to Beatrice*, Cambridge, Mass.: Harvard University Press, 1958.
—'"In exitu Israel de Aegypto"', *Dante Studies*, 78, (1960), 1–24.

Skinner, Quentin, *The Foundations of Modern Political Thought: Volume 1: The Renaissance*, Cambridge: Cambridge University Press, 1978.
—'Ambrogio Lorenzetti: The Artist as Political Philosopher', *Proceedings of the British Academy*, 72, (1986), 1–56.

Sorbelli, Albano, 'I teorici del reggimento comunale', *Bullettino dell'Istituto storico italiano per il medio evo*, 59, (1944), 31–136.

Tavoni, Mirko, 'Effrazione battesimale tra i simoniaci (*Inferno* XIX, 13–21)', *Rivista di letteratura italiana*, 10, (1992), 457–523.

Tierney, Brian, *Church Law and Constitutional Thought in the Middle Ages*, London: Variorum, 1979.

Toscano, Tobia R., 'Memoria storica e progetto politico nei canti di Cacciaguida (canti XV–XVII)', *Lectura Dantis (Potenza, 1986–1987)*, ed. Michele Dell'Aquila et al., Potenza: Congedo, (1990), 57–93.

Toynbee, Paget, *Dante Studies and Researches*, London: Methuen, 1902.

Trexler, Richard, *Public Life in Renaissance Florence*, New York: Academic Press, 1980.

Tulone, Giampiero, 'Gli "invidïosi veri" nella *Commedia* e nelle fonti dantesche', *Lettere italiane*, 52, (2000), 345–378.

Ullman, Walter, *Scholarship and Politics in the Middle Ages*, London: Variorum, 1978.

Vasoli, Cesare, 'Averroè', *Enciclopedia dantesca* vol. 1, Rome: Istituto dell'enciclopedia italiana, (1970), 473–481.

Waley, Daniel, *The Italian City-Republics*, 3rd edn, London: Longman, 1988.

Weissman, Ronald F.E., *Ritual Brotherhood in Renaissance Florence*, New York: Academic Press, 1982.

NOTES

INTRODUCTION

1 See the essay, '*Dante come personaggio-poeta della Commedia*', in Contini, 1970, pp. 334–361.

2 As Robin Kirkpatrick notes, 'it is hard, in the case of the *Commedia*, to speak (as modern critics tend to do) of an impersonal construct, where the historical author is absent or irrelevant': 1987, p. xii. In spite of this, biographical data is tantalisingly scarce for much of Dante's life, especially for his career in exile. A good biographical study is Bemrose, 2000.

3 The composition of the *Vita Nova* is normally dated to between 1292 and 1295: Bemrose, 2000, pp. 17–20.

4 Dante's direct involvement in politics began in 1295, when he was able to enroll in the Guild of Physicians and Apothecaries and so became eligible for public office. His political career in Florence ended with the sentence of exile pronounced in January 1302. See Bemrose, 2000, pp. 41–63.

5 For discussion of scholarship on Dante's theoretical writing on politics, see Chapter 2.

6 Ferrante, 1984, shares my conviction of the primary importance of the *Commedia* in assessing Dante's political thought, although my approach differs substantially from hers. Honess, 1997, *Di Fiorenza* provides an important study whose method and conclusions are far closer to my own.

7 Pertile, 2001, pp. 71–85.

8 There is a vast bibliography on the notion of *commedia* in Dante: the poet's own clearest comments on comic genre occur state that '*si vero comice [canenda videntur], tunc quandoque mediocre, quandoque humile vulgare sumatur*' ('if indeed one desires to sing in the comic style, then

sometimes the middle and sometimes the humble form of the vernacular is to be used': *DVE* II. iv. 6). See, for a general introduction,
Auerbach, 1966, pp.165–173; Barański, 1991, 1996, 2000; Pertile, 1991,
1993, 2001; Hollander, 1983.

9 D'Entrèves, 1952, p.11.
10 Quinones, 1994. Other recent, negative studies of Florence include
Anselmi, 1986; Havely, 1986; Scorrano, 1987; Ferrante also views Florence
predominantly as a model of corruption, although she makes room
briefly for the virtuous Florence of Cacciaguida: 1984, pp.281–286.
11 Florence is viewed from both negative and positive angles in this
study, especially in chps 4–6. Honess, 1997, 'Feminine Virtues' offers an
excellent study of the positive aspect of Florence in *Par.* XV–XVII; see
also Ramat, 1976; Toscano, 1990.
12 Armour, 1989; Davis, 1957, and see also 1984; Lenkeith, 1952; Scott,
1996.
13 Auerbach, 1961; Ferrante, 1984; Mazzotta, 1979.
14 Honess, 1997 *Di Fiorenza*: I understand that this study is to be published shortly.
15 Le Goff, 1982, pp.7–8.
16 Le Goff, 1988, pp.47–59.

I — DANTE AND HIS CITY

1 *Ep.* II, III,V,VI,VII; see also the references to exile in *Ep.* XII.
2 For details, including visits of various lengths to Arezzo, Forlì, Lucca,
Mantua, Milan, Padua, Pisa, Rome and Venice, see Bemrose, 2000.
3 Catto, 1980, provides an excellent brief outline on the foregoing. On
vernacular poets, see Barolini, 1984 (esp. ch. 6); on intellectual culture,
Davis, 1984 (esp. ch. 6); on urban expansion and new building, Fanelli,
1993 (esp. ch. 4).
4 The basic outline of the story appears in the oldest surviving history
of Florence, the *Chronica de origine civitatis* (ed. Hartwig, 1875), dated
to 1228 by Maissen, 1994, p.572. Rubinstein, 1942, remains a fundamental study of the myths of origin. A reliable study of the historical
Roman origins of Florence is Lopes-Pegna, 1962.
5 The future site of Florence is named '*villa Camartiae*' or 'Villa
Camarza' in the early Latin and vernacular redactions of the legend,
and the name Florence only chosen after the senate has refused
Caesar's request that the city be named Caesaria (vernacular Cesaria):
Chronica, pp.54–56.

6 Maissen, 1994, pp. 566–570; Rubinstein, 1942, p. 203.

7 *Chronica*, pp. 57–59.

8 *Chronica*, pp. 59–60. See Davis, 1988.

9 Text (often attributed to Brunetto Latini) from Davidsohn, 1908, IV. 498.

10 Villani here may be echoing Dante, *Par.* XV. 111: see Davis, 1984, p. 84.

11 Catherine Keen, 1997; Maissen, 1994.

12 *Cronica* I. 1, above.

13 Villani, *Nuova cronica*, II. 1, IV. 1, V. 7, etc. See Maissen, 1994, p. 573; Rubinstein, 1942, p. 209.

14 The relevant literature is vast. Some useful general studies include Trexler, 1980; Weissman, 1982. On aristocratic families, see Heers, 1977; Carol Lansing, 1991; on neighbourhood structures, D.V. and F.W. Kent, 1982; on guilds, Najemy, 1982.

15 Heers, 1977, pp. 144–154, 179–181; Martines, 1979, p. 35.

16 Compagni, *Cronica*. I. ii. On Dante's use of this tradition, see Najemy 1993, pp. 83–87.

17 Najemy, 1993, pp. 87–88.

18 Najemy, 1982, offers a clear and detailed analysis of Florentine governmental experiments for the period from 1280. A compelling first-hand account of Florentine politics in the same period is provided by Compagni, an active politician (1282–1301) and like Dante White (see below) in his political sympathies, in his *Cronica*.

19 Bemrose, 2000, pp. 41–43.

20 Bemrose, 2000, pp. 43–47; Najemy, 1993, pp. 81–82.

21 Bemrose, 2000, pp. 47–63.

22 Hyde, 1973, pp. 63–64, 84–87; Jones, 1997, pp. 335–343; Skinner, 1978, pp. 7–9; Waley, 1988, pp. 33–34.

23 Bartolus of Sassoferrato, *Commentaries on the First Part of the Old Digest*, in Skinner, 1978, p. 12; see Skinner's longer discussion, pp. 9–12.

24 Jones, 1997, pp. 459–466; Skinner, 1978, pp. 27–28; but cf. Holmes, 1973, pp. 111–114, 123–129.

25 Milner, 2000, pp. 71–74.

26 See Artifoni, 1986; Skinner, 1978, 1986; Sorbelli, 1944.

27 On the dating of Giovanni da Viterbo, see Najemy's summary of different arguments, 1994, p. 35. Holloway follows the complex history of the *Tresor's* translation(s) into Florentine and other vernaculars, 1993, see pp. 9–11, 64, 109, 130–132; on pp. 149, 429, she suggests the young Dante as the copyist of a Florentine MS, dated to *c.* 1285–1286.

28 Artifoni, 1986, p. 712; Skinner, 1978, p. 40; but cf. Sorbelli, 1944, p. 99.

29 Cicero, *De inventione* I. 1. Perhaps thinking along similar lines, Giovanni requires that any candidate for *Podestà* '*sit eloquentissimus et bonus orator*' ('be most eloquent and a good speaker': 11).

30 Skinner, 1986, pp. 18–20.

31 On the importance of Ciceronian rhetoric in the adversarial context of *comune* politics, and its problematic relation to the ethical theory of *peccata linguae*, see Cox, 1999.

32 Najemy, 1994; Skinner, 1986.

33 Similarly, the model letter Brunetto provides for a city to send its chosen podestaral candidate stresses that law and government place constraints on the freedom natural to humanity, but acknowledges that '*covient il autresi par necessité que nature fust sous justice et ke franchise obeist a jugement*' ('so it was imposed by necessity that nature should come under justice and freedom should obey the laws': III. lxxvii. 1).

34 '*Et si comme les gens et les habitations sont diverses, et li us et li droit sont divers parmi le monde, tot autresi ont il diverses manieres de signories; car dés lors ke Nembrot li jaians sorprist premierement le roiaume dou païs, et ke covoitise sema la guerre et les morteus haines entre les gens dou siecle, il covint as homes k'il eussent signors de plusors manieres, selonc ce que li un furent esleu a droit et li autre i furent par lor pooir*' ('And since people and places are different, and custom and law are different throughout the world, just so there are different kinds of government; for ever since Nimrod the giant first undertook kingship of the state, and since envy sowed war and mortal hatred among the people of the earth, it has been necessary that humanity have governments of several kinds, some being elected by law and others won by force': III. lxxiii. 3).

35 *Tresor*, III. lxxxii. 9; *De Regimine*, 83.

36 Najemy, 1994, p. 36. The Italian translation has traditionally been attributed to Bono Giamboni, but it was probably made by Brunetto himself: Holloway, 1993, pp. 9–10, 130–132.

37 Armour, 1983, pp. 8–9, and Bisson, 1992, pp. 3–5, offer brief summaries of the main critical theories, as background to their own interpretations.

38 The episode chimes interestingly with the legends of Florentine destruction and reconstruction in antiquity, Farinata acting like a Roman against the hostility to Florence of the Fiesolan or Totila figures of his faction-allies. The Uberti however, were normally associated with civic destruction in popular legend, for instance in the Bondelmonti murder story, and Villani even alludes to a legend that the Uberti were descendants of Florence's original enemy, Catiline (a theory Villani himself rejects: *Nuova cronica* I. 41).

39 There is no comment on the public life of the third Florentine, Jacopo Rusticucci, although he was an important Guelf leader in the 1250s and 1260s, but only on his domestic misfortune of possessing a *'fiera moglie'* ('fierce wife': l.45).

40 The tombs of Farinata and the heretics are heated by flames (*Inf.* IX. 118–120); Brunetto and the others are rained on by flames of fire (XIV. 28–39).

2 – THEORIES OF GOVERNMENT, CITIZENSHIP AND HAPPINESS

1 *Vita di Dante*, ed. Lanza, 1987, p.36. Bruni is translating from a Latin original: the authenticity of the document is naturally hard to prove, but widely accepted.

2 The reference occurs when Dante states that free will is God's greatest gift to man, *'sicut in Paradiso* Comedie *iam dixi'* ('as I have already said in the Paradiso of the *Comedy'*: I. xii. 6). In order to provide a composition date either close to *Cvo's*, or close to the Italian campaigns of Emperor Henry VII (1310–1313), scholars have in the past suggested that the words could be an interpolation either by Dante, in revising his text, or by a later scribe; recent editors however accept the reference as authentic, and consequently assign the treatise a fairly late composition date (often *c.*1316/17). See the editions of Shaw, 1995, pp.xxxviii–xxxix, and Kay, 1998, pp.xx–xxxi.

3 The literature on this aspect of Dante's political thought, and on the broader lines of the controversy, is vast. Most critical editions of the texts provide useful commentary, but see also: on Church and empire, Kantorowicz, 1957; Tierney, 1979; Ullman, 1978; on Dante's place in relation to the wider debate, Barbi, 1941; Capitani, 1965; Davis, 1957; D'Entrèves, 1952; Gilson, 1948; Goudet, 1981; Mancusi-Ungaro, 1987; Nardi, 1944, 1960, 1967; Ricci, 1970.

4 Barbi, 1941; Gilson, 1948; Goudet, 1981; Kay, 1998; Shaw, 1995; Vinay, 1950; but cf. Nardi, 1960; D'Entrèves, 1952.

5 Bartolus's tract is entitled *De dignitatibus* (*On honours*). See Donati, 1988, pp.3–4; Maurice Keen, 1993.

6 In *Cvo* too, Aristotle is *'lo Filosofo' par excellence*; in *Inf.* IV. 131 he is identified as *'il maestro di color che sanno'* ('the master of those who know').

7 Davis, 1984, chps 8–10; Skinner, 1978, pp.49–53; 1986, pp.4–5. On Dante's personal knowledge of Aristotelian texts, see Minio-Paluello, 1980.

8 On Thomism/Aristotelianism, see Busnelli and Vandelli's edition of the *Cvo*, 1934–1938. Later discussions modifying (sometimes dramatically) the picture of an 'Aristotelian' Dante include Barański, 2000 (on Neoplatonism); Boyde, 1981, 1993, 2000; Corti, 1981, 1983 (on 'radical Aristotelianism'); Gilson, 1948; Mazzotta, 1993; Nardi, 1960, 1967.

9 See, for instance, Barański, 2000; Pertile, 2001.

10 Leo, 1951.

11 Aristotle, *Metaphysics* I. i, *Eth*. I. vii.

12 See the relevant commentaries of Kay, Ricci, Shaw, and Vinay, *ad loc*; on Averroes, see Boyde, 1981, pp.276–279; Vasoli, 1970; Corti, 1981, 1983.

13 Aristotle, *Pol.*, I. ii, *Eth*. I. vii.

14 Aristotle, *Pol.*, I. ii.

15 Aristotle, *Pol*. III. ix.

16 The concept of the two goals of humanity represents another area where Vernani and others have debated Dante's possible Averroism: see Kay, Ricci, Shaw, Vinay, *ad loc*.

17 The authority of philosophers is discussed in *Cvo* IV. vi; the nature and limits of imperial authority, in IV. ix.

18 *Mon*. II. i. 2.

19 Vinay's commentary, *ad loc*.

20 The neologism '*politizare*', coined by William of Moerbecke in his Latin translation of Aristotle's *Pol.*, was adopted by both Albert the Great and Thomas Aquinas in their commentaries on the text: on its use and meanings, see Luscombe, 1992, pp.48–49; Ullman, 1978, p.113. Its appearance at *Mon*. I. xii. 9 is discussed by Nardi, 1944, pp.104–106.

21 Aristotle, *Pol.*, III. vii; also IV. ii, iv–vi, x.

22 Arisotle, *Pol.*, III. iv; also IV. vii. Shaw, *ad loc.*, notes that the direct citation may come from Aquinas's commentary on *Eth*.

23 As we saw earlier, this notion proved of particular interest to Bartolus; Donati, 1988, pp.3–4.

24 Dante specifies the conditions implied in the phrase '*l'anima ben posta*' in IV. xx. 8 and IV. xxi. 4–8; the two kinds of virtue, moral and theological, are discussed in IV. xvii and IV. xxi–xxii. As will shortly be seen, I use the pronoun 'him' advisedly: Dante offers only a strictly limited description of female moral virtues.

25 *Eth*. III. vii; though see Vasoli and De Robertis's edition *ad loc.* for discussion of the extent to which Dante deviates from Aristotle. In Italian, the virtues appear as: *Fortezza, Temperanza, Liberalitade, Magnificenza, Magnanimitade, Amativa d'onore, Mansuetudine, Affabilitade, Veritade, Eutrapelia, Giustizia*.

26 Dante gives a reasonably precise reference for his Aristotelian source –
'*nel secondo de l'Etica*', i.e. *Eth.* II. i – but editors note the difficulty of
finding any passage in Augustine that matches Dante's words closely:
Vasoli and de Robertis, *ad loc.*, note Corti's suggestion that Dante may
be alluding to an Augustinian reference in Albert the Great's commentary on the *Eth.*

27 The image also recalls Brunetto Latini's narrative poem, the *Tesoretto*
(*Little Treasure*), at the beginning of which the narrator's meditation on
Florence's loss of civic glory and values leads him to lose his way in a
'*selva diversa*' (l.190). Along the journey that follows, he undergoes
periods of instruction from various allegorical figures: Nature tells
him about natural human nobility; the Virtues, about themselves and
subsidiary qualities like *cortesia*, and about the coincidences and distinctions between social and ethical nobility.

28 Nardi comments on the blend of classical with chivalric values in *Cvo*
IV, which he sees as anticipating the prescriptions on noble conduct of
Castiglione's *Cortegiano*: 1960, p.33.

29 Twenty-five was the age set by Roman law when children could
expect emancipation from fathers or guardians.

30 More precisely, Dante specifies that Aeneas represents this age in one
section of the *Aen.*, Books IV, V, and VI: *Cvo* IV. xxvi. 8.

31 This summary is far too schematic to do justice to the vast range of
the concept of *amore* in medieval literatures: for further recent discussion (from varying perspectives), see Bloch, 1991; Boase, 1977;
Scaglione, 1991; on Dante's reception of the tradition, see Barolini,
1984; Corti, 1983; De Robertis, 1970; Durling and Martinez, 1990;
Picone, 1979.

32 Kirkpatrick, 1980, p.29; also *idem*, 1981, an article that comments on
the implications of Dante's use of the term *cortesia* (paired once again
with *amore*, l.110) in *Purg.* XIV's denunciation of political corruption
in contemporary Italy. It also offers a brief but illuminating discussion
of *Cvo*'s pairing of '*cortesia e onestade*': 1981, pp.69–70.

33 Busnelli and Vandelli comment, *ad loc.*, that Dante's definition of *lealtade*, often an equivalent of 'loyalty', suggests familiarity with its etymological links to the Latin term *legalitas*.

34 On the Ciceronian virtues, see Skinner, 1986. In the original list of
virtues, Dante notes that Aristotle classifies prudence as an intellectual
virtue, though it is often considered a moral one (*Cvo* IV. xvii. 8). In
discussing the differences between the soul's practical and its specula-
tive capacities, he lists as practical the traditional quartet of prudence,

temperance, fortitude, and justice: *Cvo* IV. xxii. 11. His division of the ages thus balances the Ciceronian moral virtues equally between youth and age, but assigns more of the Aristotelian virtues to age, suggesting that his categories have an element of fluidity – see, too, the comments on liberality below.

35 Following the traditional Ciceronian definition, prudence is summed up as comprising memory of past events, awareness of present ones, and foresight of future ones: '*buona memoria de le vedute cose, buona conoscenza de le presenti e buona provedenza de le future*' (IV. xxvii. 5).

36 Justice is specified as the intended subject of the penultimate, i.e. fourteenth, book of the treatise (IV. xxvii. 11). Scholars often assume that Dante would have focused the discussion around the *canzone* that will be discussed in my next chapter, *Tre donne intorno al cor mi son venute* (*Three ladies have come round my heart*): see Foster and Boyde's edition of the *Rime*, 1967, II. 282.

37 Ovid, *Metam.* VII. 507–660.

38 Famously, all of the figures illustrating *Senio* will in the *Commedia* be assigned places in hell: Lancelot in *Inf.* V, among the lustful; Guido da Montefeltro, in *Inf.* XXVII, among the fraudulent counsellors; Marcia, in Limbo, *Inf.* IV (although Cato himself is the guardian of ante-Purgatory, *Purg.* I). The only one to speak, Guido da Montefeltro, reveals that his political conduct prior to entering the Franciscan order was dubious, and that he continued to act deceptively even afterwards.

3 – RHETORIC, POLITICS AND EXILE

1 Barański, 1996, pp.45–57, 62; Richard Lansing, 1992.

2 Auerbach, 1961, pp.76–81, 97–98; Barański, 1996, pp.34–35, 69–77, 106–119.

3 Pertile, 2001, pp.82–84.

4 The *DVE* is generally dated to *c.*1303–1305. It was probably composed alongside the *Cvo* (*c.*1303/04–*c.*1307/08), perhaps begun slightly later and abandoned earlier: see *Cvo* I. v. 10.

5 In the book as it stands, there is virtually no consideration of prose composition: Dante simply invites prose authors to take poets' use of the vernacular as a model (*DVE* II. i. 1). Mengaldo surveys the treatise's relationship to medieval manuals from both the rhetorical tradi-

tion of the *ars dictandi/ars arengandi*, and that of the *poetrie*: after noting debts to such rhetorical traditions, Mengaldo stresses the originality of Dante's treatment and conclusions (1978, pp.44–60); see also Barański, 1996, pp.115–119. The latter elsewhere argues that Dante's programme in the *DVE* deliberately avoids the Ciceronian material central to dictaminal tradition, and underscores its ties to an original classical source in Horace: 2001, pp.15, 19–23.

6   *De vulgari*, ed. Botterill 1996, p.xv; see also Durling, 1992, p.33.

7   For Dante's calculation of the number and variety of what he terms the '*primas et secundarias et subsecundarias vulgaris Ytalie variationes*' ('primary, and secondary, and still further subordinate varieties of the Italian vernacular'), see *DVE* I. x. 7.

8   Barański, 1996, pp.63–68, 89–90.

9   Dante discusses Tuscan forms (with examples from Florence, Pisa, Lucca, Siena, and Arezzo), in I. xiii. 2–5. On Bologna, see I. ix. 4, I. xv. 2–6; on Sicily and Apulia, I. xii. 2–9; Sardinia receives a perfunctory mention at I. xi. 7.

10 For instance, Dante's gloss on the *Cvo*'s first *canzone*: '*la bontade è ne la sentenza, e la bellezza è ne l'ornamento de le parole; [...] con ciò sia cosa che la bontade di questa canzone fosse malagevole a sentire per le diverse persone che in essa s'inducono a parlare, dove si richeggiono molte distinzioni, e la bellezza fosse agevole a vedere, parvemi mestiere che per li altri si ponesse più mente a la bellezza che a la bontade*' ('the goodness [of the *canzone*] lies in its meaning, and its beauty in the elegance of its words; and since the beauty of this *canzone* was hard to understand because of the different voices that are made to speak in it, which need to be carefully distinguished, while the beauty is easy to perceive, it seemed to me that I should invite many [readers] to pay more attention to its beauty than its goodness': *Cvo* II. xi. 4–5). See also Boyde's list of the numerous occasions in the prose of the *VN* where Dante 'congratulates himself on having veiled some point in mystery' in his original lyric composition: 1971, p.120 n.2.

11 Barański, 1996, esp. chps 1–2; Pertile, 2001.

12 Like *DVE, Cvo* also devotes consideration to the differences between Latin and vernacular languages. Famously, the two treatises, despite their close composition dates, differ in their assessment of the relative nobility of Latin and the vernacular (see *DVE* I. i. 4, *Cvo* I. v. 7). Both, however, agree that the vernacular can possess qualities of great nobility and refinement.

13 On debates over angelic and animal speech in the Middle Ages, see Barański, 1996, pp.96–100.

14 In this opening discussion, Dante treats language as an arbitrary construct, where meaning is assigned '*ad placitum*' ('by convention': I. iii.
3); an interesting position in view of the statements on Adamic language that follow. Botterill comments briefly on how Dante's analysis
shows 'a number of fascinating premonitions' of twentieth-century,
Saussurian semiotic theory, but warns against over-reading the apparent similarities (*De vulgari,* ed. Botterill, p. xix).

15 On Dante's use of Genesis, especially the stories of Adam and Babel, in
the first nine chapters of *DVE*, see Barański, 1996, pp.93–114, 119–128.

16 Barański, 1996, pp.103–104; Mengaldo, 1978, pp.137–139. Dante's statement is normally interpreted as implying that God created a language
ready-made for Adam to speak; but see Corti's analysis of the two key
terms *forma* and *concreata* in this section, and her conclusion that while
God created Adam's language ability, Adam himself constructed his own
language, a language that was both natural (a vernacular) and universal
(like a *gramatica*): 1993, chp. 4, esp. pp.87–91, 107–112.

17 The phrasing is elliptical, but appears to imply the final extinction of
Adamic language in the first century AD. In *Par.* (VII. 19–120), Dante
offers a more detailed account of the widely held medieval view of
Titus's conquest of Jerusalem as divine retribution for the Jewish
rejection of Jesus as Messiah.

18 Babel remains an example of divine retribution: the abruptness and
simultaneity of its linguistic change and confusion are miraculous
signs of God's displeasure.

19 Contini, 1970, p.343; see also Barański, 1996, pp.113–114.

20 Durling, 1992, pp.31–32. Dante's survey of the different professions
involved in the Babel enterprise includes architects, overseers, engi-
neers, stonemasons and quarry-workers: *DVE* I. vii. 6–7.

21 The chapter states that '*trilingues ergo doctores in multis conveniunt, et
maxime in hoc vocabulo quod est "amor"*' ('learned writers in all three
vernaculars agree, then, on many words, and especially on the word
"love"': I. ix. 3). Dante's description of the vernacular lyricists as '*doctores*' stresses their learning and status, an important preliminary for the
arguments he will later develop regarding 'illustrious' Italian. His
interest in the languages of *oc* and *oïl* remains exclusively concerned
with their literary usage, both here and in the comparative evaluation
of Occitan, Old French and Italian literatures in his next chapter (I. x.
2). See Mengaldo, 1978, pp.76–78.

22 In more polished, 'Tuscanised' usage, the phrase might run: '*Messer, cosa
dite?*'.

23 Both the Sicilian and the Venetian phrases are lifted from verse, and Mengaldo also finds contemporary prose analogies for many of Dante's example phrases, leading him to argue that Dante's analysis of regional usage is rooted primarily in the widespread medieval taste for parody or imitation of dialect practice: 1978, pp. 150–156.

24 The 'municipal' poets Dante names are: Guittone d'Arezzo, Bonagiunta da Lucca, Gallo of Pisa, Mino Mocato of Siena, and Brunetto Latini of Florence; the few who earn his praise are *'Guidonem, Lapum et unum alium, Florentinos, et Cynum Pistoriensem'* ('Guido, Lapo, and one other, all from Florence, and Cino, from Pistoia': I. xiii. 4) – the selections of worthwhile poetry later in the text enable the Florentines to be identified as Guido Cavalcanti, Lapo Gianni, and Dante himself.

25 Durling, 1992, pp. 31–32.

26 Dante's general approval of the Hohenstaufen's determined opposition to Caesaropapism, and of their imperial vision, is evident from numerous comments on thirteenth-century Italian politics in the *Comm.*; theologically, however, the poem accuses both of serious errors, placing Frederick among hell's heretics (*Inf.* X. 119), and Manfred among the repentant excommunicates of ante-purgatory, where he confesses that *'orribil furon li peccati miei'* ('my sins were horrible': *Purg.* III. 121).

27 See the essay *'I trionfi del volgare: Dante e il plurilinguismo'*, Barański, 1996, pp. 41–77.

28 On the threefold soul, see *Purg.* XXV. 51–75; also Boyde, 1981, pp. 273–279.

29 The *canzone* is normally dated *c.* 1302–1304. Some suggest that the main body of the text was composed earlier, perhaps immediately after Dante's exile, making the second *congedo* – which has a different metrical pattern, and is absent from some manuscripts – a later addition: see notes *ad loc.* in Contini's 1984 edn, pp. 452–453. Foster and Boyde's edition offers convincing arguments in favour of 1304: 1967, II. 280–282. There are two promises in the *Cvo* that justice will form the theme of its fourteenth book (I. xii. 12, IV. xxvii. 11); since this is Dante's only *canzone* on justice, it seems probable that he intended its inclusion as the text occasioning the relevant philosophical commentary.

30 *DVE* I. xvii. 2, *Mon.* I. xi. 8–20.

31 The ladies' lament reveals that *'tempo fu già nel quale, | secondo il lor parlar, furon dilette; | or sono a tutti in ira ed in non cale'* ('there once was a time, according to their account, when they were loved; now they are treated with hostility and indifference by all': ll. 13–15). Love in turn

reveals that '*Larghezza e Temperanza e l'alte nate | del nostro sangue men-dicando vanno*' ('Generosity and Temperance and the others born of our blood go begging': ll.63–64). The virtues, however, belong to '*l'et-terna rocca*' ('the eternal fortress': l.69); with the passing of time, mortals will rediscover the qualities they currently neglect (ll.65–72).

32 On the three ladies and the source of the Nile, Foster and Boyde, 1967, II. 285–288; on justice in humanity before and after the 'Fall', Singleton, 1958, pp. 222–248.

33 Ovid, *Metam.*, I. 89–150. The virgin goddess of justice appears also in Virgil, *Ec.* IV. 5–6, paraphrased in *Purg.* XXII. 70–72; see also *Mon.* I. xi. 1. On medieval views of the relationship between Venus and Astrea – which occasionally elided the two figures – see Peters, 1991, pp.53–59. Dante's Matelda asserts (subject to a '*forse*', 'perhaps', l.141) the figuring of Eden in the classical myth of the Golden Age, *Purg.* XXVIII. 139–141.

34 Mazzotta, 1993, p.180. Foster and Boyde suggest, following Tommaseo, that Love's two arrows represent respectively love of goodness and hatred of evil: 1967, II. 288.

35 Boyde discusses Dante's blend of 'proper' and allegorical references to exile: 1971, p.148.

36 Dante does not specify the nature of the fault of which he has – per-haps – been guilty; it may be moral or theological, but the political matter of the poem as a whole, and especially of this final stanza and the second *congedo*, makes a political interpretation likely. Foster and Boyde, 1967, II. 289–291.

37 Boyde calls this 'surely [...] the most elaborate and the most intrinsi-cally difficult of all the concepts to be "signified indirectly" in Dante's lyric poetry', in his classic study of Dante's lyric style: 1971, p.147.

4 – MUNICIPAL LIMITATIONS

1 Ferrante, 1984, pp.47, 60–73; Havely, 1986, pp.107–111; Honess, 1995, pp.9–10, 17–25.

2 Ferrante, 1984, pp.46–47, also pp.60–75, 132–137; see also Di Pino, 1993, p.25.

3 Honess, 1995, pp.10–14; Le Goff, 1988, pp.47–59; Freccero, 1986, pp.11–15.

4 Singleton, 1954.

5   The poem is called polysemous ('*polisemos*'), as having both a literal
    and an allegorical meaning, in the *Epistle to Cangrande* (*Ep.* XIII. 20).
    Dante's authorship of the letter is debated: Hollander (who takes the
    letter as authentic) provides a useful survey of the key points of the
    arguments (2001). For Dante's views on allegory, see also *Cvo* II. i.
    2–14. The secondary literature on the question of Dante's views on
    and use of allegory is vast: see e.g. Barański, 1996, 2000; Charity, 1966;
    Hollander, 1969; Mazzotta, 1979, esp. chp. 6; Singleton, 1954, 1960.

6   Nardi, 1963, p.9; this reading however risks imposing too schemati-
    cally political a sense on the poem as a whole.

7   Dante frequently applies the political terminology of earthly states to
    all three regions of the afterlife: in these introductory *canti* Virgil twice
    speaks of paradise as a city (*Inf.* I. 126, 128), and also describes God as
    the emperor of paradise (*Inf.* I. 124); later in the *cantica*, Satan will be
    described as '*lo 'mperador del doloroso regno*' ('the emperor of the woeful
    kingdom': *Inf.* XXXIV. 28). Ferrante, 1984, p.46.

8   See for instance, Iannucci, 1999; Kay, 1978.

9   On both positive and negative aspects of these cities, see Armour,
    1989; Davis, 1957; Honess, [Rose] 1991, 1997 *Di Fiorenza*; Ferrante,
    1984; Lenkeith, 1952; Quinones, 1994; Schnapp, 1986.

10 On Dante's Limbo, Foster, 1977; Padoan, 1977.

11 Honess, 1995, pp.17–22.

12 Barański, 1996, p.87.

13 McLaughlin, 1997, pp.121–130.

14 Ovid, *Metam.* I. 89–150; Virgil tells how Saturn's golden rule was trans-
    ferred from Crete to Italy, *Aen.* VIII. 319–327.

15 *Daniel* 2. 31–35: the interpretation points towards perfection in a
    future age, in the Messiah's kingdom (vv. 44–45). See Mazzotta's
    detailed analysis of the Old Men, 1979, pp.23–37.

16 In the Malebolge area of lower hell the term '*contrapasso*' appears (*Inf.*
    XXVIII. 142), raising much critical discussion about whether the
    whole of Dante's underworld is founded on the principle of exact
    reciprocation between sin and punishment, or whether the term
    should be reserved only to Malebolge, to the *bolgia* where it occurs, or
    even just to the sinner who uses the term: Armour has recently
    argued, persuasively, that it should be reserved to a very limited con-
    text (2000); but see also Ferrante 1984, pp.169–170.

17 The cities of Bologna, Florence, Forlì, and Lucca, for instance, are all
    heavily represented in Malebolge; the *bolge* also contain several mem-
    bers of the clans and households of the Florentine Donati family and

of the Romagnolo Guido da Montefeltro (himself punished in the eighth *bolgia*).

18 Kirkpatrick, 1987, pp.237–239.

19 As described by Boccaccio, *Decameron* VIII. 9. In another example of the productive civic use of human waste, urine was collected by the *comune* for use by fullers in the Florentine cloth-trade.

20 The exact form of the basins is the subject of scholarly debate, as is the meaning of the apparently autobiographical reference of ll.19–21: see for instance Ottimo and della Lana, *ad loc.*; also Musa, 1964; Noakes, 1968; Tavoni, 1992.

21 Singleton's commentary, *ad loc.*, who cites Boccaccio, *Decameron* V. 7.

22 The marquis is probably Venedico's patron Obizzo II d'Este or possibly his son Azzo VIII, though this is chronologically less likely. Different early commentators cite either, and Venedico was closely connected with both: Fasoli, 1967, p.258. Obizzo d'Este has been encountered earlier in *Inf.*, where he is punished for violence and tyranny (XII. 110–112).

23 Benvenuto, *ad loc.* Singleton points out that '*salse*' was also used metaphorically to mean 'sufferings', citing a sermon of Fra Giordano da Rivalto (commentary, *ad loc.*). Its additional value as an erotic metaphor (equivalent to modern English 'saucy') would also suit the sexual sin of the *bolgia*: Raimondi, 1970, p.46.

24 On the dialect origins of '*zucca*', see the Ottimo, *ad loc.* Buti's commentary offers an alternative but also pejorative city-specific explanation for Dante's choice of expression: '*comunemente li Lucchesi ànno la testa leggiere, come la zucca quando è secca*' ('the *Lucchesi* commonly have light heads, like a dried pumpkin').

25 'I am not the Christ', *John* 1. 20. Resemblance to the Baptist carries patriotic as well as spiritual associations, as St John was the patron saint of Florence. Tavoni discusses additional parallels established in this *canto* between the protagonist and the prophet Jeremiah and SS Francis and Peter: 1992, pp.468–472, 490–494, 498–502. See also Jacoff, 1988, pp.119–120.

26 *Acts* 2. 1–4.

27 The embellishment of the florin, emblem of material values, with the image of the austere prophet often created symbolic ambiguities: Tavoni 1992, pp.503, 507–508; Catherine Keen, 1997, p.40.

28 *Matthew* 5. 19.

29 Dante's Virgil states that the prophetess Manto created a settlement on the future site of Mantua (XX. 81–93), telling the protagonist that this

is the only authentic foundation story: '*se tu mai odi | originar la mia terra altrimenti, | la verità nulla menzogna frodi*' ('if ever you hear another account of my city's origins, do not let any falsehood defraud the truth': ll.97–99). In fact, *Aen*. X. 198–200 makes Manto's son, Ocnus, the city's founder. See Mazzotta, 1979, p.90.

30 Ellis summarises different critical readings, 1998, pp.290–291; Kirkpatrick, 1987, pp.267–268; Kleinhenz, 1989, p.151 n.5.

31 Ellis, 1998, p.293.

32 *Matthew* 27. 51.

33 Kirkpatrick, 1987, pp.267–268; Kleinhenz, 1989, p.150.

34 The description alludes to Christ's condemnation of the 'sad hypocrites', *Matthew* 6.16.

35 Early commentators offer conflicting accounts of the way that the punishment functioned, and there is no external evidence that Frederick ever devised, or used, such systems of execution. The commentary tradition's eagerness to enter into gruesome detail indicates that rumours of extreme cruelty about an emperor notorious in popular imagination as a tyrant and heretic were in wide circulation, and could well have been deemed credible by Dante. The gilt-lead robes may also be associated with Christ's biblical denunciation of the Pharisees as 'whited sepulchres' and accusation that they burden the laity with observances they themselves shirk: *Matthew* 23. 4, 27. On etymological symbolism derived from the definitions of hypocrisy by Isidore of Seville and Uguccione da Pisa (who gives the derivation 'above/beneath gilding'), see Toynbee, 1902, p.108; Tulone, 2000, p.371.

36 Loderingo was one of the order's founding members; Catalano joined within months of its foundation. On the order's origins and rule, see della Lana and Benvenuto, *ad loc.*; Gozzadini, 1851, pp.24–27. Other Frati Gaudenti who appear in the *Comm.* include Frate Alberigo da Faenza (*Inf.* XXXIII. 118), and Fra Bonagiunta Orbicciani da Lucca (*Purg.* XXIV. 19, 36: see chp. 5).

37 Villani, *Nuova cronica*,VIII. 13; Gozzadini, 1851, pp.25–26.

38 See Guittone d'Arezzo's rather defensive comment on the name 'Joyful': '*Ben agia chi noi prima chiamò gaudenti, | ch' ogn' omo a Dio renduto | lo più diritto nome è lui gaudente*' ('Whoever first called us "joyful" was right, since for every man professed to God, the best name for him is joyful': poem 32. 105–107, ed. Egidi, 1940).

39 Both had previous experience as *podestà* from their secular careers: Loderingo had served in five cities during the 1250s, Catalano in seven

(Gozzadini, 1851, pp.20–21, n.118 pp.99–100). After entering the order, Catalano and Loderingo acted jointly as *podestà* in Bologna in 1265 and 1267; Loderingo also held a joint term of office with Iacopo Tavernieri in 1263.

40 Villani, *Nuova cronica* VIII. 13.

41 Villani, *Nuova cronica*, VIII. 13–17: the chronicler's stress on the Brothers' '*falsa ipocresia*' ('false hypocrisy': VIII. 13) suggests that his account may in fact be influenced by knowledge of Dante's *Inf.* XXIII. For evidence that Catalano and Loderingo's Florentine activities were based on explicit orders from Pope Clement IV, see Pietrobono, 1961, p.16; Russo, 1971, pp.25–27.

42 Fanelli, 1993, pp.20, 37, 252–253. On the city's Roman origins and monuments, see Villani, *Nuova cronica* II. 1.

43 Dante-character's earlier meeting with the shade of Farinata stressed that the Ghibelline leader had protected the whole city from a similarly partisan programme of destruction (*Inf.* X. 91–93) – comparison thus shows up the Brothers' irresponsibility more strongly.

44 Guido da Pisa appears to be the first commentator to introduce the query: '*aut ipsis fratribus compatiendo, aut eis aliquis inproperare volendo*' ('either feeling compassion for these friars, or wishing to impute some misconduct to them').

45 Benvenuto da Imola and the Anonimo Fiorentino, *ad loc.*; Raimondi, 1970, p.56.

46 On Caiaphas's hypocrisy, see Kirkpatrick, 1987, p.282; Raimondi, 1970, p. 8 n.1.

47 Raimondi, 1970, pp.59–60.

48 Ferrante, 1984, pp.191–193.

5 – CREATING COMMUNITY

1 Le Goff, 1984, esp. chp. 10; also Armour, 1983, p.137.

2 Armour, 1989; Mazzotta, 1979; Pertile, 1998; Scott, 1996.

3 Ferrante, 1984, pp.46–47, 56–57, 198–201; the chapter on purgatory is entitled 'Society in Transition' (pp.198–252).

4 Barolini, 1984, provides a systematic study of the *Comm.*'s poets; see also Ferrante, 1984, pp.203–204, 237–243.

5 Armour, 1989, pp.112–148; Ferrante, 1984, pp.205, 244, 251–252; Scott, 1996, pp.64–67, 134–136, 181–184.

6 Pertile, 1998, pp.13–21; Scott, 1996, pp.48–49.

7 Davis, 1957; Lenkeith, 1952.

8 Ryan, 1982; who also comments on Virgil's vulnerable moments in *Inf.*

9 Virgil concentrates in his speech on the adult, pagan souls of Limbo, especially the heroic figures who occupy its central castle, although Limbo also contains the souls of unbaptised infants still subject to the taint of original sin (*Purg.*VII. 31–33).

10 Dante draws on a strong poetic tradition of vernacular political invective. Barolini (1984, pp.179–182) has shown that throughout this sequence he closely echoes a lyric on Pisan politics by Guittone d'Arezzo, *Magni baroni certo e regi quasi* (*Great lords indeed and almost kings*), poem 47 (ed. Egidi, 1940), composed *c.*1285.

11 The Gloss to the *Corpus Iuris* describes Italy as '*non [...] provincia, sed domina provinciarum*' ('not a province, but the mistress of the provinces'): Ercole, 1913, p.172 n.2. The phrase also echoes *Lamentations* 1.1, the obvious source for the description of widowed Rome: 'How doth the city sit solitary, that was full of people! how is she become as a widow, she that was was great among the nations, and princess among the provinces, how is she become tributary!'. Guittone d'Arezzo, in *Magni baroni*, calls Pisa '*la migliore | donna de la provincia e regin anco*' ('the best lady of the province and its queen': ll.70–71).

12 Marco Lombardo's discourse on the eclipse of imperial authority also employs the *Cvo*'s image of the *freno* (rein) of law, *Purg.* XVI 93, 94.

13 The allusion to Marcellus might refer to the hero of the Second Punic War, Dante ironically comparing local faction-leaders to a famous defender of Roman liberty. Alternatively, Marcellus could be Pompey's ally against Julius Caesar in the Roman Civil War, giving a more straightforward allusion to the dangers of political faction and anti-imperialism. The majority of early commentators opt for the latter; but Scott makes an interesting case for the former: 1996, p.107. On Dante's detestation of the term *parte*, signifying organised and institutionalised division within the body politic, see Peters, 1977.

14 Dante comments on his affection for Italian/Florentine in *Cvo* I. x–xiii and *DVE* I. vi. 3.

15 Dante's fondness for textile metaphors in relation to language is evident from the *DVE*'s classification of words by wool qualities, II. vii. 2–7; see Gorni, 1979, pp.20, 25–27.

16 Marco Lombardo, too, comments on the enduring validity of Justinian's neglected codes: '*le leggi son, ma chi pon mano ad esse?*' ('the laws are there: but who puts his hand to them?': *Purg.* XVI. 97).

17 The image of Florence as an *inferma* with shifting *membre* recalls Guittone d'Arezzo's *Magni baroni*, which also represents a city as '*infermata*' ('sick' 1.69) and '*dimembrata*' ('dismembered': 1.76). Like Dante, Guittone proposes taking the political example of Rome as a countermeasure to tyranny (ll.103–107). Barolini, 1984, pp.179–182.

18 Barolini, 1984, pp.160–161, 171; Ferrante, 1984, p.214; Scott, 1996, p.99.

19 Barolini, 1984, pp.153–173; Scott, 1996, pp.109–127.

20 Poem 26, ed. Boni, 1954.

21 Barolini, 1984, pp.153–173. As Barolini notes, Sordello is a fairly minor poet, and in *DVE* Dante does not cite from his verse directly, as he does from other Occitan poets, including Bertran de Born: 1984, pp.161–163, 179.

22 Barolini, 1984, pp.179–182. Similarities between this lyric and the '*Ahi serva Italia*' passage were noted above. On Guittone, *DVE* I. xiii.1.

23 As Barolini points out, Sordello's poem is aggressive and 'had it been acted on, would have resulted in fighting in every corner of Europe' (1984, p.172); Dante's inter-textual citation takes the contrary course of denouncing princely competition and violence, and commending the harmony they achieve *post mortem* in purgatory.

24 Guittone in *Magni baroni* appeals to Pisa's rulers to '*essa sanare*' ('heal her': 1.88), noting that the citizens weep at her plight (1.73).

25 Parker emphasises that the widow would have had little choice in the question of her second marriage, in which she was subject to her brother Azzo VIII d'Este's decisions as to the organisation of family politico-dynastic alliances through her renewed marital availability after her first husband's death: 1993, pp.136–138, 141–144.

26 It is worth noting, in the context of this matrimonial critique, that several members of her family, the Este, appear in *Inf.* on account of familial and sexual impropriety: see *Inf.* XII. 112, XVIII. 56.

27 More precisely, Nino asserts that his own cockerel would have made a superior ornament to the widow's tomb, which carries her husband's family crest (ll.79–81). The allusion anticipates the interest in the effects of stability or faction on female burial shown in *Par.* XV. 118–119: see chp. 6.

28 See Benvenuto da Imola, *ad loc.* The Malaspina territories lay within the region of the Lunigiana: in *Par.* XVI. 73, the city of Luni becomes an emblem for the decline of human societies and the passing of time, in contrast to the present insistence on the durability of political traditions.

29 Scott, 1996, pp.179–180. On Statius and Virgil, and their respective roles in the *Comm.*, see Barolini, 1984, esp. pp.201–269; Ferrante, 1984, pp.194–195.

30 See Freccero's study of the *piaghe* that political events have inscribed on Manfred's body (*Purg.* III. 108, 111, 119), and of the meaning of the seven Ps (1986, pp.199, 205); also Tavoni's reading of the '*suggel*' of *Inf.* XIX. 21 in the light of the '*sigillo*' (*Par.* 107) of St Francis's stigmatisation: 1992, pp.490–493.

31 Poems 72–74 (Dante's) and 72a–74a (Forese's) in Foster and Boyde. Cursietti, 1995, has suggested the entire *tenzone* to be a forgery; in the debate that has followed, I find his opponents' arguments convincing: See Alfie, 1998, for a fuller discussion, with useful bibliography.

32 Forese died on 28 July, 1296; Statius, *c*.96 AD.

33 Corso, as Singleton notes *ad loc.*, was assassinated in 1308 when attempting to flee his former faction-associates, who had turned against him. In imagining Corso '*a coda d'una bestia tratto*' ('dragged at the tail of a beast': XXIV. 83), like a criminal being taken to execution, Forese creates an imagined *pittura infamante* of his brother like the images of executed criminals used by the *comuni* to disgrace the memory of their enemies.

34 The bibliography on the stylistic issues raised by Bonagiunta's words is vast: see Barolini, 1984, pp.40–57, 85–153; Durling and Martinez, 1990, pp.53–70; Pertile, 1993, 1994.

35 If Dante's authorship of the *Fiore* (and perhaps the *Detto d'amore*) is accepted, his past record as a 'comic' poet becomes more substantial: Barnes, 1997; Boyde, 1997.

36 Kirkpatrick, 1990.

37 The *pargoletta* interpretation is proposed by Benvenuto and the Anonimo Fiorentino (poems 34 and 36 in Contini's 1946 edn, 64 and 66 in Foster and Boyde, 1967); Gentucca as a female name, by Buti.

38 Guinizelli poem IV, ed. Contini, 1995.

39 Indeed Pézard (1950) famously interprets Brunetto's sin as not sexual but linguistic perversion, in preferring French to Italian.

40 A third possibility would leave Cino da Pistoia as the best Italian, since he was accorded the parallel place to Arnaut as the supreme love poet of the *lingua di sì* in *DVE*, but there is little additional support for this hypothesis in the passage.

41 However, when Arnaut's shade speaks a little later, the words Dante attributes to him employ not Daniel's own challenging *trobar clus* style, but an easily accessible *trobar leu*: Pertile, 1993, p.48.

42 Dante echoes the historical Arnaut's poetic signature: *'eu son Arnauz c'amas l'aura'* ('I am Arnaut, who gather the wind': *Ab gai so conde e leri (To the joyful sound in clear and elegant style)*, 43–45; poem 10, ed. Perugi, 1978). Arnaut's opening words, *'tant m'abellis vostre cortes deman'* ('your courteous question so pleases me': l.140) recall the lyric by Folquet of Marseilles (see *Par.* IX. 37–42), *Tant m'abellis l'amoros pessamens (The thought of love so pleases me)*, poem 2, ed. Stronski, 1910.

43 Pertile, 1993, pp.47–50.

6 – IDEALS OF CITY LIFE

1 Honess, 1994, p.43–44, 46–47.

2 Ferrante entitles her chapter on the *Par.* 'The Ideal Society' (1984, pp.253–310); see especially her opening comments, pp.253–259.

3 Virgil describes Ripheus as *'iustissimus unus | qui fuit in Teucris et servantissimus aequi'* ('the most outstandingly just of the Trojans and the one most devoted to right'), *Aen.* II. 426–427; his unorthodox salvation by Dante has been the object of extensive critical commentary.

4 The assessment forms one of Dante's 'prophecies' of events still in the future at the *Comm.*'s fictional date of 1300. Count Henry of Luxembourg was elected emperor in 1308, and came to Italy in 1310 to begin an active campaign for the revival of imperial authority; after initial successes, mounting opposition impeded his progress, and he died of fever in 1313 *en route* to confront his Angevin and Guelf opponents in southern Italy.

5 All three texts mention Aeneas, the Decii, Cincinnatus, Scipio, and Caesar: see the two closely matched passages, *Cvo* IV. v, *Mon.* II. v. The dating of the two treatises was discussed in chp. 2.

6 Charles Martel died aged twenty-four, in 1295, just on the threshold of the age of *Giovinezza* represented in the *Cvo* by Aeneas: Peters, 1991, pp.62–63.

7 Dell'Aquila, 1990, pp.49–50.

8 See Peters' discussion of the 'two Venuses' of medieval astrology and mythography: 1991, pp.55–59.

9 Aristotle, *Pol.* I. i, VII. viii–ix. There are close parallels between Charles's development of Aristotelian arguments, and the *Cvo*'s demonstration that *'l'uomo abbisogna di molte cose, a le quali uno solo sat-*

isfare non può' ('man has many needs, which a single individual cannot satisfy on his own': *Cvo* IV. iv. 1).

10 Loius rose to be Bishop of Toulouse, and was later canonised. Peters, 1991, p.67.

11 Cacciaguida's birth-date must be extrapolated from the astrological allusions of *Par*. XVI. 34–39; while the calculation is problematic, most critics prefer the date 1091. The allusion to his crusading activity under the Emperor Conrad dates his death on the battlefield to the Third Crusade, 1147 (*Par*. XV. 139–148).

12 The phrase '*sanguis meus*' echoes Anchises' address to Aeneas, *Aen*. VI. 835. Honess, 1994, pp.45–46; Schnapp, 1986, pp.64, 142–147, 206–215.

13 '*Terza e nona*', the offices named, recall the numerical patterning of threes and nines in the *VN*, in which the anthropomorphised city space was sanctified by the presence of Beatrice, and 'widowed' by her absence (*VN* XXVIII.1), using the same imagery derived from *Lamentations* as was applied to Rome in *Purg*.VI. 112–113, as we have seen.

14 The *buon tempo antico* topos: see Davis, 1984, pp.88–93; Schnapp, 1986, p.43; Toscano, 1990, pp.73–74.

15 Limentani comments that Dante 'ignores the bright side of the picture' with a pessimism that 'no historian would accept as accurate' (1985, pp.148–149), while Figurelli describes his attitude to commercial activity as moral repugnance (1965, p.655); see also Davis, 1968, pp.74–77; Pertile, 1998, p.20; Ramat, 1976, p.125.

16 A point emphasised by Honess, 1997.

17 Charles Martel earlier explained that the spirits of the higher spheres appear to the pilgrim as lights because of their intense joy in God. He employs a textile-related image that however emphasises the naturalness of the 'clothing' of light by figuring it not as a manufactured silk garment, but as a natural phase of the silk-moth's life-cycle: '*la mia letizia mi tien celato | che mi raggia dintorno e mi nasconde, | quasi animal di sua seta fasciato*' ('my happiness keeps me concealed, which rays around me and hides me, like a creature bundled inside its own silk': *Par*.VIII. 52–54). The image draws on the ancient tradition figuring the soul as a butterfly, used also in *Purg*. X. 124–126.

18 Parker, 1993, pp.136–139, 141–142.

19 Honess, 1997, 'Feminine Virtues', pp.113, 118.

20 *Cvo* IV. iv. 2, *Mon*. I. v. 5.

21 Male activity will however emerge as a central concern in *canto* XVI, when Dante-character introduces a specifically political line of questioning.

22 Honess, 1994, pp.49–50, 1997 'Feminine Virtues', p.119; Schnapp, 1986, p.43.

23 In the foundation legends, Troy's descendants founded Rome, and Florence was founded by Romans and populated partly by Fiesolans, after Rome's destruction of that city.

24 Approximately forty-three families are identified by patronymic, family crest, or other allusion; there are also references to single individuals, or to famous episodes in civic history, that extend the frame of political reference.

25 For instance, Figurelli, 1965, p.656; Momigliano, 1976, p.49.

26 Modern research shows that Dante's list of families in decline or emerging as *parvenus* is not entirely accurate, but underwrites personal concerns in his own political agenda, especially related to the issues of social and moral nobility and to constitutional developments: Carpi, 1990, pp.243–250.

27 Dante's disapproval of this development is clear from his disparaging comments on Giano della Bella, chief formulator of the 1293 anti-magnate Ordinances: *Par.* XVI. 127–132; see chp 1.

28 The negative emphasis that Florence is *not* weeping reverses the familiar imagery of *Lamentations*, applied to Florence in the *VN* after Beatrice's death, and to Rome in *Purg.*VI. 112–113.

29 Under anti-magnate legislation, proscribed families could regain the right to participate in the priorate and in popular government by renouncing their noble station and changing surname and coat of arms. Many of the 'extinguished' families mentioned by Cacciaguida, such as the della Sannella (*Par.* XVI. 92), Guidi (l.122), and Importuni (l.133), have in fact not died out, but changed their identity in this manner. The image suggests that a parallel process of nobility lost along with changed heraldry has affected the city as a whole.

30 Aristotle, *Pol.* III. 3: but where Aristotle simply comments that the expansion of the city and the mixing of its population change the city, Cacciaguida deduces that this change is *for the worse.*

31 The whole of *Mon.*'s third book is dedicated to enquiring whether imperial power depends directly from God, or from an intermediary, i.e. the papacy; the former proposition is firmly endorsed, and the book upholds the principle of the absolute separation of powers between the supreme secular authority, the emperor, and the supreme spiritual authority, the pope.

32 Schnapp, 1986, pp.48–49.

33 Quinones, 1994, pp.17–18, 128, 130–133; Schnapp, 1986, p.54.

34 Catherine Keen, 1997, pp.31–32, 38–41; Schnapp, 1986, pp.153–169. Early commentators such as Benvenuto and della Lana emphasise the ambiguities of the patronage of Mars over Florence: the god/planet is associated as much with valour, resistance and *virtù* as with aggression; there are corresponding ambivalences in the symbolism of St John the Baptist, whose image appeared on the florin and whose biblical eccentricity could have negative implications for the city under his protection. Carpi, 1990, pp.252–260; Tavoni, 1992, pp.409, 503–509.

35 On the pejorative implications for Dante of the term '*parte*', see Peters, 1977, pp.115–119.

36 Honess, 1994, pp.53–55.

37 *Matthew* 3.3.

38 Pertile, 2001, pp.71–85.

39 Mazzotta, 1979, p.299.

INDEX